the TRUE BELIEVER

Asa MAHAN

WHITAKER
HOUSE

All Scripture quotations are taken from the King James Version of the Holy Bible.

Boldface type in the Scripture quotations indicates the author's emphasis.

The True Believer:
Character, Duty, and Privileges

ISBN: 978-1-62911-004-2
eBook ISBN: 978-1-62911-028-8
Printed in the United States of America

Whitaker House
1030 Hunt Valley Circle
New Kensington, PA 15068
www.whitakerhouse.com

Library of Congress Cataloging-in-Publication Data (Pending)

1 2 3 4 5 6 7 8 9 10 11 21 20 19 18 17 16 15 14

CONTENTS

PREFACE

The design of the following discourses is stated with sufficient explicitness on the contents page. An answer to the inquiry *What are the true character, duties, and privileges of the children of God in this life?* has now become one of the great and pressing wants of the church. Happy will it be for Zion if those whom the Holy Spirit has made overseers of the flock of God (see Acts 20:28) will instruct her rightly in respect to such inquiries. I indulge the fond hope that these discourses, prepared with no little prayer for divine illumination—and the preparation of which has so deeply refreshed my own spirit—may do something to forward so desirable a result. Zion is the chosen dwelling place of my heart. I have no interests or plans that are not fully identified with her purification, blessedness, and enlargement. Never may I be permitted to write a single line for the public eye or ear for any other end. The reason these discourses are given to the public is the full conviction that the church imperiously needs to be instructed in the knowledge of the great and precious truths these discourses were designed to elucidate.

Some years ago, the substance of all of them but the last, which has never before been given to the public, was published in the *Oberlin Evangelist*. Since their appearance in that publication, I have been often and earnestly solicited to furnish them in a volume by themselves. As a response to such requests, they have been carefully revised and corrected and are now presented in a form in which I am willing they should meet the public eye.

But two classes of readers will *fully* appreciate what is here written—those who are earnest inquirers after the great salvation in all its fullness and those who have a present experience of that fullness in their own hearts. To such, especially, the work is commended with the fervent hope and prayer that their numbers in the churches may be multiplied a thousandfold till the "*redeemed of the* Lord *shall return, and come with singing unto Zion; and everlasting joy shall be upon their head*" (Isaiah 51:11). Among that happy throng, perhaps, this work will be remembered by here and there an individual as one of the instruments by which his feet were guided and established in the highway of holiness. This is the only form of ambition I now know. If the reader will derive as great blessedness and profit in reading as I have in preparing this work, I will never have occasion to regret the loss of my labor. One of the most pleasing features of the doctrine therein set forth is the fact that he who proclaims it receives while he is thus watering others, if possible, greater fullness of joy than he who embraces it when proclaimed.

1

THE GOSPEL PLAN

"Whether therefore ye eat, or drink, or whatsoever ye do, do all to the glory of God."
—1 Corinthians 10:31

"In all thy ways acknowledge him, and he shall direct thy paths."
—Proverbs 3:6

"Be careful for nothing; but in every thing by prayer and supplication with thanksgiving let your requests be made

known unto God. And the peace of God, which passeth all understanding, shall keep your hearts and minds through Christ Jesus."
—Philippians 4:6–7

"Thou wilt keep him in perfect peace,
whose mind is stayed on thee: because he trusteth in thee."
—Isaiah 26:3

"Thou shalt call his name JESUS:
for he shall save his people from their sins."
—Matthew 1:21

"Jesus said unto him, If thou canst believe,
all things are possible to him that believeth."
—Mark 9:23

The design of the present discourse is not to give a particular explanation of the passages above cited or to deduce any one specific principle from them as the basis of my remarks. Instead, it is to present some reflections of a general nature that are designed to throw light upon the gospel plan—reflections that have suggested themselves to my mind on reading these and kindred passages of Scripture. I need not here particularly remind the reader that all God requires of any being on earth or in heaven is comprehended in one word—*love*—and that every particular precept is only a specific exemplification and application of this one principle.

With this thought distinctly before the mind of the reader, I remark that love, in all its forms, implies devotion to the interest of its object. In the form of natural affection, it implies this. Parental affection, for example, implies devotion to the feelings and interests of children. In the form of benevolence, such as is required by the moral law, love implies supreme devotion to the great interests and objects of benevolence existing in the universe around us. As exercised toward God, it implies supreme respect for and delight in His character, implicit confidence in His veracity and faithfulness, unreserved obedience to His authority, and the consecration of our entire being to His kingdom and glory. As exercised toward the creatures of God, it implies the devotion of our powers to all their interests, temporal and spiritual, according to their relative importance, such as Christ Himself manifested when He was on earth. The person who exercises this love lives and moves and has his being for this object. (See Acts 17:28.) *"Pure religion and undefiled before God and the Father"* (James 1:27) will manifest itself, not merely in devotion to the spiritual and eternal interests of men, but also in *"visit*[ing] *the fatherless and widows in their affliction, and... keep*[ing] *himself unspotted from the world"* (verse 27).

It is the fundamental design of Christ, in the plan of redemption, that the principles of the gospel—or the law of love—will be carried out and exemplified by the believer in every condition and relation in life. In other words, he will eat, drink, and clothe his body; demean himself in the family, in the church, and before the world; and regulate all his interests and transactions with his fellow men under the influence of the same Spirit of love by which Christ was induced to become poor for our sakes, that we, through His poverty, might be made rich. (See 2 Corinthians 8:9.) We understand distinctly the Spirit by which Christ Himself was influenced in every condition and relation in life and by which a minister of the everlasting gospel ought to be influenced in the duties of his sacred calling. The design of Christ is that every believer will be influenced by the same motives in every condition and relation in life. *"Whether therefore ye eat, or drink, or whatsoever ye do,* ***do all*** *to the glory of God"* (1 Corinthians 10:31). *"In all thy ways acknowledge him"* (Proverbs 3:6). These are the fundamental requisitions by which Christ designs and expects that we will regulate our entire conduct before God and the world.

In some particular sphere in life, every individual is required and expected to glorify God by devoting all his powers and interests to the divine glory and conforming his entire deportment in that sphere to the principles of the gospel. On account of natural endowments and the arrangements and dispensations of divine providence, one person is adapted to and required to do more in one sphere in life, and another in another. But the farmer, the mechanic, the merchant, the husband, the wife, the parent, and the child are to glorify God by conforming their entire deportment and transactions with their fellow men to the same principles of pure and perfect love as the minister of the gospel is expected to regulate his conduct in his sacred calling. Every man, whatever his sphere in life may be, is expected to make it his supreme object to conduct himself in such a manner that the greatest possible amount of glory will result to God and the greatest good to men. In the particular sphere in which a person is for the time being called to move, *there* is the time and the place in which he is to glorify God. If he is at home, within the domestic circle, or abroad on a journey or engaged in any of the ordinary or special transactions of life, it is by ordering his whole deportment in these particular circumstances in conformity with the principles of the gospel that God is to receive honor from him.

Such are the fixed arrangements of divine providence and grace. If we do not thus glorify God in each particular sphere in which we are called to move, we do not glorify Him at all. He can receive no honor from us in any sphere whatever. Suppose, for illustration, a professed Christian is, as in this respect he ought to be, very punctual in his attendance upon the services of the sanctuary on the Sabbath and upon all the meetings for social prayer, and in all these services, he appears exceedingly devout. If you should meet him nowhere else, you might, whatever his real character may be, receive a hallowed influence from his example because you would think his external appearance a reflection of the state of his heart. But should you see that man in some business transaction in a settled plan to overreach you, what influence would his appearance in the house of God and the circle for social prayer now exert upon you? As long as that sin remains upon that individual, unconfessed and unrepented of, it is impossible for him to glorify God in your estimation in any other sphere, whatever his appearance and conduct there may be. The same principle holds equally true in all cases whatsoever. The man who does not glorify God in every sphere in which he is called to move does not glorify Him in any.

A fundamental design of the redemption of Christ was and is to provide and reveal grace. By availing ourselves of grace, we may *"serve God acceptably with reverence and godly fear"* (Hebrews 12:28) in every particular sphere in which we are called to move. In this consists our completeness in Christ. In making provisions for our redemption, He remembered us in every particular sphere and condition in which we are called to move. As a Savior, He presents Himself as able and willing to meet all our necessities and to render us, in every relation in life, all that God requires us to be.

Hence, I remark that if Christ does not save us by rendering us, in our different spheres and relations in life—as parents and children, as husbands and wives, as citizens and members of the household of faith—what He requires us to be, He does not save us at all. If He saves us, He does it by destroying in us the *spirit of disobedience* and inspiring us with the *spirit of obedience* to the commands of God. The man imbued with such a spirit will have respect to all God's commandments in every relation in life. If Christ saves us, He does it by destroying our selfishness and rendering us benevolent like Himself. The person possessed of such a spirit (and none others know Christ as a Savior at all), who loves his neighbor as himself, will not overreach or defraud his neighbor in any matter. All his business transactions with him will be an exemplification of the law of love.

Hence, I also remark that if our faith does not fasten upon Christ, to render us in our different spheres what God requires us to be, we do not, in any true sense, exercise faith in Him as a Savior from sin. It is in these circumstances and relations that our sins are found. Here we sin, if we sin at all. Here, then, our faith must fasten upon Christ to be thus saved from our sins, or we do not know Him by faith as such a Savior.

Another fundamental principle of the gospel plan is this: In every condition and relation in life, we are authorized and required to look to Christ for special wisdom and grace to render us, in those particular circumstances, all God requires us to be. This we are to do with the assured expectation that, in conformity with his promise, while we acknowledge Him in all our ways, He will direct our paths. (See Proverbs 3:6.) He will instruct us, teach us the way we should go, and guide us by His eye. (See Psalm 32:8.)

While we thus consecrate our entire being to God, He kindly assumes the guardianship of all our interests, temporal and spiritual. While we are *"careful for nothing; but in every thing by prayer and supplication with thanksgiving let* [our] *requests be made known unto God"* (Philippians 4:6), His word stands pledged that *"no good thing will he withhold"* (Psalm 84:11) from us and that the *"peace of God, which passeth all understanding, shall keep* [our] *hearts and minds through Christ Jesus"* (Philippians 4:7). Our exclusive business, the only thing about which we are to be careful, is to hearken to God's Word and do His will. His business is to see that all our real interests are secure, all our real wants supplied, and our souls kept in perfect peace. Such is a brief outline of the gospel plan. The way is now prepared for some important remarks that arise from our thoughts thus far, remarks designed to throw still further light upon this subject.

We see the relationship between the moral principles and precepts and the doctrines of the gospel. The former constitute the rules of action by which we regulate our heart and conduct in all the circumstances and relations of life. The latter embody those motives and influences, designed and adapted by infinite wisdom and love, to secure obedience to the moral precepts of Christianity. This is the design of every doctrine of the gospel, and this is the relationship between the doctrines and moral precepts of Christianity.

We see, in the light of this subject, the essence of the perfection of the gospel. It consists in the absolute perfection of its moral precepts and in the equally perfect adaptation of its doctrines and influences to secure obedience to its moral precepts.

Any other view of the gospel than this makes it an imperfect gospel.

We also perceive the essence of the perfection of Christ as a Savior. It consists in His perfect ability and willingness to meet entirely every demand of our being in every condition and relation in time and eternity. It consists in His ability and willingness to remedy all the consequences of past sins, to secure us in the future against the power of sin and all its incentives, and to cause His followers to *"stand perfect and complete in all the will of God"* (Colossians 4:12). Such a Savior we sinners imperiously need, and if Christ was in any respect deficient in these characteristics, He would be an imperfect Savior.

We may understand the nature of evangelical faith. The believer, in the exercise of such faith, recognizes himself as complete in Christ in every condition, relation, and sphere in life. To his mind, *"all the promises of God in him are yea, and in him Amen, unto the glory of God by us"* (2 Corinthians 1:20).

His great inquiry is, *What has God promised?* When he understands the blessing really embraced and offered in any promise, his faith at once fastens upon Christ so he may have that promise in all its fullness accomplished in his own experience. Then he has no more doubt about whether he will realize its fulfillment than he has about the truthfulness of God. He never staggers at any promise of God through unbelief. (See Romans 4:20.) When called to move in any particular sphere or relation in life, he at once looks to Christ for grace and wisdom to meet fully every responsibility. This he does, expecting to receive of Christ's fullness and *"grace for grace"* (John 1:16) as his circumstances require. Such is true evangelical faith. Reader, is this the confidence you have in Him?

We may see the nature of unbelief. Unbelief assumes three forms:

1. It denies the truth of revelation altogether. This is *infidelity*.
2. It admits the truth of revelation but denies the fact that provisions are made and revealed in the gospel to enable the believer to *"stand perfect and complete in all the will of God"* (Colossians 4:12) in this life. Or it admits the adequacy of the provisions of grace and then affirms that they sustain such a relation to us that no believer ever did or ever will so avail himself of them in this life in order to render the obedience required. This is *unbelief*—as manifested by those who oppose the doctrine of Christian perfection.
3. Unbelief in the third form admits the provisions of grace and the possibility that we might avail ourselves of them but withholds the faith required. This is *practical unbelief*.

We may also notice the symptoms of unbelief or those indications by which any man may determine whether he is under its influence:

1. The absence of a confirmed and settled peace of mind is a sure indication of unbelief. *"They that trust in the Lord shall be as mount Zion, which cannot be removed"* (Psalm 125:1). *"Thou wilt keep him in perfect peace, whose mind is stayed on thee"* (Isaiah 26:3). Faith recognizes in Christ a full and perfect and present supply for every necessity. Where is the place for anxiety in such a mind? Remember, reader, that if your peace is not *"as a river, and thy righteousness as the waves of the sea"* (Isaiah 48:18), it is because of your unbelief.

2. Present disquietude in regard to the future is a sure indication of unbelief. Faith recognizes in Christ a full supply of every necessity in every possible situation in our present and future. It therefore casts all its cares upon the Lord with the most peaceful assurance that every want will be met as it occurs. (See Psalm 55:22.) Anxiety finds no place in such a mind. Will you bear it in mind, reader, that all disquietude about the future, whether about our temporal or spiritual interests, finds its origin exclusively in unbelief?
3. Continued failure in good resolutions is another certain indication of the presence and prevailing influence of unbelief. Faith is the victory that overcomes the world. (See 1 John 5:4.) It resolves upon obedience and, by the grace of God, renders that obedience. Unbelief is overcome by the world. It "resolves, and resolves, and dies the same." Or, rather, despite its resolutions to the contrary, it slides back with a *"perpetual backsliding"* (Jeremiah 8:5). Reader, how is it with you? Do your often repeated and as often broken resolutions proclaim the fact that you are in unbelief?
4. Another very common indication of unbelief is the idea that in our circumstances and relations in life something peculiarly unfavorable opposes our sanctification, and thus, when our condition is changed, we will be more holy. How perfectly evident is it that the faith of such persons rests not upon Christ but upon external circumstances? In other words, here are the certain indications of unbelief. Faith recognizes for itself an infinite fullness in Christ for every condition, relation, and circumstance in life.

5. The complaint of a *hard heart* is another sure indication of unbelief. God has promised He will *"take the stony heart out of* [our] *flesh, and will give* [us] *an heart of flesh"* (Ezekiel 11:19). Faith lays hold of the promise and realizes its fulfillment in actual experience. Unbelief, on the other hand, retains the heart of stone as a fearful weight upon the soul. The conscious presence, therefore, of such a heart is a certain indication of unbelief.

6. A want of a felt, conscious assurance that God hears and answers us when we pray is another certain indication of unbelief. Faith introduces the soul into the very audience chamber of the Most High. It uses the name of Christ with the most fixed and peaceful assurance of being heard and of receiving the petitions desired of Him. Unbelief, on the other hand, shuts the soul from God and depresses it with the gloomy consciousness that God does not hear and will not answer.

Christian, when you pray with the feeling that God does not hear you, will you admit the fact that the cause is unbelief in your own heart? Say not that past sin is the cause. Past sin originated in unbelief, and God always hears the prayer of penitence and faith, whatever the past may have been.

The common impression is that our sinful propensities and the number and power of our temptations and besetments to sin are so strong we cannot hope to be sanctified in this life; this is a certain indication of the widespread influence of unbelief. The language of unbelief in this case is that Christ, as a Savior, is not *able* to deliver us from the world, the flesh, and the devil—or that he is not *willing,* which is the worst imputation that can possibly be cast upon His character. To say Christ is able or willing to save us from all sin when, and only when, He has us beyond the reach of all temptation is saying very little, surely, to His credit as a Savior. It is the cruelest imputation that unbelief ever casts upon His character. Christian, how often have you thus wounded Him in the house of His friends?

I might mention other symptoms of unbelief, but these are sufficient to enable the reader to determine whether he is under its fearful influence.

We can now see why the religion of the majority of professing Christians waxes and wanes with external circumstances. This is the case with a very great proportion of the church. If religion is revived around them, they are excited and active. If it declines, the love of many waxes cold. (See Matthew 24:12.) They lie down and slumber with the rest. What is the cause of such a state of things? Here I will give three answers:

1. The religion of such persons is not a religion of love. If it was so, as soon as religion began to decline, instead of going with the multitude, they would begin to "*sigh and...cry for all the abominations*" (Ezekiel 9:4) being done around them.
2. Theirs is not a religion of faith. Faith does not look at the things we see, which are temporal, but at the things that are unseen and eternal. (See 2 Corinthians 4:18.) The religion of faith, therefore, is independent from external circumstances for its strength and continuance. It endures "*as seeing him who is invisible*" (Hebrews 11:27).
3. It is not Christ but external circumstances that sustain and influence such persons. "*Jesus Christ the same yesterday, and to day, and for ever*" (Hebrews 13:8). Those who are really sustained and influenced by faith in Him will, indeed, be as "*mount Zion, which cannot be*

> *removed"* (Psalm 125:1). When circumstances around them are unfavorable, *"he giveth more grace"* (James 4:6), because *"as thy days, so shall thy strength be"* (Deuteronomy 33:25).

What then must we think of the condition and prospects of a great proportion of professing Christians? Let the reader attentively examine the ninth chapter of Ezekiel and there learn who, and who only, have the mark of God on their foreheads.

> *And he called to the man clothed with linen, which had the writer's inkhorn by his side; and the LORD said unto him, Go through the midst of the city, through the midst of Jerusalem, and set a mark upon the foreheads of the men* ***that sigh and that cry*** *for all the abominations that be done in the midst thereof. And to the others he said in mine hearing, Go ye after him through the city, and smite: let not your eye spare, neither have ye pity: slay utterly old and young, both maids, and little children, and women: but come not near any man upon whom is the mark; and begin at my sanctuary.* (Ezekiel 9:3–6)

One solitary class, as we see, was spared—those who, amid abounding wickedness, "sighed and cried for the abominations" (see verse 4) being done around them. In all the churches of the living God, this one class only now stands approved in His sight as *"heirs together of the grace of life"* (1 Peter 3:7). Reader, when *"judgment must begin at the house of God"* (1 Peter 4:17), where will you appear?

The true spirit of the gospel, which distinguishes the sincere believer from all other men, next claims our attention. It is all comprehended in this—implicit faith or confidence in every truth of God; firm reliance upon all His *"exceeding great and precious promises"* (2 Peter 1:4); and filial, unreserved obedience to all His commandments. Such an individual only really fears one thing, and that is sin. As from the pains of the second death, he flies from it himself and from all incentives and allurements to it, and in the deep sincerity of his heart, he sighs and cries when others perpetrate it. This, reader, is the true Christian. This was the spirit of Him whose name we bear, and we must remember, *"If any man have not the spirit of Christ, he is none of his"* (Romans 8:9).

I not infrequently meet with the question of how we should obey the great precept *"Whether therefore ye eat, or drink, or whatsoever ye do, do all to the glory of God"* (1 Corinthians 10:31). How should we demean ourselves in respect to food, drink, dress, and the business relations and transactions in life, for example, so that we will therein glorify God? We are now prepared with a specific answer to such inquiries, which are of vast importance to everyone who would have respect to all God's commandments.

Let us suppose that an individual, in all his business transactions and arrangements, maintains a strict adherence to the principles of integrity and to the demands of the great law of love—*"Thou shalt love thy neighbor as thyself"* (Matthew 19:19)—and that he seeks the guidance of wisdom from above in all that Providence commits to his trust. Such an individual will glorify God in his business transactions as really and truly as the minister does in the most hallowed duties of his sacred calling. Thus every individual may glorify Christ in all the varied circumstances and relations in life. The application of the principle under consideration to the regulation of our conduct in respect to food, drink, and dress, is manifest.

> *Every creature of God is good, and nothing to be refused, if it be received with thanksgiving: for it is sanctified* [its

> appropriate use is a service, rendered virtue in us and acceptable to God] *by the word of God and prayer.*
> (1 Timothy 4:4–5)

The great truth here presented is this: Every object God created, He brought into being for a certain end. When we use each object for the end for which it was created, with respect for what is right and according to the will of the great Giver of all, we honor God in its use. Our mental and physical constitution was created for a certain end, an end of which no one is ignorant. Food, drink, and apparel are requisite to this end. When from a sacred regard and in strict subordination to this end, we gratify and regulate these propensities—never in obedience to the demands of pride, custom, or appetite, or violating the laws of life and health—we then glorify God in our bodies and spirits, which are His. (See 1 Corinthians 6:20.) Thus, while we acknowledge God in all our ways, everywhere, and in all things, He directs our paths to His own glory. (See Proverbs 3:6.) One of the most melancholy features of the prevailing religion of the present time is the almost total divorce of the fear of God and respect for His laws from the ordinary transactions of life. How few remember that *every* work is to be brought into judgment, with every secret thing, whether it is good or evil. It is a fearful thing, reader, to defile the temple of God, and that temple, remember, is the mortal body you now inhabit. (See 1 Corinthians 3:17.) Reader, does God thus receive glory from you? *"He that is faithful in that which is least is faithful also in much: and he that is unjust in the least is unjust also in much"* (Luke 16:10).

We see how individuals lose the presence of Christ when they leave their closets (the house of God) and engage in business when on a journey or when brought into new and untried circumstances. The reason is because they do not admit Christ has provided special grace for them in those particular circumstances, or they do not avail themselves of that grace. If this were so, the peace of God, which passes all understanding, would keep their hearts and minds at all times and under all circumstances. (See Philippians 4:7.) Christ will be with you, Christian, as the joy, the rest, the life, and the peace of your soul, whenever and wherever you have faith to apprehend and receive Him. Whenever your faith abandons Him, then He leaves you in darkness and the shadow of death.

We see how it is that many professors of religion destroy their influence as Christians when they are not at all aware of the fact. It is through the *temper* and *spirit* they manifest in the particular spheres of active life they are called to move in. For example, a clerk in a store who was under deep conviction of sin and apparently on the point of submission to God was turned backward and rendered an infidel when he detected his employer, a professed Christian, in an attempt to defraud a stranger out of six cents in the sale of a trifling article. The exhortations to repentance from that merchant could have no influence over that young man after the disclosure of such a spirit. How many children are hardened into an incurable obstinacy against religion because of the ill temper of their parents in the domestic circle? Reader, is the blood of no deathless spirit sprinkled upon your garments because of your conduct in some unguarded hour? Does religion so influence you in every sphere and relation in life that your entire deportment is a standing reproof against sin and not an excuse for it?

We may understand the great defect in the gospel, as apprehended by the mass of Christians at the present time. One glaring and melancholy defect is that Christ is contemplated almost exclusively as a Savior from *hell* and not as a Savior from *sin*—as a *justifying* but not a *sanctifying* Savior. Another is that the gospel, as now apprehended, has comparatively little to do with men in their particular and varied relations in life. They expect the gospel to influence them in the closet and on the Sabbath but to have very little to do with them in the ordinary transactions of life.

The gospel, when thus contemplated, can have but little influence upon Christians themselves or upon the world through them. On the other hand, when Christ is recognized and received—as the parents' and the child's, as the husband's and the wife's, as the farmer's, the mechanic's, and the merchant's Savior—when every believer in every sphere and relation in life looks to Christ as a special Savior to him in that particular sphere in which he is called to move—*then* will the power of the gospel be felt in the church and through the church upon the world. This, reader, is the gospel of Christ. Christ has come as a Savior to us in every condition and relation in life. The promises and provisions of His grace cover our entire necessities, here and hereafter. There is no condition or relation in life where His grace is not extended and where it will not be sufficient for us if we have faith to receive it. Remember, *"the just shall live by faith"* (Hebrews 10:38). Remember, also, the fearful declarations, *"If ye will not believe, surely ye shall not be established"* (Isaiah 7:9) and, *"If any man draw back, my soul shall have no pleasure in him"* (Hebrews 10:38).

Such, I repeat, is the gospel of Jesus Christ. Such a Savior is Jesus Christ to all who will receive and trust in Him. Do you love this gospel? Have you faith to receive such a Savior? If you can thus receive Him, not one "jot or tittle" of all that He has spoken and promised will fail in its accomplishment in your blessed experience. (See Matthew 5:18.) *"If thou canst believe, all things are possible to him that believeth"* (Mark 9:23).

> So let our lips and lives express
> The holy Gospel we profess;
> So let our works and virtues shine,
> To prove the doctrine all divine.[1]

1. Isaac Watts, "So Let Our Lips and Lives Express," 1707.

2

THE BELIEVER'S CONFIDENCE

"This is the confidence that we have in him, that, if we ask any thing according to his will, he heareth us: and if we know that he hear us, whatsoever we ask, we know that we have the petitions that we desired of him."
—1 John 5:14–15

In the preceding verse, the apostle informs us that his object in writing was to impart to believers a knowledge of the fact that they have eternal life in Christ and to induce in them the continued exercise of faith in the Son of God. *"These things have*

I written unto you that believe on the name of the Son of God; that ye may know that ye have eternal life, and that ye may believe on the name of the Son of God" (1 John 5:13). In the text, he imparts to us a knowledge of the *nature* of that faith we are required to exercise in Christ. *"This is the confidence that we have in him"* (1 John 5:14); that is, this is the nature of that confidence or faith the true believer exercises in Christ. It is the assurance that whenever we ask of God anything according to His will, He will hear us and bestow upon us the blessings we desire of Him. This is true faith, as it looks to God, through Christ, for the supply of all real necessities. In discussing this subject, I propose to elucidate the following propositions:

1. The meaning of the phrase *"according to his will"* as used in the text
2. The relations of Christ to the believer when He asks for blessings according to the will of God
3. The nature of the confidence referred to in the text
4. The infinite obligations resting upon us to exercise such confidence

According to His Will

The term *"will"* as applied to God is used in various and quite different senses in the Bible. Sometimes it is applied to the divine purposes or determinations. For example, Jesus said, *"Even so it is not the will* [purpose, determination, or intention] *of your Father which is in heaven, that one of these little ones should perish"* (Matthew 18:14). It is also applied to the commands of God—*"doing the will of God* [obeying the commands of God] *from the heart"* (Ephesians 6:6). It is sometimes used in a sense still different to designate the promises of God or the benevolent feelings of His heart. Thus, the Spirit "*maketh intercession for the saints according to the will of God*" (Romans 8:27). In other words, He intercedes for objects that correspond with the divine promises and the benevolent feelings of the divine mind. That the phrase "*according to his will*" is used in this last sense in the text, including, of course, that which is conformable to the commands of God, I argue from the following considerations.

It is absurd to understand the phrase as meaning "the secret purposes of God." The meaning of the phrase would then be, "If we ask anything according to His will," that is, those blessings God had previously determined to bestow upon us, "we will be heard and have the blessings we desire." But such blessings we will enjoy whether we ask for them or not. Prayer would thus be utterly useless. The question, also, of whether our prayers would be according to the divine will would be accidental and not depend at all upon the question of whether prayer, in respect to its spirit and object, corresponds with the divine will as expressed in the commands and promises of God.

Christ was not appointed as Mediator between God and man so that we, through Him, may secure the accomplishment of the secret purposes of God. Faith can never fasten upon Christ for any such object. He was appointed as Mediator, however, so that through Him the believer may secure in himself the accomplishment of the "*exceeding great and precious promises*" (2 Peter 1:4). Whenever, therefore, the prayer of the believer fastens upon any blessing available to our faith through the promises, he then asks for what is "*according to the will of God,*" as the phrase is used in the text. Such prayer is everywhere represented in the Bible as pleasing in the sight of God and, of course, as corresponding with the divine will as expressed not only in the promises but also in the divine requirements.

But an important question here arises: What are the blessings that are *"according to the will of God"* in the sense in which the phrase has now been explained? I answer in this way: any blessing, whether temporal or spiritual, that would be to us, in our circumstances, a real good. Whenever we ask for any such blessing, we ask for that which is *"according to the will of God."* This is evident from two considerations:

1. All such blessings are available to our faith in the promises. *"They that seek the Lord shall not want any good thing"* (Psalm 34:10). *"Any good thing"* is anything whatever that would be to them, in their circumstances, a real good. *"My God shall supply* ***all your need*** *according to his riches in glory by Christ Jesus"* (Philippians 4:19).
2. When the believer, in the simplicity of faith, prays for any such blessings, he asks for that which corresponds with the benevolent feelings of God's heart. A child asks an affectionate parent for some blessing that the parent sees would be to the child a real good. That petition, of course, meets a ready response in all the deep and tender sympathies of the parental heart. So it is with the believer when his prayer fixes upon anything that God sees would, if bestowed, be a real blessing to the petitioner. Such petition corresponds with all the benevolent feelings of God's heart of infinite and boundless love. The believer, then, asks for that which is *"according to the will of God"* in the sense of the text when he prays for anything that would be to him, in his circumstances, a real blessing.

Christ and the Believer

We will now consider the relations of Christ to the believer when he asks for things *"according to the will of God."*

In all such petitions, He permits us to use His name.

> *Verily, verily, I say unto you, Whatsoever ye shall ask the Father in my name, he will give it you. Hitherto have ye asked nothing in my name: ask, and ye shall receive, that your joy may be full.* (John 16:23–24)

> *And whatsoever ye shall ask in my name, that will I do, that the Father may be glorified in the Son. If ye shall ask any thing in my name, I will do it.* (John 14:13–14)

> *Ye have not chosen me, but I have chosen you, and ordained you, that ye should go and bring forth fruit, and that your fruit should remain: that whatsoever ye shall ask of the Father in my name, he may give it you.* (John 15:16)

Christian, have you comprehended the infinite privileges and boundless influence with God that Christ has conferred upon you in permitting you to use His name when you approach the throne of grace? Suppose Christ to be now upon the earth as He was eighteen hundred years ago. He comes to you and requests you to make known to Him your wants, assuring you He will then *"pray the Father for you"* (John 16:26), that these wants may be fully met. You comply with His request. Christ kneels with you and fervently beseeches the Father that, for the sake of His Son, He will confer these blessings upon you. Would you not feel absolute assurance that His prayer would secure the good desired? Now, in permitting you to use His name at the throne of grace, Christ has conferred upon you all the influence there—in respect to all necessities, temporal and spiritual—that He Himself would have in the circumstances supposed.

A poor beggar calls for the supply of his wants upon a man who has great treasures in a bank. He writes a check and directs the petitioner to go to the bank and in his name draw for the amount specified. How much influence has that beggar now at the bank, in reference to the sum named in that check? Just as much as the individual whose name he is permitted to use. So when Christ says to you, *"Ask in my name,"* He has conferred upon you, in reference to all appropriate objects of prayer, all the influence that He Himself has at the throne of grace. He has put into your hands a check upon the bank of heaven, signed by His own name—a check covering all your necessities, both temporal and spiritual, in time and eternity. He has required you by virtue of His name to draw upon the Father till every want of yours is perfectly met—till your cup of blessedness is full and overflows forever. *"Hitherto have ye asked nothing in my name: ask, and ye shall receive, that your joy may be full"* (John 16:24).

Christ not only permits us to use His name when we approach the throne of grace, but He, as our great High Priest, stands in the presence of the Father and intercedes for us. *"Wherefore he is able also to save them to the uttermost that come unto God by him, seeing he ever liveth to make intercession for them"* (Hebrews 7:25).

Suppose the beggar, in the case above, says to his benefactor, "I have no doubt that your name would be sufficient to gain my object if I could secure a hearing. But they know me only as a beggar and will at once drive me from their presence without hearing me at all."

His friend, to allay his fears, says, "I will go with you, and when you present your paper, I will request them to give you a hearing, assuring them that my name is appended to the paper that you present."

So when Christ says to the believer, "Ask in My name," He adds, "I also will pray the Father for you so that your petitions may be heard and answered." Such are the relations of Christ to the believer whenever he approaches the throne of grace for the supply of any real necessity.

The Nature of This Confidence

This confidence implies two things:

1. A full assurance that the use of Christ's name, together with His intercession, will gain the ear and heart of God so as to secure a hearing to our requests.

"And this is the confidence that we have in him, that, if we ask any thing according to his will, he heareth us" (1 John 5:14). Thus the beggar, while conscious of utter poverty and destitute of all influence at the bank, rests with perfect fixedness in the assurance that his friend's name, together with his personal influence, will secure him a favorable hearing. The same is true of faith in Christ. Its language is this: "Though infinitely guilty and vile in myself, and utterly destitute of all influence at the throne of grace, should I approach it in my own name, and while it would be infinitely dishonorable in God to listen to me for a moment, should I thus approach, yet I know and am assured that the name of Christ, together with His intercession in my behalf, will reach the ear and heart of God so that He will listen with deep and tender interest to my requests." And, Christian, what an infinite privilege is here revealed to us, the privilege of

knowing that when we pray, we are in the very audience chamber of the Most High, in the Holy of Holies of His sacred presence. We are uttering our petitions directly into the ear of the infinite God, who is listening with deep and attentive interest to all our requests, and every want we disclose strikes a chord that vibrates to the very center of His heart. Faith in Christ renders all this a felt reality to the believer. It enters as a fundamental element into the confidence we have in Him.

2. A certain assurance that the name of Christ, together with His intercession, will not only reach the ear and heart of God, so as to secure a favorable hearing, but also secure the blessings we desire of Him.

"*If we know that he hear us, whatsoever we ask, we know that we have the petitions that we desired of him*" (1 John 5:15). The beggar, as he contemplates the name of his benefactor, together with his personal influence now exerted in his behalf, says with joyful assurance, "I know that I will not only be heard but will also obtain the object I am seeking." So faith in the heart of the believer uses the name of Christ and rests in His intercession with the fixed assurance that His name and intercession will be all-influential to secure the supply of every real necessity, whatever it may be. In Christ all fullness dwells. (See Colossians 1:19.) Faith recognizes itself as complete in Him in respect to every real want here and hereafter. The believer, in the exercise of faith, under the deepest sense of his own infinite vileness and ill-desert, uses the name of Christ and rests in His intercession with the full assurance that in so doing he will realize in his own experience the entire fulfillment of the promise "*They that seek the Lord shall not want any good thing*" (Psalm 34:10). When his mind fixes upon any blessing, temporal or spiritual, and is assured that the possession of it would be to him, in his circumstances, a real good, he feels the most perfect assurance that through the name and intercession of Christ he can obtain that blessing from God.

Such, Christian, is the nature of faith in Christ. Let me ask you, Is this the character of the confidence which you have in Him? You never pray without assuring your heavenly Father that you present every petition in the name of Christ. With what feelings do you use that dear and venerable name? Is it with the peaceful assurance you will be able to secure the petitions you desire of Him? So far as you are destitute of this felt assurance of the power of His name to secure a full supply of all your need, so far you are under the influence of cruel unbelief. Let me repeat the question, Christian: What is the character of the confidence *you* have in Christ? Do you feel in your heart that the privilege of using the name of Christ and availing yourself of His intercession at the throne of grace has placed you in such relations to God that, from this time forth, you need not want any good thing, that you may now ask and receive till your joy is full, till your cup of blessedness overflows forever? This is true faith, as it uses the name of Christ at the throne of grace.

Why We Must Exercise Such Confidence

You know absolutely, Christian, God's power to bestow. You know perfectly that He is able to meet, fully and entirely, every want of yours in time and eternity. Now, when Christ has told you to go in His name to His Father and draw upon Him till your joy is full, when He has promised Himself to intercede for you, when you thus approach the throne of grace—what excuse have you for not going with the fullest assurance that every want will be met and that He will not withhold any good thing from you? (See Psalm 84:11.) Do you feel the pressure of some special want? You know that that particular necessity God is perfectly able to meet. Christ has told you to carry your desire to His Father and, in the name of the Son of His love, ask Him to meet it. Why, then, should you not comply with the injunction of Christ with the most perfect assurance that you will have the petition that you desire of Him?

The appointment of Christ as Mediator has removed all obstacles, so far as God is concerned, to the bestowment of any blessing in His power to bestow. As soon as you are ready by faith to receive the good thus provided for and offered to you, no reason in the universe exists why any real blessing should be withheld from you. Of this you are aware. Why, then, should you not use the name of Christ and rest in the efficacy of His intercession with perfect assurance that when you ask, you will receive till your joy is full (see John 16:24), that whatever you ask of the Father in Christ's name, He will give to you? Where is the excuse for unbelief?

The mediation of Christ renders it in the highest sense honorable in God to bestow the richest possible blessings in answer to requests presented in the name of Christ. Whenever blessings are bestowed on Christ's account, even upon the chief of sinners, no injury results to the character of God or to the interests of the universe, but infinite glory results to Christ. The richer the blessings thus bestowed, the higher the honor conferred upon Him.

When it is known that the bank always meets the drafts of an individual, whatever the amount may be and by whomsoever the draft is presented, this is the highest honor such an institution can confer upon such an individual. The individual presenting the draft is not honored at all, but the individual who holds the account. So when God bestows blessings upon us on Christ's account and in answer to requests presented in His name, He honors not us but Christ. When it is known that the name of Christ, even when presented by the chief of sinners, secures the richest blessings in God's power, then the highest conceivable glory goes to Christ. In the presence of such truths, Christ says to you, "Go to the Father in My name, and ask what you will, and it will be done for you." What excuse, then, have you for not using the name of Christ and resting in His intercession with the most perfect confidence that God will supply all your needs according to His riches in glory by Christ Jesus?

In the gift of Christ for our redemption, God has given the most perfect demonstration of the feelings of His heart toward us. He has shown clearly that there is no blessing in His power to bestow—nothing in existence that would bless us—that He does not desire to give us. *"He that spared not his own Son, but delivered him up for us all, how shall he not with him also freely give us all things?"* (Romans 8:32).

Now, to doubt the efficacy of Christ's name, to open the ear and move the heart of God so as to secure a supply of any necessity He is able to meet—what is it but to call in question the love of God as manifested in all the mysteries of redemption? Christian, are you not under infinite obligations to exercise this confidence? To doubt under such circumstances is to call into question the efficacy of Christ's name and intercession with God to secure the blessings we need, which are promised to all who ask in reliance upon the efficacy of His name and intercession.

Suppose the beggar above referred to, while on the way to the bank with the check of his friend in his hand, and that friend himself by his side, manifests great fears and apprehensions lest he will not be heard and obtain the good he is seeking. Suppose he expresses such fears and apprehensions to the multitude around him as he passes along. What is he doing but dishonoring his friend and benefactor by proclaiming a distrust of the efficacy of his name and influence to secure the good which he has promised? The injured man, after hearing his name dishonored a while, says to the object of his compassion, "Sir, please return to me that check. I do not choose to have my name thus dishonored. You may now obtain a supply of your necessities elsewhere."

Christian, dare you, by unbelief and doubting, when asking in the name of Christ—knowing He stands before His Father to intercede for you so that you will have what you desire of Him—thus dishonor your Savior? Can you expect He will ever allow you to use His name again? Is not this the most grievous and aggravated sin you can possibly be guilty of?

To doubt, under such circumstances, is to question the Word of God. Christ has said, *"Ask, and ye shall receive"* (John 16:24) and, *"If ye shall ask any thing in my name, I will do it"* (John 14:14). Using the name of Christ without expecting to receive the petitions you desire of Him—what is it but calling into question the Word of Christ? Christian, can you endure the thought of doing it? Unbelief does this. To ask in the name of Christ while doubting whether you will obtain the good you ask does this. Will your soul, Christian, be cut off from the infinite blessedness prepared for you because of doubting not only the efficacy of Christ's name and intercession but also His positive Word? No, take the name of Christ, and in reliance upon His intercession, *"Come boldly unto the throne of grace, that* [you] *may obtain mercy, and find grace to help in time of need"* (Hebrews 4:16).

Remarks

We are now prepared to contemplate one of the great mysteries of redemption. It is this: In himself, the Christian has nothing. No being in the universe is poorer, more *"miserable, and poor, and blind, and naked"* (Revelation 3:17). Yet in Christ, because of the Christian's relation to Him, he has all things. No being in the universe is richer. No being has greater power with God or can obtain greater blessings from Him. And all this takes place on principles perfectly honorable to God and equally consistent with the interests of the universe.

A man in one of our eastern cities experienced financial catastrophe. His credit was gone. His family was reduced to poverty, and he was involved in liabilities amounting to several hundred thousand dollars. He delivered his whole estate into the hands of his creditors and stood penniless, and worse than penniless, before the world. He had a brother, however, who was known in that city as possessing great wealth. From this brother, he received a power of attorney to transact business in the brother's name. On the authority of that brother, through the influence of his name, which he was permitted to use, he at once commenced business as one of the most efficient and prosperous merchants in the city. "In myself," said this individual to a friend of mine, "I have no credit at all. No man will trust me with a single bale of goods; yet I am really worth all that my brother is worth. I can make any purchases and upon the same terms that he can. I sometimes illustrate this fact by first offering to purchase of an individual on my own credit. He will not trust me a farthing. I tell him that I wish to obtain the goods on my brother's account. I can then purchase every article in his store."

So it is with the Christian. If he approaches the throne of grace in his own name, God thunders eternal terrors upon him.

But if he approaches in the name of Christ, God bows His ear and listens with infinite tenderness to his request. He opens all the treasures of eternity and bids the suppliant to ask what he will, and it will be done for him. No angel before the throne has a title to an estate more vast. No one can obtain greater blessings from God than he. "*O the depth of the riches both of the wisdom and knowledge of God! how unsearchable are his judgments, and his ways past finding out!*" (Romans 11:33). In the mysteries of redemption, infinite extremes meet. Yet such are the ways of God to men. Such, Christian, are your privileges consequent on your relations to Christ.

You may now, Christian, be ready to ask on what conditions all this blessedness may be yours! If you would enjoy all the good provided for you through the grace of Christ, there must be, on your part, in the first place, a deep sense of need. In yourself you have nothing to recommend you to God but infinite guilt, poverty, and wretchedness. Christ expects you to feel and acknowledge this when you appear at the throne of grace in His name. There must be implicit confidence, too, in the efficacy of Christ's name and intercession to obtain for you any blessing you need. Christian, do you feel this when you use the name of Christ at the throne of grace? Can you repose in that name as all-efficacious to procure for you any blessing you need? There must also be an actual application to God in every time of need and in respect to every necessity in full reliance upon the efficacy of the name and intercession of Christ to secure a full supply of every want. On these simple conditions, "*God shall supply all your need according to his riches in glory by Christ Jesus*" (Philippians 4:19). There is not a want of yours, temporal or spiritual, during the interminable future before you that He will leave unsupplied.

In the light of this subject, we may understand the kind of expectation demanded of us when we pray for spiritual and temporal blessings. In respect to the former, we know certainly that the possession of all such blessings in all their fullness must be a good to us. Whenever, therefore, we approach the throne of grace in the name of Christ for such blessings, we are to expect to receive the identical blessings for which we pray. The absence of such expectation is unbelief.

But when we pray for temporal blessings, we do not, in many instances, certainly know that the possession of the particular object for which we pray would be a blessing to us. We are always to pray, therefore, for such blessings, expecting that the *want* that directed the mind to the particular object in view will be met in the best possible manner. But whether it will be met by the bestowment of the particular thing specified in prayer or something else, here we are not to indulge any positive anticipations. This question God's wisdom is to decide.

A very extensive and dangerous error into which a large portion of the church has fallen here demands a passing notice. The error is this: There is great danger, it is thought, of raising expectation too high, especially in young converts, in respect to the amount of blessedness in Christ that the Christian may enjoy in this life. How careful many cold professors are to impress the young convert with the conviction that the blessedness of his first love will not long continue—that however clear the light now shines upon him may be, the days of darkness will be many and long continued. This is done to prevent the depth of gloom consequent on having previous expectation too highly raised.

Now, in respect to all finite objects, this is no doubt a wise precaution. How often, for example, is the influence of a minister greatly injured because of public expectation having previously been raised too high respecting him? But in respect to the infinite and boundless grace and love of God, precisely the reverse is always true. Here expectation cannot possibly equal the reality. "*Eye hath not seen, nor ear heard, neither have entered into the heart of man, the things which God hath prepared for them that love him*" (1 Corinthians 2:9). And when we approach the throne of grace in the name of Christ and in humble reliance upon His intercession, instead of there being any danger of our coming with expectations too highly raised, we ought to come with the most peaceful and assured expectation of obtaining "*exceeding abundantly above all that we ask or think*" (Ephesians 3:20). Who can measure the boundless love of God? Who can measure, in anticipation, the amount of blessedness the name of Christ can draw from that ocean of love when that name is used by a strong and unwavering faith at the throne of grace? Never let us entertain a thought of raising expectation too high while faith in the name of Christ keeps the heart and mouth open wide to receive the fullness that infinite love has prepared for us.

A question of this kind may here arise in the minds of some: If the Christian can obtain all real blessings through the name and intercession of Christ, why should we not ask for the instantaneous conversion of the whole world, expecting to secure that result? I answer: That could be obtained if it was on the whole best for the Christian, best for the world, and in itself possible. But God has told us the best way to have the world converted. It is by "*the foolishness of preaching*" (1 Corinthians 1:21) along with the sanctification and consequent perfect blessedness of the church. Through such instruments, and such alone, is it proper to pray that the world may be converted to God.

> *Arise, shine; for thy light is come, and the glory of the* Lord *is risen upon thee. For, behold, the darkness shall cover the earth, and gross darkness the people: but the* Lord *shall arise upon thee, and his glory shall be seen upon thee. And*

> *the Gentiles shall come to thy light, and kings to the brightness of thy rising.* (Isaiah 60:1–3)

You see, Christian, the reason you do not possess all that fullness of joy and peace that is your privilege to enjoy through the name and intercession of Christ. The want of this blessedness arises from one of two causes or both combined.

1. A lack of desire and preference for this very good

How few individuals would be satisfied to know that they will possess just that amount of temporal good, for example, and no more and no less than what infinite wisdom and love sees would be best for them? Yet unless you are in this precise state of mind, it is impossible for God to bless you. You do not possess the amount of spiritual blessings that faith in the name of Christ would procure you, because you do not appreciate their value sufficiently to seek them with all your heart.

2. A lack of confidence in the efficiency of Christ's name and intercession to secure such blessings

> *Let him ask in faith, nothing wavering* [doubting whether God will bestow the blessing asked]. *For he that wavereth [doubts] is like a wave of the sea driven with the winds and tossed. For let not that man think that he shall receive any thing of the Lord.* (James 1:6–7)

Nothing can grieve the heart of our Savior so much, nothing can be so offensive to God, as to have the name of Christ used at the throne of grace with the expectation that it will avail little to secure the blessings we need. Christian, is not this the great cause of that deep and impenetrable gloom that covers your mind if you are now in darkness? Have you appreciated the value of the privilege conferred upon you in being permitted to ask in His name? Have you reposed confidence in the efficacy of that name to procure the blessings you need and especially to fill your cup of blessedness and cause it to overflow continually? Whenever you approached the mercy seat with due confidence in the efficacy of the name of Christ to secure the petitions you desired of Him, were you sent empty away? Have you not always received exceedingly and abundantly above all that you asked or thought?

You may now, Christian, answer the question, whether you have real genuine faith in Christ or not. You know that it is your privilege to ask of the Father, in the name of Christ, for any blessing you need. What confidence do you have in the power of that name to secure the ear and move the heart of God? Do you believe—and is this truth a felt reality to your mind—that you may now, through the name of Christ alone, secure not only a hearing at the throne of grace but also a full supply of every necessity here and hereafter? Is this the confidence that you have in Christ? If so, you have the faith the gospel requires. If not, you are under the influence of unbelief. If you ever present a request to God in the name of Christ without expecting that He will hear you and that you will have the petitions you desire of Him, that prayer is put up, not in faith, but in unbelief.

We may now understand the reason of the peace-giving power of faith. A merchant, we will suppose, in looking over his books, finds that on each of ten successive days, claims amounting to a hundred thousand dollars will be brought against him and that each of these claims must be promptly met or he becomes a hopeless bankrupt. He finds his own resources wholly inadequate to such exigencies. His heart sinks into utter despondency. Just at this moment, he receives a letter from his father, a man of untold wealth, informing him that in anticipation of difficulties in which he might be involved, he had deposited in the bank for his use ten million dollars, and he may now draw at will any amount he may need. How instantly does this thick gloom give place to the highest animation and joy? He is no longer appalled at the greatness of his liabilities, because he knows that he has available resources that are more than sufficient to meet them. So the Christian, as soon as his faith fixes upon Christ, knows that whatever his necessities may be, he can, in the name and through the intercession of Christ, draw upon the resources of infinite love till at all times and under all circumstances his joy is full, till all his wants, however vast and multiplied, are perfectly met. The natural and necessary result is peace as a river and righteousness as the waves of the sea. (See Isaiah 48:18.) Faith in Christ removes every care and keys the mind in perfect peace, because it reveals boundless available resources to meet every possible exigency. *"Therefore will we not fear, though the earth be removed, and though the mountains be carried into the midst of the sea"* (Psalm 46:2). Why? *"The Lord of hosts is with us; the God of Jacob is our refuge"* (verse 7). When the believer looks only at himself and contemplates his condition as a sinner, the greatness of his guilt, the vastness of his necessities, the strength of his sinful propensities, and the number and power of his enemies, he will be appalled. But when the eye of faith turns to Christ, all fear and all apprehension arising from these causes are swallowed up and lost in the boundless resources that then open upon the enraptured vision.

How reasonable the precepts *"Be careful for nothing"* (Philippians 4:6), *"Rejoice in the Lord alway"* (Philippians 4:4), and so forth. How possible obedience to such precepts appears when contemplated in the light of this subject. Who can describe the infinite sweetness that dwells in that divine declaration, *"Ye are complete in him"* (Colossians 2:10)? Why should we not *"be careful for nothing*" and "*rejoice in the Lord alway*" when every demand of our being is so perfectly met in the infinite fullness of Christ? Christian:

> Why that look of sadness?
> Why that downcast eye?
> Can no thought of gladness
> Lift thy soul on high?
> O, thou heir of heaven,
> Think of Jesus' love,
> While to thee is given,
> All his grace to prove.[2]

We may now understand the true meaning of the command, "*Let us therefore come boldly unto the throne of grace*" (Hebrews 4:16). The beggar, as he thinks of the name attached to the check he holds in his hand and of the friend by his side who is to be surety for him at the bank, says to himself, "I know I will obtain my object." So the Christian, when he thinks of the name he is permitted to use at the throne of grace and of the Intercessor who stands to plead for him there, says in the simplicity and energy of his faith, "I know that whatsoever I ask, I will have the petition I desire of Him." This humble but fixed confidence he has in the efficacy of Christ's name and intercession to procure any blessing he needs constitutes the boldness with which he approaches the throne of grace.

It may be important for us to contemplate the doctrine of Christian perfection and the opposite doctrine as they appear in the light of this subject. The former doctrine maintains that in Christ, through faith in His name, there are available resources to the believer to meet every demand of his being throughout his endless existence. It is simply a reflection of the great truth

2. Thomas Hastings, "Hope Thou in God," 1832.

that *"ye are complete in him"* (Colossians 2:10). The opposite doctrine, on the other hand, maintains that a state of entire sanctification in this life would be a real good, the richest blessing that God could bestow, and that for this blessing, we are to approach the throne of grace and, in the name of Christ, ask the Father to confer it upon us. At the same time, it maintains that it is a dangerous error for us to indulge the expectation that the name and intercession of Christ will be efficacious to obtain this blessing. We may use the name of Christ in respect to any other blessing, expecting to receive it, but in respect to the positive promise of God to sanctify us wholly and preserve us blameless unto the coming of our Lord Jesus Christ (see 1 Thessalonians 5:23), it maintains that we are to use the same dear name with the certain expectation of *not* having the petitions we desire of Him.

Christian, when nearest to my God in the most hallowed moments of all my Christian experience, I know that doctrine cannot be true. And may I not say that in the depth of your soul, you know it also? Are these the *"good tidings of great joy"* (Luke 2:10) that He who was anointed of God to bind up all who are brokenhearted has to proclaim to those who are bound in servitude to sin—that He will never break from their necks the yoke of Satan till He takes them out of the world? Christian, the gospel *"speaketh better things"* (Hebrews 12:24) to the weary and tempest-tossed believer. It says to him, *"Ask, and ye shall receive, that your joy may be full"* (John 16:24) and, *"Let us therefore come boldly unto the throne of grace, that we may obtain mercy, and find grace to help in time of need"* (Hebrews 4:16).

A few words to my impenitent readers will close this discourse. Sinner, your necessities are infinite, and if you long remain under them, they will sink you down into eternal death.

Provisions now exist in the gospel to meet all those necessities. You also may approach the throne of grace, in the name of Christ, and obtain eternal redemption. But if you refuse to *"seek ye the LORD while he may be found"* and *"call ye upon him while he is near"* (Isaiah 55:6), how changed must your condition soon be! Soon there will be *"a great gulf fixed"* (Luke 16:26) between you and all that is pure, holy, and blessed in the universe. Soon you may to all eternity call for the least conceivable blessing, and it will not be granted you. Will that time, reader, ever come with you? Will this be your fearful doom, and will that doom receive an infinite aggravation from the recollection of what you might have been had you availed yourself of the present opportunity? *"If thou be wise, thou shalt be wise for thyself: but if thou scornest, thou alone shalt bear it"* (Proverbs 9:12).

3

FULLNESS OF JOY

"Hitherto have ye asked nothing in my name: ask, and ye shall receive, that your joy may be full."
—John 16:24

In introduction to the train of thought I will pursue in the present discourse, I will make the following observations:

1. The gospel will be, to all who truly embrace it, a life-giving and a peace-giving gospel.

> *All thy children shall be taught of the Lord; and great shall be the peace of thy children.* (Isaiah 54:13)

The redeemed of the Lord *shall return, and come with singing unto Zion; and everlasting joy shall be upon their head: they shall obtain gladness and joy; and sorrow and mourning shall flee away.* (Isaiah 51:11)

Come unto me, all ye that labour and are heavy laden, and I will give you rest. Take my yoke upon you, and learn of me; for I am meek and lowly in heart: and ye shall find rest unto your souls. For my yoke is easy, and my burden is light. (Matthew 11:28–30)

Peace I leave with you, my peace I give unto you: not as the world giveth, give I unto you. Let not your heart be troubled, neither let it be afraid. (John 14:27)

Howbeit when he, the Spirit of truth, is come, he will guide you into all truth: for he shall not speak of himself; but whatsoever he shall hear, that shall he speak: and he will show you things to come. (John 16:13)

The spirit of the Lord God *is upon me; because the* Lord *hath anointed me to preach good tidings to the meek; he hath sent me to bind up the brokenhearted, to proclaim liberty to the captives, and the opening of the prison to them that are bound.* (Isaiah 61:1)

2. The peace the believer receives through the gospel will be at all times and under all circumstances full, permanent, and uninterrupted.

Whosoever drinketh of the water that I shall give him shall never thirst; but the water that I shall give him shall be in

him a well of water springing up into everlasting life.
(John 4:14)

These things have I spoken unto you, that my joy might remain in you, and that your joy might be full.
(John 15:11)

The sun shall be no more thy light by day; neither for brightness shall the moon give light unto thee: but the Lord *shall be unto thee an everlasting light, and thy God thy glory. Thy sun shall no more go down; neither shall thy moon withdraw itself: for the* Lord *shall be thine everlasting light, and the days of thy mourning shall be ended.*
(Isaiah 60:19–20)

3. *This blessedness is represented in the Bible as the common experience of the early Christians.*

Whom [Jesus Christ] *having not seen, ye love; in whom, though now ye see him not, yet believing, ye rejoice with joy unspeakable and full of glory.* (1 Peter 1:8)

The Bible says it is through this fullness of joy in the believer, when seen and apprehended by the world, that the world will be converted to Christ.

Arise, shine; for thy light is come, and the glory of the Lord *is risen upon thee. For, behold, the darkness shall cover the earth, and gross darkness the people: but the* Lord *shall arise upon thee, and his glory shall be seen upon thee. And the Gentiles shall come to thy light, and kings to the brightness of thy rising.* (Isaiah 60:1–3)

This fullness of joy is presented in the Bible, not only as the privilege of the believer, but as a sacred duty. *"Rejoice in the Lord alway: and again I say, Rejoice"* (Philippians 4:4). *"Finally, my brethren, rejoice in the Lord"* (Philippians 3:1).

Hence we see, Christian, that to the extent that you are destitute of this fullness of joy, to that same extent you are disqualified for the great work to which God has called you. *"The joy of the LORD is your strength"* (Nehemiah 8:10). If the joy of the Lord does not dwell in you in all its fullness, your strength in His service will be weakness.

Hence we also perceive that any professed view of the redemption of Christ that does not fill up the Christian's cup of blessedness and cause it to overflow continually cannot be from heaven. To suppose this is to suppose the gospel to embrace palpable contradictions; such an idea defeats one of the revealed purposes of redemption. The object of the present discourse will be to illustrate the following propositions:

1. The state of the individual whose joy is full in the sense of the text
2. The objects embraced in the command and promise *"Ask, and it shall be given you"* (Matthew 7:7)
3. The obligations resting upon all believers to ask and receive this fullness of joy
4. The spirit with which this blessedness should be sought

The State of Fullness of Joy

The fullness of joy here referred to implies a degree of blessedness corresponding with the capacities of the subject in the circumstances of our present existence. The term *full,* in its ordinary acceptation, denotes this much to whatever subject it is applied. To be particular, I would remark:

1. Fullness of joy does not of necessity imply the entire absence of external affliction.

On the other hand, the design of the Savior is that the peace-giving power of the gospel will be rendered preeminently conspicuous when it fills the believer's cup of blessedness even in the furnace of affliction.

> *When thou passest through the waters, I will be with thee; and through the rivers, they shall not overflow thee: when thou walkest through the fire, thou shalt not be burned; neither shall the flame kindle upon thee.* (Isaiah 43:2)

How glorious the gospel appears when it is seen to possess the power not only to fill the believer's cup of blessedness in the midst of such afflictions, but to cause him even to rejoice in tribulation and to render him in the midst of "*persecution, or famine, or nakedness, or peril, or sword*" (Romans 8:35). "*We are more than conquerors through him that loved us*" (Romans 8:37). We may readily conceive that an individual might be brought into such a relation to external afflictions that they will constitute an important ingredient of his fullness of joy.

It would be in itself a great calamity to an individual to have the house containing his whole estate consumed by fire. Suppose, however, that the conflagration reveals to him treasures a hundred times more valuable than all he before possessed—treasures that, but for that calamity, he would never have discovered. The otherwise untoward event ever after becomes a source of great blessedness to him. A true patriot also would rejoice in the loss of all his worldly possessions if, by that means, his country could be saved. So the Christian, when by faith he perceives that all his *"light affliction, which is but for a moment"* is working out for him *"a far more exceeding and eternal weight of glory"* (2 Corinthians 4:17)—when he perceives also that by these same afflictions Christ is honored and His kingdom advanced—then, indeed, he rejoices in tribulation. The believer's love for Christ also may, and ought to be, so great as to render all afflictions endured for His sake the source of the highest blessedness. It was so with the early believers. Among the sources of their purest gratitude and joy was the fact that they were *"counted worthy to suffer shame for his name"* (Acts 5:41).

2. *Neither does fullness of joy imply the entire absence of all physical suffering.*

For the reasons above stated, the mind may be brought into such a relation to physical sufferings that they may constitute important ingredients in its cup of blessedness. A young man was called to undergo a surgical operation through which there was but a faint probability that he would survive. Before it commenced, he was told that if at any time there should be a cessation in the operation, he might know that it was unsuccessful and that he would die under it. At length, for reasons not anticipated by the operators, there was a pause. It was to the subject a moment of inconceivable suspense and agony. He dared not speak. That might be death to him. But was not the deep silence around the certain indication of speedy dissolution? Soon, however, a painful sensation indicated the operation had been resumed. He said that the painful sensation was to him the most blissful feeling he had ever experienced. The mind of that young man was brought into such a relation to bodily pain of a certain kind that it was a source of the highest blessedness to him.

Now, the gospel is able to bring the mind into a similar relation to physical suffering of every kind that we are called to endure in this life, and this it does accomplish for all who exercise the faith that is required. *"Thou wilt keep him in perfect peace, whose mind is stayed on thee"* (Isaiah 26:3). The Bible does not promise to the believer perfect freedom from physical suffering. It does, however, on the condition of simple faith, promise perfect peace or entire fullness of joy. Consequently, it promises to bring the believer into such a relation to all physical suffering that it will not be a source of real unhappiness but will constitute one of the sources of that perfect peace into which steady and unwavering faith introduces the mind.

James Brainerd Taylor speaks of bodily pain as a source of great blessedness to him, while his faith was reposing upon the bosom of Christ. Christ brought the mind of Paul into such a relation, not only to external afflictions, but to physical sufferings, that he took pleasure in them. The same was true of early saints. The same is true, I repeat, of every believer whose faith is steadfast and unmovable in the promises of God.

3. The fullness of joy referred to in the text does not imply the total absence of what may be called mental sorrow.

Perfect blessedness is the state that results from conscious obedience to all God's commandments. Among the divine requirements we find a class of precepts like the following: *"Rejoice with them that do rejoice, and weep with them that weep"* (Romans 12:15). To pour out our hearts, then, for objects that demand tears of us is not inconsistent with fullness of joy but is, rather, essential to it.

Let me say here that every person who is deeply read in Christian experience is fully aware that feelings of deep and tender sympathy for the afflicted and oppressed—that tears poured out like water over past sins and over sinners exposed to the pangs of the second death, and that what may be called agonizing prayer for the redemption of lost men—are among the streams of pure and perfect blessedness that flow through a truly sanctified mind. To such a mind, such feelings and exercises are by no means unwelcome guests. They disturb not its deep repose upon the bosom of bliss. On the other hand, they set in motion those profound and tender emotions that draw the soul into a state of blessedness more complete than could otherwise be enjoyed.

4. Neither does fullness of joy imply that the mind is always in a state of the highest conceivable ecstasy.

Present circumstances and capacities of the mind do not permit it to always be in this state. Nor have we any evidence that this is the fixed and unvarying form of the blessedness of heaven. There is, in a deep and pervading serenity of mind, a blessedness as full and perfect as in ecstatic joy. The mind may pass and repass from one of these states to the other; the character of the blessedness in such respects may almost continually vary and its joy always be full. What, then, does the fullness of joy referred to imply?

5. It implies the conscious absence of everything that would be to the mind a real evil.

"There shall no evil befall thee, neither shall any plague come nigh thy dwelling" (Psalm 91:10). Suppose the mind is brought into such a conscious relation to God and the universe that this precious promise, in all its fullness, is fulfilled in its experience, and the mind itself is perfectly aware of the fact. It then possesses one of the essential elements of the fullness of joy under consideration.

6. This state implies the conscious available possession of everything that would be to the mind, in its present state, a real blessing and that is necessary to meet perfectly every real want, every real demand of its being, here and in eternity.

"All things work together for good to them that love God" (Romans 8:28). *"All things are yours; whether Paul, or Apollos, or Cephas, or the world, or life, or death, or things present, or things to come; all are yours; and ye are Christ's; and Christ is God's"* (1 Corinthians 3:21–23). Whenever the mind comes into such a conscious relation as this to God and to all beings and objects in time and eternity, its joy will be full. Its positive enjoyment will be as great as its present capacities and circumstances permit. What blessedness more pure, full, and perfect can we conceive of than this?

7. In short, the fullness of joy referred to in the text implies the same blessedness, in kind and degree, as far as our capacities permit, that Christ enjoyed when on earth.

"Peace," says Christ, *"I leave with you, my peace* [the peace I enjoy] *I give unto you"* (John 14:27). This, Christian, is the fullness of joy offered to you in the gospel. This is the blessedness; it is both your duty and your privilege to enjoy.

The Objects Embraced in "Ask, and Ye Shall Receive, That Your Joy May Be Full"

This command and promise do not embrace and offer to us everything that, for the time being, may *appear* to us to be a good. On account of our limited knowledge, the possession of certain things may appear to us necessary to the fullness of our joy, while God may know that they are not. Thus, Paul felt for a time that the removal of the thorn in his flesh was necessary to his complete blessedness, while to the mind of God, the highest happiness of the apostle required the continuance of the thorn. (See 2 Corinthians 12:7–9.)

But this command and promise do embrace and offer everything God sees necessary to our perfect blessedness, everything really necessary to the entire fullness of our joy. God knows perfectly what things are necessary to meet every demand of our being. Whatever He sees to be necessary to this end, we are authorized and required to look to Him for, in the name of Christ, with the certain expectation of receiving it at His hands. *"Ask, and ye shall receive, that your joy may be full"* (John 16:24). Christian, whatever is necessary to fill your cup of blessedness and keep it full is here offered to you. This is the table that infinite love has spread for us here in this wilderness. Let not unbelief reject the good thus tendered to us, because it is so great. Let us not stagger at the promise of God but be strong in the faith, giving glory to God. (See Romans 4:20.)

The Obligation to Ask and Receive Fullness of Joy

This fullness of joy was left us by our Savior, as a legacy, when He ascended to His Father and our Father, to His God and our God. (See John 20:17.) *"Peace I leave with you, my peace I give unto you: not as the world giveth, give I unto you"* (John 14:27). *"These things I speak in the world, that they might have my joy fulfilled in themselves"* (John 17:13). Whatever Christ has thus left us, we have no right to reject. We wrong our own souls, our Savior, and the world if we do it.

Christ requires this of us. *"Ask* [a positive command], *and ye shall receive, that your joy may be full"* (John 16:24). *"Let the peace of God rule in your hearts, to the which also ye are called in one body"* (Colossians 3:15). Here we are not only required to let the peace that God enjoys rule in our hearts, but it is also declared that the enjoyment of this blessedness is one of the great objects of our sacred calling as Christians. Christian, if you were convicted of such sins as falsehood, theft, or blasphemy, you would be overwhelmed with a sense of guilt and shame before God and men. Did you ever reflect on the truth that when your joy is not full and when the peace of God does not rule in your hearts, you are living in disobedience to requirements equally sacred? You have no more right to be filled with care and perplexity; you have no more right to let that aching void within remain unfilled with joy unspeakable and full of glory than you have to blaspheme the worthy name by which you are called.

Unless Christians possess this fullness of joy, Christ's testimony about the effects of believing in Him can never appear to the world as a reality.

> *He that believeth in me, though he were dead, yet shall he live: and whosoever liveth and believeth in me shall never die.*
>
> (John 11:25–26)

> *He that believeth on the Son hath everlasting life.*
>
> (John 3:36)

> *Whosoever drinketh of the water that I shall give him shall never thirst; but the water that I shall give him shall be in him a well of water springing up into everlasting life.*
>
> (John 4:14)

Christian, you profess to exercise the very faith in Christ that is here referred to. You profess to have drunk of the waters He gives. Does your experience correspond with the above declarations of Christ? If not, that experience affirms to the world that His testimony is not true. As you would have the Savior appear to the world as a faithful and true witness, you are bound to comply with the requirement of the text, *"Ask, and ye shall receive, that your joy may be full"* (John 16:24).

The honor of Christ, as the head of the church, requires that all believers possess this fullness of joy. You enter a family circle and find that the presence of the husband and father is a source of the highest blessedness to his household and is essential to their fullness of joy. How that husband and father is honored, in your estimation, by such a fact. On the other hand, suppose you find his presence a source of gloom and terror to that circle, that they are blessed only when he is absent. What dishonor does such a fact attach to the character of the head of that family!

Now Christ sustains the same relation to the church that the husband or father does to the family circle. If He is seen to be her life—if in His presence her joy is full and in His service her peace is as a river and her righteousness as the waves of the sea—then He, as the head of the church, receives the highest honor before the world. But if the opposite is true of her experience in the service of Christ, if His yoke and burden appear to weigh her down into a state of gloom and despondency, the highest conceivable dishonor results to Christ before the world. The reproaches that ought to fall upon her fall upon Him. Who will honor the dear and venerable name of Christ when it has ceased to be a source of pure and perfect blessedness to His own friends? What infinite guilt must rest upon us if we thus dishonor our Savior when He has permitted and required us to come to the throne of grace and, in His name, "ask and receive till our joy is full." (See John 16:24.)

This fullness of joy in Christ is indispensable to the most energetic action in His service. *"The joy of the Lord is your strength"* (Nehemiah 8:10). When the presence of Christ has rendered our blessedness complete, when it is a felt reality to our minds that we may at all times and under all circumstances approach the throne of grace and in the name of Christ ask and receive a full supply of every necessity, then indeed in His service, whatever burdens He lays upon us, we can mount up on wings as eagles, run and not be weary, and walk and not faint. (See Isaiah 40:31.) But just as far as the peace of God does not rule in our hearts, so far we are weak and powerless in His service. If then, Christian, you would be *"strong in the Lord, and in the power of his might"* (Ephesians 6:10), stand at the throne of grace and, in the name of Christ, ask till your joy is full.

Our influence with the world requires that we ourselves possess this fullness of joy. How valuable must that gospel appear to sinners when it is seen, under every variety of condition, to fill up the believer's joy and cause it to overflow continually. How valuable must the name of Christ appear to the sinner when he sees that by and through that name, at the throne of grace, the believer can and does obtain a complete supply of every necessity.

Christian, you can recommend that gospel and that dear and venerable name to the sinner with great power and confidence when such has been their visible influence in your experience! Do remember that to the extent that they have failed to prove valuable in your experience, their estimated value will be diminished when you recommend them to the world.

The Spirit with Which This Blessedness Should Be Sought

The great question is: In what attitude of mind does it become us, guilty and vile as we are, to appear in the presence of

God to ask such a blessing at His hands? When we contemplate the feelings of Mary as she washed our Savior's feet with her tears and wiped them with the hair of her head, surely similar feelings become ours when we approach the feet of our Father in heaven and ask Him now to fill our cup of blessedness and cause it to overflow forever. When also we contemplate the feelings of the aged apostle when he exclaimed, *"Behold, what manner of love the Father hath bestowed upon us, that we should be called the sons of God"* (1 John 3:1), surely similar feelings become ours when we ask of God a full and perfect supply of every necessity in time and eternity. With what feelings, then, we should approach the throne of grace to ask such infinite and boundless blessings as these!

It becomes us to appear in the attitude of the deepest penitence and contrition and with the most humble and hearty confession of our guilt and vileness in His sight. In no other attitude, surely, does it become sinners to ask God to fill our cup of blessedness and cause it to overflow forever.

There must be a proper appreciation of the infinite grace and kindness of God in the bestowment of such blessings upon such creatures. Were you now, Christian, to present your cup to your Father in heaven and to ask Him to fill it with unmingled blessedness, could you appreciate the infinite grace and kindness manifested in meeting such a request? Would your gratitude and love in any degree correspond with the blessings received?

We must ask with the most implicit confidence in God's ability and willingness to confer upon us the very fullness of joy that we ask and in the fact that it is our privilege to receive it. A great many persons, when we tell them that it is the privilege of the believer to be kept in perfect peace in this life, will not admit it. They will not admit that provisions exist in the gospel for our fullness of joy or that God is willing or intends to confer any such blessing upon the believer in this life. Such persons are not in an attitude to receive *"the things which God hath prepared for them that love him"* (1 Corinthians 2:9).

And let me say here that if we thus limit the grace of God, we wrong our own souls. But if we will not stagger at the promise of God through unbelief but will be strong in the faith, giving glory unto God, and be fully persuaded that what He has promised He is able also to perform (see Romans 4:21), then, Christian, there is no good thing that He will withhold from us (see Psalm 84:11). We may ask what we will, and it will be done unto us. (See Mark 6:23.)

We must ask in the name of Christ with the most peaceful assurance and expectation that His name will secure the blessing we seek. Christ has set before us an open door to the throne of grace and has required us to come boldly and to ask and receive till our joy is full. Under such circumstances, we must *"ask in faith, nothing wavering"* (James 1:6); otherwise, we should not expect to receive anything from the Lord. (See James 1:7.) Now, Christian, can you do this? Can you spread out your entire necessities before God with the assurance that He, for Christ's sake, will meet them all? *"Open thy mouth wide, and I will fill it"* (Psalm 81:10). *"Whatsoever ye shall ask the Father in my name, he will give it you"* (John 16:23). Christian, *"believest thou this?"* (John 11:26). *"If thou canst believe, all things are possible to him that believeth"* (Mark 9:23).

While we thus ask God to meet all our necessities, we must present our whole being as a willing sacrifice to Him to be employed in His service. On no other condition have we a right to ask or expect such fullness of the Lord. *"Having therefore these promises, dearly beloved, let us cleanse ourselves from all filthiness of the flesh and spirit, perfecting holiness in the fear of the Lord"* (2 Corinthians 7:1). Let us present our bodies as a living sacrifice, holy and acceptable unto the Lord, which is our reasonable service. (See Romans 12:1.) Christian, are you willing to do this? Are you willing to suffer the loss of all things for Christ (see Philippians 3:8) and let God dwell in you and walk with you as your God, you being His son or His daughter forever? If you can do this with all your heart, then, in the name of the Lord, let me assure you that…

> *Because thou hast made the Lord, which is my refuge, even the most High, thy habitation; there shall no evil befall thee, neither shall any plague come nigh thy dwelling.*
> (Psalm 91:9–10)

> *Surely he shall deliver thee from the snare of the fowler, and from the noisome pestilence. He shall cover thee with his feathers, and under his wings shalt thou trust: his truth shall be thy shield and buckler.* (Verses 3–4)

Remarks

We may now understand what the appropriate objects of prayer are. Anything the mind apprehends as a good is an appropriate object of prayer. When the removal of any particular evil or the possession of any particular blessing, whether temporal or spiritual, appears as a good to the mind, we are to make known our requests to God. The same will hold true in respect to prayer, both for ourselves and others.

We may also understand the nature of the sovereignty God exercises in respect to prayer put up in faith for such objects. He does not, as many seem to suppose, exercise an arbitrary sovereignty in giving or withholding the object prayed for. He always answers the prayer of faith by meeting the want that prompted the request and meeting it by giving the blessing most perfectly adapted to meet it. If the particular object specified in prayer is better adapted than any other to meet this want, this particular object is granted. But if some other object will best accomplish this end, this will be given instead of the one specified—which is only to say that it is the spirit of the prayer that is answered and not the letter.

Thus, when Paul prayed that the thorn in his flesh might be taken away, God saw that the promise *"My grace is sufficient for thee"* (2 Corinthians 12:9) would be a greater blessing and would more perfectly meet the want that prompted the prayer than the removal of the evil specified—or the promise together with the removal of the evil—could be. Hence, the want was met by the bestowment, not of the particular thing specified, but of something else better adapted to meet that want. This is the sovereignty, and the only sovereignty, I suppose, that God exercises in respect to the prayer of faith. When we ask bread, He does not give us a stone. When we ask a fish, He does not give us a serpent! Nor does He ever deny our requests.

"Every one that asketh receiveth" (Matthew 7:8), and we always receive that which is best adapted to meet the want that prompted our request. What a blessed sovereignty this is to have infinite wisdom and love always answer prayer by the bestowment of the blessing best adapted to meet the want that prompted the prayer.

In the light of this subject, we may contemplate the power of the gospel to bless the believer in every condition of life. The text was originally and primarily addressed to the twelve apostles, and it disclosed to them the blessedness they were authorized to expect while prosecuting the great work Christ had devolved upon them. Let us look for a moment at the external circumstances through which they would be called to pass. Christ, in the first place, was to be removed from them, and by this means, all their long-cherished plans of worldly aggrandizement were to be wholly defeated. They were likewise to be wholly cut off from those prospects of worldly acquisitions of every kind upon which mankind place so much value. They were also to become the objects of the universal contempt and curses of mankind and were to stand before the world as the offscouring of all things. They were finally to be subjected to the greatest sufferings and cruelties and even to death itself. Those who killed them would think they did God service. Everything, in short, in their external circumstances did exist and was to exist to render them comfortlessly wretched. Yet in the midst of such circumstances, Christ promised them a perfect fullness of joy. *"Ask, and ye shall receive, that your joy may be full"* (John 16:24). What power must there be in a religion that can not only render men perfectly blessed under such circumstances but can also make those very circumstances into sources of blessedness to their minds.

This power the gospel possessed eighteen hundred years ago, and reader, the power it possessed then, it possesses now. *"Jesus Christ is the same yesterday, and to day. and for ever"* (Hebrews 13:8). His gospel is also the same. He is as able and willing to bless you through that gospel as He was to bless His ancient disciples. Nothing but unbelief separates you from all this blessedness.

Let us contemplate the actual condition of the church as contrasted with her high and blessed privileges. A pastor in one of our eastern cities, an opposer of the doctrine of Christian perfection, once remarked that the individual who had for years been regarded as one of the most consistent Christians in that city was, in his opinion, one of the most unhappy men in it. A minister in another city, in reply to some remarks on the condition of the church, said that there were two brethren in that city who, he was sure, did know the gospel as a life-giving and peace-giving gospel. I replied that I had seen one of these men, who, a short time since, had informed me that as a Christian, he was exceedingly unhappy and unblessed and that he knew of no other Christian in a better state.

The ministers and elders of a leading Presbytery had met for prayer and religious conversation some years since. The brother who presided commenced the relation of Christian experience, saying that the uniform character of his experience was that of despondency, and he closed by remarking that nothing but fear prevented his leaving the ministry. The other members, with the exception of the pastor and elders of a single church, who had embraced different views of the gospel from their brethren, followed in a similar strain.

A question here arises, *Is this a fair representation of the state of the great mass of our churches?* What is the uniform confession of a vast majority of the church throughout the length and breadth of the land? What do her favorite hymns indicate in respect to her spiritual state? Is it not true that those hymns that were designed for backsliders are the standing hymns through which the church expresses her permanent condition? Take the following stanzas as examples:

Where is the blessedness I knew,
When first I saw the Lord?
Where is the soul-refreshing view
Of Jesus and his Word?

What peaceful hours I once enjoyed!
How sweet their memory still!
But they have left an aching void
The world can never fill.[3]

Look how we grovel here below,
Fond of these trifling toys;
Our souls can neither fly nor go
To reach eternal joys.[4]

These and similar hymns were designed for backsliders and express the very feelings with which they ought to return to God. But does not the church sing them as indicative of her permanent state? Now what an appalling state of things do such facts indicate! What fearful backsliding and apostasy! What dreadful abandonment of the Spirit of God and of the consolations of His presence and love! One would almost think God must be a wilderness to Israel. Yet the gospel was designed to be to all believers *"a place of broad rivers and streams"* (Isaiah 33:21). *"In the Lord Jehovah is everlasting strength"* (Isaiah 26:4), and He has promised that

> *They that wait upon the Lord shall renew their strength; they shall mount up with wings as eagles; they shall run, and not be weary; and they shall walk, and not faint.*
> (Isaiah 40:31)

Yet the church complains that she "can neither fly nor go, to reach eternal joys." God has declared that *"the path of the just is as the shining light, that shineth more and more unto the perfect day"* (Proverbs 4:18). The church complains that the path has been waxing more and more obscure ever since she entered it.

3. William Cowper, "O for a Closer Walk with God," 1772.
4. Isaac Watts, "Come, Holy Spirit, Heavenly Dove," 1707.

O *"tell it not in Gath, publish it not in the streets of Askelon...lest the daughters of the uncircumcised triumph"* (2 Samuel 1:20).

We may now see how it is that the church often proclaims her own disgrace and disgraces her Lord and Savior when she is not aware of the fact. Suppose that, as one enters a family circle, he hears the husband and wife complaining of a want of enjoyment in each other's society, speaking of the time soon after their union as the most happy period they had enjoyed together and affirming that the remembrance of that period had left an aching void in their hearts that nothing to be met within their present associations could fill. Would not each of these individuals, by such disclosures, proclaim the other's shame in the most flagrant manner conceivable? Yet the church can give utterance, before God and the world, to precisely similar sentiments respecting her union with her Savior and her God—and do it without blushing and without the least apparent apprehension that in so doing she is proclaiming her own disgrace and dishonoring her Maker and her Redeemer. It would seem we have been so long accustomed to dishonoring our Savior that it has almost, in our estimation, ceased to be a crime. Did you ever reflect, Christian, that the highest dishonor you can cast upon your Savior is to proclaim to the world that the period of your first love is the most blessed portion of your Christian experience and that when you first saw the Lord you were most blessed in Him? Well may the Lord say, "Be ashamed and confounded, every one of you, because you have thus dishonored your Redeemer, the Holy One of Israel." (See Isaiah 45:16.)

We may now understand one of the grand secrets of the success of the gospel, as preached by the apostles and early Christians. Take a single passage in illustration:

> *Blessed be God, even the father of our Lord Jesus Christ, the Father of mercies, and the God of all comfort; who comforteth us in all our tribulation, that we may be able to comfort them which are in any trouble, by the comfort wherewith we ourselves are comforted of God. For as the sufferings of Christ abound in us, so our consolation also aboundeth by Christ.* (2 Corinthians 1:3–5)

They proclaimed the gospel as a full and perfect remedy for every evil, as able to meet entirely every necessity to our condition as creatures and sinners. They did this also with the most implicit confidence in the power of the gospel to produce such results, because they had, in every variety of condition, tested its power and experienced such results from it in their own souls. Now is it at all wonderful that a gospel—every promise and declaration of which was thus verified in the visible experience of those who proclaimed it—should be *"mighty through God to the pulling down of strong holds"* (2 Corinthians 10:4). Is it wonderful that men proclaiming such a gospel with such an experience of its efficacy should turn the world upside down. (See Acts 17:6.)

Permit me here to express the solemn conviction that no one is qualified to preach this gospel or to urge its reception upon sinners who has not a similar experience of its power. The manifest and palpable want of this experience on the part of those who now proclaim it is the sole reason why it is not as mighty in their hands as it was in the hands of its first advocates.

We may now notice the question, whether a state of entire sanctification is in this life attainable in such a sense as to be an object of rational expectation. To determine this, we need only to answer two questions:

1. Are we authorized to pray in the name of Christ that "the very God of peace may sanctify us wholly"? (See 1 Thessalonians 5:23.)
2. Is the bestowment of this blessing or the attainment of this state essential to the fullness of the believer's joy?

There is not a real Christian on earth who will not answer each of these questions in the affirmative. Then, if there is a blessing in the universe that we are authorized to pray for with the expectation of receiving—in view of the command *"Ask, and ye shall receive, that your joy may be full"* (John 16:24)—it must be this. For none other is so indispensable to the fullness of our joy. If the opposers of this doctrine can prove either that we are not authorized to pray in the name of Christ for complete sanctification in this life or that this blessing is not essential to the fullness of our joy, then the doctrine falls to the ground. If they cannot do this, the doctrine is founded upon a rock, and the gates of hell can never prevail against it.

Another important test that we may apply to this and the opposite doctrine to determine which must be in accordance with the Word of God here presents itself to our contemplation. One of these doctrines, as all admit, must be true. It will also be admitted that the doctrine that must be true is the belief that is best adapted to render the joy of the believer full. Let us test these two doctrines in the light of these self-evident principles. According to both, we are authorized to pray, in the name of Christ, for entire sanctification in this life. According to both, the attainment of this state is indispensable to the fullness of our joy. If the doctrine of Christian perfection is true, we are authorized and required to pray in the name of Christ for perfection in holiness, expecting to receive the blessing for which we pray. If the opposite doctrine is true, we are to pray in the name of Christ for the same identical blessing, with the absolute certainty of *not* receiving it. Which belief, let me ask, is most favorable to fullness of joy? If the latter is true, is not the declaration *"Ask, and ye shall receive, that your joy may be full"* (John 16:24) the perfection of absurdity?

I close this discourse with a solemn question to every believer in Christ. You know, my brother, that Christ has set before you a wide-open door to the throne of grace. He has required you to come and ask in His name till your joy is full. Will you comply with this command of your blessed Lord? Remember, nothing grieves Him more or dishonors Him before the world to a greater degree than to have one of His redeemed ones unblessed. Will you stand at the throne of grace till He restores unto you the joys of His salvation and upholds you by His free spirit (see Psalm 51:12), and then go forth to teach transgressors His ways so that sinners may be converted to Him (see Psalm 51:13)? *"If ye know these things, happy are ye if ye do them"* (John 13:17).

4

LIFE ETERNAL

"And this is life eternal, that they might know thee the only true God, and Jesus Christ, whom thou hast sent."
—John 17:3

The term *life*, in its most general sense, designates "that state of animals and plants or of organized being in which its natural functions are performed or in which its organs are capable of performing their functions." In the Bible, when applied to the mind, it designates "existence in a state of perfect blessedness." *"I am come that they might have life, and that they might have it more abundantly*" (John 10:10). By the phrase "*life eternal,*" as used in the text, we are to understand a state of blessedness as great as the capacities of the subject permit and endless in its duration. The knowledge of God and of Jesus Christ referred to in the text implies:

1. An apprehension of the real character of the "*only true God, and Jesus Christ, whom* [He] *hast sent,*" especially as that character is revealed in the great plan of redemption
2. A knowledge of this character in the relations God sustains with us as sinners redeemed, sanctified, and saved by His grace

A single fact will illustrate the thought here presented. Two men, the one aged and the other in the meridian of life—the former in a state of poverty and affliction, the latter possessed of affluence—met on the plains of Italy. As they entered into conversation, each became greatly interested in the other's character and history. Soon, however, a fact was stated by one of the parties that simultaneously revealed to each the endearing relation he sustained to the other, and with the exclamations "My father!", "My son!", they were instantly locked in each other's arms. How immeasurably heightened was the interest each felt in the other's character when that character was contemplated in the light of the endearing relation of father and son. So it is with the believer. Were he brought into such circumstances that the infinite perfections and glory of God should be distinctly apprehended by him, irrespective of any relations existing between him and God, the divine character would, even then, be an object of inconceivable interest to his mind. But how immeasurably heightened is this interest when, in the presence of such apprehensions, the believer can say, "This is my Father and my God. He is my shield and my exceeding great reward"?

(See Genesis 15:1.) On this point I will have occasion to speak again in the progress of the present discourse.

This knowledge implies the harmony of the soul with the entire character of God, as thus apprehended. Fallen spirits have intellectual apprehensions of the character of God full and distinct. But because of the opposition of their hearts to Him, He is to them *"a consuming fire"* (Hebrews 12:29). To know God as an object of supreme love and delight is the knowledge referred to in the text.

With these observations, I would remark that the following truths are clearly revealed in the text and context:

First, the possession of this knowledge, in connection with the state of mind above referred to, is life eternal. In other words, it induces a state of blessedness as great as the capacities of the subject permit and endless in its duration.

Second, Christ bestows eternal life upon those who love Him by communicating to them knowledge of the character of the only living and true God and of Himself, as sent of God, as the Savior of the world. When we ask Christ to confer eternal life upon us, it is the same thing as asking Him to impart to us this knowledge. This is the fountain of the water of life, of which He freely gives to all who are thirsty. (See Revelation 21:6.)

Third, Christ has received unlimited power and authority from the Father to confer this knowledge and consequent perfect and eternal blessedness upon all who have been given to Him by the Father; that is, upon all true believers. For all such, and such only, have been given to Christ for this purpose.

> *As thou hast given him power over all flesh, that he should give eternal life to as many as thou hast given him. And this*

> *is life eternal, that they might know thee the only true God, and Jesus Christ, whom thou hast sent.* (John 17:2–3)

Fourth, Christ is now able and willing to impart this knowledge and consequent blessedness to all who will believe in Him; *"Come unto me, all ye that labour and are heavy laden, and I will give you rest"* (Matthew 11:28). *"I will give unto him that is athirst of the fountain of the water of life freely"* (Revelation 21:6).

Fifth, this knowledge, the possession of which is life eternal, no person in existence can impart to us but Jesus Christ. That knowledge that Christ is empowered to bestow, no other being can bestow, nor can we derive it from any other source. *"No man knoweth the Son, but the Father; neither knoweth any man the Father, save the Son, and he to whomsoever the Son will reveal him"* (Matthew 11:27). The attention of the reader is now invited to a consideration of the following propositions:

1. To all who love God, a knowledge of the "only living and true God, and of Jesus Christ, whom He hath sent, is eternal life" (See John 17:3.)
2. The condition on which Christ will impart this knowledge and consequent blessedness to us

Possession of This Knowledge Will Be Eternal Life

In other words, it will induce a state of blessedness as great as the capacities of the subject will permit and endless in duration. It transforms the whole moral character into a perfect resemblance to that of Christ. The infinite and perfect blessedness of God results from the conscious possession of infinite and perfect holiness. Just so far as the believer enters into a conscious possession of a character like that of God, as revealed in the plan of redemption, so far, to the extent of his capacities, he possesses the pure and perfect blessedness that God Himself enjoys. Now the possession of the knowledge here referred to results in the full and conscious possession of such a character.

"We all, with open face beholding as in a glass the glory of the Lord, are changed into the same image from glory to glory, even as by the Spirit of the Lord" (2 Corinthians 3:18). Let Christ lift the veil, Christian, and show you His glory, as He is able and willing to do by His Spirit, and you would be like Him. Your whole moral character will be transformed into His likeness. The natural result will be that His joy would be fulfilled in you. (See John 17:13.) The blessedness He enjoys would be yours to the full extent of your capacities. And this would be life eternal. This would be the life eternal that God enjoys and that the pure spirits around His throne possess.

Such knowledge of God, such apprehension of the infinite glory and love of Christ, induces the continued exercise of that perfect love that is the consummation of blessedness. The highest happiness of which we are susceptible arises from the strong and continued exercise of the benevolent affections. Any object that can call forth these affections and induce their strong and continued exercise will render us in the highest degree blessed. Now there is but one object in existence that is capable of doing this. It is a revelation of *"the knowledge of the glory of God in the face of Jesus Christ"* (2 Corinthians 4:6). Let the Spirit of God take of the things of Christ and show them to the believer; let Him impart to him full and distinct apprehensions of His glory. Let the Most High cause all His goodness to pass before him—and the result is that *"the fountains of the great deep"* of feeling and affection in the soul are *"broken up"* (Genesis 7:11). The tide of love rolls on with a power perpetually increasing. The heart's purest, strongest, and best affections forever roll around one blissful center. This *"perfect love casteth out fear"* (1 John 4:18), and in the continued flow of the benevolent affections, the blessedness of the soul can be measured only by the extent of its capacities. Christian, this is life eternal.

Those deep and tender emotions excited by a fixed contemplation of the glory of God as it shines in the face of Jesus Christ render the blessedness of the soul as great as its capacities permit. The emotions excited by a continued contemplation of objects beautiful, grand, or sublime are of the most "happifying" nature that the mind experiences. Men will cross the ocean and circle the earth to enjoy those deep and expanding emotions that a perception and contemplation of the sublime scenery of nature awakens. Men have often expended fortunes to secure the enjoyment of the emotions awakened by a contemplation of the sublime objects of the different continents. When the emotions of delight awakened by the contemplation of finite objects—however beautiful, grand, or sublime in themselves—are compared to those awakened by the contemplation of the infinite, such as the infinite and boundless love and glory of God, they are almost beyond compared. Take one or two examples in illustration:

Mr. Tennent had occasion to take a journey that would occupy a whole day. Before he started, he entered his closet and besought the Lord to manifest Himself to him on the way. As he mounted his horse, the veil was lifted, and he beheld with open face the glory of the Lord. He had those full and distinct apprehensions of the love and glory of God that filled the whole sphere of moral and intellectual vision. In these divine contemplations, his mind was occupied during the entire day in a state of such fixedness that he was wholly insensible to all things else around him. At length his horse stopped at the place of his destination without the exertion of any conscious direction on the part of the rider. So wrapped was he in the visions of the divine glory that it required much effort on the part of the people in the house to recall him to a consciousness of the scenes around him.

Now, I suppose that during that day the emotions awakened by such contemplations rendered the mind of that man of God as blessed as his capacities permitted. Nor could his powers long have endured such a crushing weight of glory. Take another example:

A man of God of a similar spirit to Tennent, on retiring one morning to his place of private devotion, gave directions to a domestic to call him down at the expiration of three hours, as he was then to receive a visit from some friends. At the specified time, the domestic found him in such fixed contemplations of the divine glory that he returned without disturbing him. At the end of three hours more, he returned and found his master in the same state as before. So perfectly absorbed was his whole mind in those visions of the breadth and depth and length and height of the love of Christ that passes knowledge as to render him wholly unconscious of the presence of any other object. Again, he retired, and after three hours, returned once more and found the man of God in the same fixed contemplations as formerly. God was causing all His goodness to pass before him. On being then aroused, his first inquiry was whether it was possible that the time had come for the arrival of his friends. He had been so fixed with those spiritual apprehensions as to be entirely unconscious of the lapse of time.

Many persons, such as Mrs. Edwards, and Dr. Payson near the close of life, have had similar manifestations of the divine love and glory. Now, while the soul is borne upward and onward with the tide of emotion awakened by such contemplations, nothing but an increase of capacity can render its happiness greater. Considering that a revelation to the mind of the light of the knowledge of the glory of God in the face of Jesus Christ is adapted to hold all the powers of our being in a state of perpetual fixedness, in which the tide of blissful emotions rise and swell forever with constantly accumulating power, how true the declaration of our Savior is—"*This is life eternal, that they might know thee the only true God, and Jesus Christ, whom thou hast sent*" (John 17:3).

It is not to be expected that Christians will, at all times and under all circumstances, have these overwhelming visions of the divine glory. Our present capacities do not permit it. But, Christian, we would impress this truth deeply upon your mind—that it is your privilege, as well as your duty, to have those perpetual apprehensions of the divine glory that will render your blessedness at all times and under all circumstances full. Let Christ once lift the veil and show you His glory, and the deep emotions of love and delight that will swell your bosom will render the life eternal referred to in the text a blessed reality in your experience. Christ is able and willing, yes, infinitely desirous to do this for you. If you will seek Him with all your heart, He will be found by you. He will bring you out of darkness into God's marvelous light. (See 1 Peter 2:9.) God Himself will walk in you and dwell in you (see 2 Corinthians 6:16), and with an open face, you will behold, as in a glass, His glory (see 2 Corinthians 3:18). And thus,

> *The sun shall be no more thy light by day; neither for brightness shall the moon give light unto thee: but the* Lord *shall be unto thee an everlasting light, and thy God thy glory. Thy*

> *sun shall no more go down; neither shall thy moon withdraw itself: for the* Lord *shall be thine everlasting light, and the days of thy mourning shall be ended.*
>
> (Isaiah 60:19–20)

The fact that the knowledge under consideration must be eternal life may be shown also by a reference to the relations that the individual thus knowing God recognizes as existing between him and God. Let us suppose that while an individual has a full and distinct apprehension of the infinite perfections and glory of God, such as the Spirit only can impart, he becomes perfectly conscious that every attribute of divinity stands pledged to secure and advance his eternal blessedness and that throughout eternity God is to employ the resources of His own infinity to render him in the highest degree holy and happy. Let him also become as fully sensible of the fact that, in consequence of the relations existing between him and God, he is brought into such relations to the arrangements of universal providence that not an event will ever transpire throughout the universe that will not work together for his good—in short, that all things are his, whether the world, or life, or death, or things present, or things to come, all are his, and he is Christ's, and Christ is God's. (See 1 Corinthians 3:21–22.) To know God with the consciousness of sustaining such relations to Him as these, this surely must be life eternal.

As a further illustration of this thought, let us now contemplate a few cases recorded in the Bible. What must have been the feelings of Abraham in view of the following declaration of God to him: *"Fear not, Abram: I am thy shield, and thy exceeding great reward"* (Genesis 15:1)? How could he have endured a greater weight of blessedness than he enjoyed in the contemplation of such relations to God?

Take also the following incident in the life of Moses:

> *And Moses said unto the LORD, See, thou sayest unto me, Bring up this people: and thou hast not let me know whom thou wilt send with me. Yet thou hast said, I know thee by name, and thou hast also found grace in my sight. Now therefore, I pray thee, if I have found grace in thy sight, show me now thy way, that I may know thee, that I may find grace in thy sight: and consider that this nation is thy people. And he said, My presence shall go with thee, and I will give thee rest. And he said unto him, If thy presence go not with me, carry us not up hence. For wherein shall it be known here that I and thy people have found grace in thy sight? is it not in that thou goest with us? so shall we be separated, I and thy people, from all the people that are upon the face of the earth. And the LORD said unto Moses, I will do this thing also that thou hast spoken: for thou hast found grace in my sight, and I know thee by name. And he said, I beseech thee, show me thy glory. And he said, I will make all my goodness pass before thee, and I will proclaim the name of the LORD before thee.* (Exodus 33:12–19)

Now, I suppose the blessedness of Moses here was full. This to him was life eternal. And, Christian, we wish to impress your mind with the conviction that you may know God so as to be as perfectly blessed in Him as Moses and Abraham were.

What also must have been the feelings of the prophet when the plan of redemption opened in prophetic vision upon his mind. "*Unto us a child is born, unto us a son is given: and the government shall be upon his shoulder: and his name shall be called Wonderful, Counsellor, The mighty God, The everlasting Father, The Prince of Peace*" (Isaiah 9:6). How could his blessedness have been greater than when his mind was swallowed up with the unfolding of such mysteries as these?

Contemplate now the feelings of the aged Simeon when, under the inspiration of the Holy Spirit, he entered the temple, assured that the promised Messiah, the Babe of Bethlehem, the *"Wonderful, Counsellor, The mighty God, The everlasting Father, and The Prince of Peace,"* was there. As he took the Babe in his arms with a full apprehension of the fact that that He was the incarnate God, *"a light to lighten the Gentiles, and the glory of thy people Israel"* (Luke 2:32), is it at all wonderful that he exclaimed, *"Lord, now lettest thou thy servant depart in peace, according to thy word: for mine eyes have seen thy salvation, which thou hast prepared before the face of all people"* (Luke 2:29–31)? I suppose he then enjoyed as much of heaven as was possible without bursting this tenement of clay. In his mind, the truth of the assertion *"This is life eternal...*[to] *know thee the only true God, and Jesus Christ, whom thou hast sent"* (John 17:3) was a living, felt reality. It will be so in your experience, Christian, when the Spirit of God takes the things of Christ and shows them to you.

Similar feelings pervaded the mind of John the Baptist when he saw Jesus coming to him and exclaimed, *"Behold the Lamb of God, which taketh away the sin of the world"* (John 1:29).

> *Again the next day after John stood, and two of his disciples; and looking upon Jesus as he walked, he saith, Behold the Lamb of God!* (John 1:35–36)

John seemed to have received a full and distinct apprehension of the mysteries of redemption. The relations he sustained to Christ were revealed with perfect distinctness to his mind, and in their light, his joy was unspeakable and full of glory. O to lay the hand upon the head of such a victim and there confess our sins with the certain knowledge that "*the chastisement of our peace was upon him*" and that "*with his stripes we are healed*" (Isaiah 53:5). This is the death of sin; this is life eternal.

Think also of the feelings of the apostle when he penned the following lines:

> *And the Word was made flesh, and dwelt among us, (and we beheld his glory, the glory as of the only begotten of the Father,) full of grace and truth.... And of his fulness have all we received, and grace for grace.* (John 1:14, 16)

The Christian, when overwhelmed with a sense of his infinite guilt and ill-desert, with appalling thoughts lifts the eye to the God before whom we must all appear. At this moment, the inspired declaration presents itself to his mind, "*We have an advocate with the Father, Jesus Christ the righteous*" (1 John 2:1). To know Christ is sustaining such a relation as this to us, what is it but life eternal?

Contemplate now the following exclamation of an inspired apostle: "*Behold, what manner of love the Father hath bestowed upon us, that we should be called the sons of God*" (1 John 3:1). A missionary had employed a pundit to aid him in the translation of the Scriptures. The missionary read a passage, and then the pundit translated it into his native tongue. When the passage above cited was read, the pundit stopped, and after thinking a moment, said, "You have not read that passage right."

The missionary read again, "*Behold, what manner of love the Father hath bestowed upon us, that we should be called the sons of God.*"

"Why," said the astonished heathen, "you have not read that passage right."

As the passage was read a third time, the pundit dropped his pen and wept. He could not translate such words. The thought had never entered his mind before that such a being as man could sustain such a relation to the infinite God. What, then, must be the blessedness of that mind that apprehends distinctly the perfection and glory of God with a full consciousness of the fact that he sustains such a relation to such an infinite being? This, surely, is life eternal. And because we sustain such a relation to God as this, Christ Himself is not ashamed to call us brethren, saying, "I will declare My Father's name among my brethren." (See Hebrews 2:11–12.) Again He said, *"Go tell* ***my brethren*** *that they go into Galilee, and there shall they see me"* (Matthew 28:10) and, *"Go to* ***my brethren****, and say unto them, I ascend unto my Father, and your Father; and to my God, and your God"* (John 20:17). To know the only living and true God and Jesus Christ, whom He sent, in such relations as these, *"this is life eternal"* (John 17:3).

The Conditions for Receiving This Knowledge and Blessedness

We must set our hearts supremely upon its attainment.

> *My son, if thou wilt receive my words, and hide my commandments with thee; so that thou incline thine ear unto wisdom, and apply thine heart to understanding; yea, if thou criest after knowledge, and liftest up thy voice for understanding; if thou seekest her as silver, and searchest for her as for hid treasures; then shalt thou understand the fear of the Lord, and find the knowledge of God....Then shalt thou understand righteousness, and*

judgment, and equity; yea, every good path.

(Proverbs 2:1–9)

"Ye shall seek me, and find me, when ye shall search for me with all your heart" (Jeremiah 29:13). The great mass of professing Christians walk on in darkness without finding God simply because they never set their hearts upon finding Him.

A friend of mine, speaking of a certain sister in Christ, said, "That sister knows what it is to have fellowship with God, and I doubt not you will find her prepared to sympathize with you in reference to your views of the infinite and boundless love of Christ. Years ago, she received such apprehensions of the great mysteries of redemption as few obtain in this life. She became fully sensible," he said, "that it was her privilege to know God as she never had known Him and to enjoy Him as she never had enjoyed Him. She then fixed her whole heart upon attaining this state. She besought the Lord night and day with strong crying and tears to manifest Himself to her by showing her His glory. As she came from her closet one Sabbath morning to accompany her family to church, an accident occurred that she saw would occasion a delay of two or three minutes. She felt that interval was too precious to be lost. She hastened to her closet and spent the time in the most fervent prayer that God would manifest Himself to her soul. As she entered the house of God, He did manifest Himself to her to such an extent that her mind was almost overpowered with the weight of glory and blessedness that pressed upon her. Since that, while I knew her, she seemed to be continually sitting at the feet of Christ with a full realization, in her own experience, of the truth of the declaration '*This is life eternal, that they might know thee the only true God, and Jesus Christ, whom thou hast sent.*'" Those who thus seek God find Him, and none others do find Him.

Think of the African who, as Mr. Buck in his *Religious Anecdotes* informs us, crossed the ocean to hear about the "Christian's God that paid the debt." In his own country, he became sensible of his condition as a sinner. At the same time, the thick and impenetrable gloom of despair settled down upon his mind, because he was in total darkness in respect to the way of pardon and eternal life. In this state, he was accustomed to sit under the shade of a particular tree and weep aloud in view of his lost and hopeless condition. A wicked sailor who heard his cries one day told him to "go to England and there hear about the Christian's God that paid the debt." Without a moment's delay, he sought the nearest port and took the first ship he could find that was bound for London. On the voyage, he continually besought the sailors and all on board to tell him about "the Christian's God that paid the debt." But none could unfold the mystery. On his arrival at London, he passed up and down the streets beseeching the multitude that passed to tell him about the Christian's God that paid the debt. Some gave him money, others heaped abuse upon him, but none pointed him to *"the Lamb of God, which taketh away the sin of the world"* (John 1:29). At length he gave it up in despair, and as the shades of evening came on, he sat down on one of the public greens and began to utter the same mournful cries that he had been wont to utter in his native land. His cries attracted the notice of an evangelical clergyman who was on his way to a public lecture. As the man of God inquired the cause of his grief, the other said, "Do tell a poor man about the Christian's God that paid the debt."

"Come with me," said the minister, "and I will tell you." He took the inquirer into the church and gave a history of the plan of redemption, representing sin as the debt and Christ, by His incarnation and atonement, as paying the debt.

"I have found it," cried the African, as the mystery was unfolded to him. As the minister came down from the pulpit, after the congregation had retired, he found the stranger entirely unconscious of visible objects, so perfectly absorbed was his whole soul in the mystery of mysteries that had dawned upon his mental vision. He had sought the Lord with all his heart, and He was found of him, and now his cup was full.

Now, reader, if you do not know God in such a sense that your blessedness in Him is also full, you are as really in darkness and as utterly dependent upon divine teaching for the light of life as that African was. If you will seek God as he sought Him, He will be found of you, too. If you do not thus seek Him, you will never see the light; you will wander on in darkness without knowing at what you stumble. If you continue to walk in darkness without seeking God with all your heart, when you know that you may enjoy His marvelous light, what else can you expect but that the darkness around you will thicken into the gloom of eternal midnight? Reader, will you seek the Lord with all your heart until He is found of you?

If you would attain this knowledge, Christian, set your heart supremely upon the object for which Christ imparts it to you. If Christ should enable you to behold, as with open face, the glory of the Lord, you might be *"changed into the same image from glory to glory, even as by the Spirit of the Lord"* (2 Corinthians 3:18). In other words, you might be free from sin and rendered pure and holy, like God. Would you, above all things, prize this state, together with the blessedness that results from its possession? If so, you may seek the Lord with the assurance that you will find Him and that in finding Him you will find eternal life.

You must seek this knowledge with the most perfect assurance that its possession will in fact be life eternal. Do you believe that if Christ should admit you, as it were, into the holy of holies of His sacred presence and permit you to behold, with unveiled face, the glory of the Lord, your blessedness would be full? Can you seek such a knowledge as such a good? If so, be assured that in seeking you will find Him and that in finding Him your joy will be unspeakable and full of glory.

Seek this knowledge with the profoundest humility and teachability. A philosopher of Germany became sensible of his condition as a sinner and set himself to study the Bible for the purpose of understanding the way of life therein revealed. But impenetrable darkness hung over the sacred page. At length he requested a poor peasant, whom he knew as a very ignorant but highly spiritual man, to sit down with him and teach him the way of life as revealed in the Bible. Thus humble and teachable must you become if you would find God. Is this, reader, the spirit that you breathe? Are you ready to be taught and led by anyone, even a child or a beggar, if he can only lead you to Christ?

Seek the counsel and secure an interest in the prayers of those who have the fullest and richest experience of that knowledge of the only living and true God and Jesus Christ, the possession of which is life eternal. Lay open to them your whole heart and, having received their counsel, engage them to...

> *bow* [their] *knees unto the Father of our Lord Jesus Christ, of whom the whole family in heaven and earth is named, that he would grant* [them], *according to the riches of his glory, to be strengthened with might by his Spirit in the inner man; that Christ may dwell in* [their] *hearts by faith; that* [they], *being rooted and grounded in love, may be able to comprehend with all saints what is the breadth, and length, and depth, and height; and to know the love of*

> *Christ, which passeth knowledge, that* [they] *might be filled with all the fulness of God.* (Ephesians 3:14–19)

Brother, take this course while you also seek the Lord with all your heart, and He will do for you exceeding abundantly above all that you ask or think.

Seek this knowledge in devout dependence upon the teachings of the Holy Spirit. Seek and expect His teachings with a humble confession of your darkness and ignorance in the most prayerful study of the Bible and attendance upon all the means of grace. If you will do this, rest assured that you will find God. He will bring you out of darkness and into His own marvelous light, and you will have a blissful experience of the truth of the words of Christ "*This is life eternal, that they might know thee the only true God, and Jesus Christ, whom thou hast sent*" (John 17:3). And now, Christian, do you want eternal life enough to seek it with all your heart? Will you now enter into a solemn covenant with your own soul that you will never rest until you have a full and rich experience of that knowledge of God that is life eternal?

Remarks

We may now understand the meaning of such interesting and important passages of the Bible as the following:

> *Enoch walked with God.* (Genesis 5:22)

> *I will dwell in them, and walk in them; and I will be their God, and they shall be my people.* (2 Corinthians 6:16)

> *I will not leave you comfortless: I will come to you.* (John 14:18)

He that loveth me shall be loved of my Father, and I will love him, and will manifest myself to him. (John 14:21)

We will come unto him, and make our abode with him. (John 14:23)

As these are among the most interesting and important declarations and promises of the Bible, it is of great importance that we correctly apprehend their meaning. Perhaps I can best convey my understanding of the meaning of these passages by a reference to two or three examples.

During the great revivals in the days of President Edwards, a little child was observed by her parents to be exceedingly sorrowful and sad, often in tears, and she spent a great portion of the time alone in her closet. At length the mother asked the child the cause of her sadness. "Why, mother," said the child, "God won't come to me. I call to Him, but He won't come to me." Sometime after this, the child came out of her closet, and with inexpressible joy beaming in her countenance, she exclaimed, "Mother, He has come; God has come!" Now, reader, if you can conceive distinctly of the state that child described in the phrase "God has come" and then suppose it permanent in the experience of the believer, you can understand the meaning of these passages.

Before, when she called, God did not seem to hear. It seemed as if He was distant, and it was impossible to get to Him. Now He seemed to be directly present to the soul, and she had a perfect consciousness that He heard and answered her requests and that she was the object of His infinite love and favor. When the soul enters into such a relation to God as this, God has come to that person. He has made His abode with him, and He dwells in him and walks in him. Christian, has God thus come to you?

Look now at the following extract from a letter of Dr. Payson when he was a blissful inhabitant of the land of Beulah:

> The Sun of righteousness has been gradually drawing nearer and nearer, appearing larger and brighter as He approached, and now He fills the whole hemisphere, pouring forth a flood of glory, in which I seem to float like an insect in the beams of the sun; exulting, yet almost trembling, while I gaze on this excessive brightness, and wondering, with unutterable wonder, why God should thus deign to shine upon a sinful worm. A single heart and a single tongue seem altogether inadequate to my wants: I want a whole heart for every separate emotion, and a whole tongue to express that emotion. But why do I speak thus of myself and of my feelings? Why not speak only of our God and Redeemer? It is because I know not what to say. When I would speak of them, my words are all swallowed up. I can only tell you what effects their presence produces, and even of that I can tell you but very little.

Let this state become permanent with the Christian, not only on the bed of death but at all times, in sickness and in health, in life and in death, and then, like Enoch, he will walk with God. He will have a full and blessed experience of the meaning of the above passages. He will know the only living and true God, and Jesus Christ whom He sent (see John 17:3), in the sense of the text.

Look now at the scene that transpired in the experience of James Brainerd Taylor when he received the blessing of entire sanctification—

> At this very juncture, I was most delightfully conscious of giving up all to God. I was enabled to say, "Here, Lord,

take me, take my whole soul, and seal me Thine—Thine now, and Thine forever. If Thou wilt, Thou canst make me clean." There then ensued such emotions as I never before experienced—all was calm and tranquil, solemn; and a heaven of love pervaded my whole soul. I had a witness of God's love to me and of mine to Him. Shortly after I was dissolved in tears of love and gratitude to our blessed Lord. The name of Jesus was precious to me. 'Twas music in my ear. He came as a King and took full possession of my heart, and I was enabled to say, "I am crucified with Christ; nevertheless, I live; yet not I, but Christ liveth in me." Let Him, as King of kings and Lord of lords, reign in me—reign without a rival, forever. The Lord hath done great things for me, whereof I am glad, and for which I would praise His holy name. Not unto me—not unto me; I am nothing—Jesus is all. To His name be the glory! He is the author and finisher of faith. I know and am as fully assured of my acceptance with God, as I can be of my own existence—that is, if love, joy, and peace, are evidence of reconciliation. I have a hope full of glorious immortality. The perfect love of God casteth out all fear of death, of the grave, of judgment, of hell. Filial fear—fear of offending my heavenly Father and my brethren, possesses me. Surely, I am a miracle of grace; a sinner saved by grace—free, sovereign grace. I feel that I love the Lord because He first loved me. And even now I am favored with the gracious presence of *Immanuel*. How suitable and delightful is His name—"God with us." Yes, and *formed within us* the hope of glory.

Christian, has Christ thus manifested Himself to you? Have He and the Father made their abode with you? Does He commune with your spirit? Before you call, does He answer you? And while you are speaking, does He say to your soul, "Here am I"?

We may also understand the real condition of the great mass of professing Christians. They are in the same state that that child was when God would not come to her—except with this fearful difference: They are not sorrowing after the Lord as she was. Like Job, they know not where they might find Him and come even to His seat. (See John 23:3.)

> *Behold, I go forward, but he is not there; and backward, but I cannot perceive him: on the left hand, where he doth work, but I cannot behold him: he hideth himself on the right hand, that I cannot see him.* (Job 23:8–9)

Christian, for the universe, I would not be in such a relation to God as this. Do not rest a moment till you have found God. Call to Him till He answers you, till He comes to you and makes His abode with you.

In the light of this subject, we may gain a clear conception of one of the highest evidences of the divine origin of the Scriptures. It is the perfect adaptation of all the truths and principles of the gospel to the capacities of all who embrace it, whether learned or ignorant, and however great or small their capacities. Let the tall seraph, who for ages has adored and burned before the eternal throne, turn his contemplation upon the mysteries of redemption, and all his powers are put on the stretch to comprehend "*what is the breadth, and length, and depth, and height; and to know the love of Christ, which passeth knowledge*" (Ephesians 3:18–19).

Let a Newton, also, as his mind has just descended from a boundless range among the suns and worlds that are scattered abroad through the immensity of space, or as it ascends from the deep profound of nature, where it has been holding devout converse with her hidden laws, turn aside to see this great sight, and the unfolding glories of redemption perfectly fill the whole compass of his moral and intellectual vision. To his great mind, also, the love of Christ passes knowledge. Now let the child, the peasant, or the almost idiot apprehend the same gospel and how perfectly it adapts itself to his capacities. All who apprehend and embrace it, it beautifies with salvation (see Psalm 149:4) and renders their blessedness full. All, of every capacity, are complete in Christ. Here every demand of their beings is met perfectly and forever.

I think I will never lose the impression I received when a child on reading the story of poor Joseph who was so destitute of intelligence as to be hardly capable of a single distinct idea on any subject. He was providentially led into the house of God one Sabbath, where a discourse was preached from the text *"This is a faithful saying, and worthy of all acceptation, that Christ Jesus came into the world to save sinners; of whom I am chief"* (1 Timothy 1:15). From that moment, that great truth, adapting itself to the capacities of the subject, took possession of his mind and ever after held all his powers in the same blissful fixedness that it did those of Paul. It was *"in him a well of water springing up into everlasting life"* (John 4:14). By night and by day, at home and abroad, this faithful saying dwelt upon his heart and his tongue and rendered the small sphere in which his intellect ranged a little heaven. At length, his minister heard he was sick, nigh unto death, and hastened to see him. "Joseph," said the minister, "How do you do? Are you happy?"

"Happy, happy," was the reply. *"This is a faithful saying, and worthy of all acceptation, that Christ Jesus came into the world to save sinners; of whom I am chief."* With infinite sweetness, he pillowed his dying head on that divine thought, and the last words that trembled upon his pallid lips were, *"This is a faithful saying, and worthy of all acceptation, that Christ Jesus came into the world to save sinners; of whom I am chief."* Now, reader, a gospel that thus adapts its blessed truths and influences to all capacities—that thus beautifies and blesses all that embrace it—must be from heaven. It must have come warm from a heart of infinite love.

Permit me here to suggest a thought that appears to me of great importance in studying the truth of God. Suppose you meet with an individual who has made great attainments in holiness and whose peace in Christ is as a river and whose righteousness is as the waves of the sea (see Isaiah 48:18), such a case, for example, as J. B. Taylor. Find out, now, just those views of the gospel from which this holiness and blessedness result, and you have found the pure truth of God. Such a person may hold many errors; from these, however, his holiness and happiness never resulted.

We see when it is that any one is prepared to proclaim the gospel, either as a minister or in the private walks of life. It is when this gospel is in him a well of water springing up into everlasting life. (See John 4:14.) It is when, and only when, he has that knowledge of the only living and true God and Jesus Christ, whom He sent, the possession of which is, in his own experience, eternal life. *"Restore unto me the joy of thy salvation; and uphold me with thy free spirit. Then will I teach transgressors thy ways; and sinners shall be converted unto thee"* (Psalm 51:12–13).

We see how to make all self-denials and sacrifices in the service of Christ not only easy but also sources of great blessedness. It is to attain through the Spirit such apprehensions of the glory of God as it shines in the face of Jesus Christ (see 2 Corinthians 4:16) as will induce us to *"count all things but loss for the excellency of the knowledge of Christ Jesus"* (Philippians 3:8). When we come into such a relation of Christ as this, every yoke He lays upon us will be easy and every burden light. Christian—if you knew Christ as you might and ought to know Him, the loss of all things and even death itself, for His sake, would be a privilege to you.

We may also understand why the great mass of Christians derives so little benefit from the preaching of the gospel. Two reasons may be assigned:

A very great portion of such ministrations have very little tendency to increase either the holiness or happiness of the hearer and seem to be prepared without any very definite reference to either of these objects. The preachers themselves are not greatly blessed in the gospel, and how is it possible for them, in this state of mind, to present it as a source of great blessedness to others?

But another and still more important reason is that few Christians attend upon the Word with an intense desire and expectation of receiving that knowledge of God, the possession of which is eternal life. How seldom, Christian, do you visit the sanctuary with your heart set upon beholding as in a glass the glory of the Lord and being changed into the same image from glory to glory? (See 2 Corinthians 3:18.) No wonder, then, that you leave the sacred place unblessed. *"And ye shall seek me, and find me, when ye shall search for me with* ***all*** *your heart"* (Jeremiah 29:13).

In the light of this subject, we may know when our views of any of the doctrines of the Bible accord with the mind of the Spirit. It is when we have obtained such apprehensions of such truths as are in the highest degree adapted to purify the heart and render our blessedness in Christ complete. Christ came into the world to bless us in turning every one of us from our iniquities. (See Acts 3:26.) Every revelation He has given is adapted, when rightly apprehended, to secure these results. Every correct view of any revealed truth, therefore, is adapted to sanctify the soul and fill it with *"quietness and assurance for ever"* (Isaiah 32:17). Christian, have you attained to such apprehensions of the gospel as this? Is the knowledge you possess of the only living and true God and Jesus Christ, whom He sent, eternal life to you? If not, will you not ask yourself whether your views of the gospel must not undergo some modifications before you can attain to a real knowledge of the glory of God as it shines in the face of Jesus Christ?

We may now understand the different ways in which the enthusiast and fanatic and the individual who is really taught of the Spirit explain the Bible. The former abandons all the laws of interpretation and receives, as the teachings of the Spirit, any meaning a wild and disordered imagination may attach to the sacred text. The latter receives nothing that is not justified and demanded by the laws of interpretation properly applied. Yet through the Spirit, he receives those apprehensions of the truth that no man who relies simply upon such laws to gain a meaning of the sacred text can obtain. *"The things of God knoweth no man, but the Spirit of God"* (1 Corinthians 2:11). *"No man can say that Jesus is the Lord, but by the Holy Ghost"* (1 Corinthians 12:3). That is, no man can make that affirmation, with an apprehension of what is really embraced in it, unless such apprehensions are imparted to him by the Holy Spirit.

We may now understand why the Bible is, to the great mass of the church, as a sealed book, why they feel so little interest in reading it and derive so little consolation from its life-giving truths. It is this: They have so little experience of the teachings and illumination of the Spirit of God. If the Spirit were to lift the veil and show them the things of Christ, as He would do if His divine illuminations were sought with all diligence, they would find themselves at once upon the banks of that *"river, the streams whereof shall make glad the city of God"* (Psalm 46:4), where also grows the tree of life that yields fruit every month and whose leaves are for the healing of the nations. (See Revelation 22:2.)

They would find themselves the blissful inhabitants of the land of Beulah. The Celestial City would be full in view, and the Sun of Righteousness, gradually drawing nearer and nearer and appearing larger and brighter as He approached, would fill the whole hemisphere, pouring forth a flood of glory in which they would seem to float like insects in the beams of the sun—exulting yet almost trembling while they gaze on this excessive brightness and wonder with unutterable wonder why God should thus deign to shine upon a sinful worm. In their own experience, they would know the truth of the divine declaration *"This is life eternal, that they might know thee the only true God, and Jesus Christ, whom thou hast sent"* (John 17:3).

Now, Christian, has not Christ been long enough a stranger and a sojourner to you? Have you not long enough called Him yours without knowing Him? Will you not now set your heart, through the Word and teachings of the Spirit, upon *knowing* your God and Savior? From this time forth, let this be the fixed purpose of your heart—to know all of Christ that you possibly can know, to enjoy all of Him that you possibly can enjoy, and to do all for Him that you possibly can do. Then will your light go forth as brightness and your salvation as a lamp that burns. (See Isaiah 62:1.)

5

CHRIST'S WITNESSES

"Ye are my witnesses, saith the Lord, *and my servant whom I have chosen: that ye may know and believe me, and understand that I am he."*
—Isaiah 43:10

"Ye shall receive power, after that the Holy Ghost is come upon you: and ye shall be witnesses unto me both in Jerusalem, and in all Judea, and in Samaria, and unto the uttermost part of the earth."
—Acts 1:8

In a very important sense, all Christians are Christ's witnesses. It is chiefly through the instrumentality of such testimony also that the world is to be brought back to God. It is in this relation that I design to contemplate the Christian in the present discourse. A witness is one who bears testimony to facts of which he has personal knowledge. In determining the weight to be given to the testimony of a witness, two circumstances are taken into the account—his competency and his credibility. A person, in order to be competent to give testimony in any instance, must be of a suitable age, possessed of a sane mind, and have a personal knowledge of the facts about which he testifies. The opinion of a witness is not asked, but the facts of which, from personal knowledge, he can give testimony.

The credibility of a witness is determined by such considerations as the following:

1. His character for veracity.
2. The presence or absence of considerations of a personal nature tending to bias his judgment or to induce him to give false statements.
3. Consistency, or the want of it, in his statements. Suppose a witness, in one part of his story, palpably contradicts what he has stated in a former part. This would destroy his credibility.
4. Consistency between the facts stated and the conduct of the witness. For example, suppose a witness professes to regard a certain individual as a man of great worth when it should appear that he had always *treated* him as a worthless character. Such a fact would wholly destroy his credibility.
5. The concurrence of several witnesses imparts the highest credibility to testimony.

In presenting Christians as Christ's witnesses, I will direct the attention of the reader to the following propositions:

1. The ways the testimony of the apostles and early Christians differs from or resembles the testimony of Christians in all ages
2. What the actual experience of Christian must be in order for their testimony to be for and not against Christ
3. The obligation resting upon Christians to give full testimony for and not against Christ

The Differences and Resemblances

There is one respect, now, in which Christians can bear no part with the apostles and early Christians in the testimony they bear for Christ. I refer to the facts recorded in the Bible—facts of which the latter were eyewitnesses. Take this single statement as an example:

> *I delivered unto you first of all that which I also received, how that Christ died for our sins according to the scriptures; and that he was buried, and that he rose again the third day according to the scriptures: and that he was seen of Cephas, then of the twelve: after that, he was seen of above five hundred brethren at once.* (1 Corinthians 15:3–6)

Now the business of those here referred to as witnesses for Christ was to affirm to the world that, as here stated, they had heard Christ, seen Him with their eyes, looked upon Him, and handled Him with their hands. (See 1 John 1:1.) So of many other facts recorded in the Bible. Those who were eyewitnesses of those facts were to testify to the world the things which they had seen and heard. In this kind of testimony, no Christian in any subsequent age can bear any part whatever. They can only report to the world the testimony that the original witnesses have handed down to them.

But there is another kind of testimony for Christ equally and, if possible, still more important, which Christians in every age are required to bear in common with the apostles and early Christians.

They are required to bear testimony to the truth of whatever the Bible affirms of Christian experience. In other words, whatever results the Bible affirms will follow from embracing the gospel, every Christian, in consequence of having realized these results in his own experience, is required to stand as a witness before the world to confirm the testimony of God. For example:

> *Come unto me, all ye that labour and are heavy laden, and I will give you rest. Take my yoke upon you, and learn of me; for I am meek and lowly in heart: and ye shall find rest unto your souls. For my yoke is easy, and my burden is light.*
> (Matthew 11:28–30)

Christians are required to give testimony to the world from their own experience that the result of taking Christ's yoke and bearing His burden is the very rest and peace here promised. So in respect to all the *"exceeding great and precious promises"* (2 Peter 1:4) and declarations of Scripture pertaining to the results of embracing the gospel by faith, Christians are required to give testimony to the world from experience that all such promises and declarations are *"yea, and in him Amen"* (2 Corinthians 1:20). So far as they are able to give such testimony, so far, and so far only, are they qualified to stand before the world as witnesses for Christ. So far as their experience corresponds with such declarations and promises, so far is that testimony honorable to Christ. So far as it does not correspond with or is opposed to such declarations and promises, so far it is dishonorable to Christ or against Him before the world.

Here permit me to remark that Christians are required not only to give formal testimony for Christ in these respects but, in their visible experience and example before the world, to be epistles (or witnesses) of Christ, *"known and read of all men"* (2 Corinthians 3:2). It should also be remembered that Christians are, in fact, at all times and in all circumstances, giving their testimony either for Christ or against Him in their example before the world. Their very profession has made them a *"spectacle unto the world, and to angels, and to men"* (1 Corinthians 4:9). They are, therefore, in their conversation and deportment, always giving their testimony in favor of or against God's truth. How solemn the position that man assumes who, before the world, professes himself a child of God. He stands as a medium of communication between God and the world—a medium to transmit the beams of the sun of righteousness—or, by obstructing those rays, to perpetuate and render more dark the darkness that covers the earth.

The Actual Experience of Testifying For and Not Against Christ

In the very act of professing himself a Christian, a man presents himself to the world as a competent witness for Christ with all the knowledge and other qualifications requisite to render his testimony worthy of confidence. He professes to have embraced the gospel as required and to have tested, in his own experience, its power to produce the results attributed to it in the Bible when thus received. He, therefore, voluntarily presents himself to the world as a witness who is fully qualified to testify to the world regarding whether all the promises of the Bible to those who embrace the gospel are, or are not, *yes* and *amen* in Christ Jesus. (See 2 Corinthians 1:20.) What, then, must the Christian be in his religious experience in order that he may be found a true and not a false witness for Christ?

He must be pure in heart and life. In professing ourselves Christians, we profess to be those who *"lay hold upon the hope set before us"* (Hebrews 6:18). Now the Bible affirms that *"every man that hath this hope in him purifieth himself, even as he is pure"* (1 John 3:3). Christian, what is the influence of your hope? Does it lead you to seek the purity that God possesses? If such is its manifest influence, you are a true witness for Christ. If not, your testimony to the world is a standing affirmation that the above declaration of God is not true. What a fearful thing it is for one to profess to have this hope and not to present to the world an exhibition of and a testimony to its purifying power and influence.

In professing ourselves Christians, we also affirm to the world that we exercise the faith that the gospel requires. The Bible affirms of faith that it *"worketh by love"* (Galatians 5:6), purifies the heart (see Acts 15:9), and overcomes the world (see 1 John 5:4). As we profess to exercise this faith, we profess ourselves qualified to stand as witnesses and to testify to the world whether the influence of faith corresponds with the above declarations of Scripture. If, from its conscious and visible effects upon ourselves, we can affirm that the gospel is *"the power of God unto salvation to every one that believeth"* (Romans 1:16), our testimony is for Christ. If not, it is against Him. It is a perpetual affirmation to the world that such declarations as the above respecting the influence of faith are not true.

Again, in professing ourselves Christians, we affirm to the world that Christ is in us and we are in Him, according to the meaning the Bible attaches to such phraseology. The Scriptures affirm, on the one hand, *"If any man be in Christ, he is a new creature: old things are passed away; behold, all things are become new"* (2 Corinthians 5:17) and, *"Whosoever abideth in him sinneth not"* (1 John3:6). On the other hand, they affirm that if Christ is in us, *"the body is dead because of sin; but the Spirit is life because of righteousness"* (Romans 8:10), and that we will be all-powerful against the temptations of the devil. *"Greater is he that is in you, than he that is in the world"* (1 John 4:4).

Christian, what are the effects of your abiding in Christ and His abiding in you, as developed in your experience? Do they correspond with the above declarations of the Bible? To the extent that you are possessed of conscious and manifest purity, to that extent your testimony is for the truth of God and the honor of Christ. To the extent, on the other hand, that sin in any form has dominion over you, to that extent your testimony is against the truth of God and to the dishonor of Christ.

Once more, in professing ourselves Christians, we affirm that we have the spirit of Christ. *"If any man have not the Spirit of Christ, he is none of his"* (Romans 8:9). What is the fruit of the Spirit, as affirmed by the Word of God? *"The fruit of the Spirit is love, joy, peace, longsuffering, gentleness, goodness, faith, meekness, temperance: against such there is no law"* (Galatians 5:22–23). *"They that are Christ's* [who have His Spirit] *have crucified the flesh with the affections and lusts"* (verse 24). You affirm that you are Christ's and that His Spirit dwells in you. Can you testify to the world that the fruit of the Spirit, as developed in your experience, corresponds with these affirmations of the Bible? Are you found a true or a false witness for Christ?

We come, then, to this solemn conclusion. To the extent, and only to the extent, that we are pure and holy in heart and life is our testimony about the effects of embracing the gospel honorable to Christ. To the extent that sin in any form or degree dwells within us or has dominion over us, to that extent we are found false witnesses for Christ.

To be found true and not false witnesses for Christ, we must possess, through the gospel, great and constant peace of mind. As Christians, we profess to love the law of God. We should not think of calling ourselves Christians if we do not believe we love it. The Bible's declaration is, *"Great peace have they that love thy law: and nothing shall offend them"* (Psalm 119:165). As Christians, we profess to stay ourselves upon God and to trust in Him. The Bible affirms that *"thou wilt keep him in perfect peace, whose mind is stayed on thee: because he trusteth in thee"* (Isaiah 26:3). In declaring ourselves Christians, we affirm our belief in Christ. The Bible asserts that those who believe in Christ, in consequence of believing in Him, *"rejoice with joy unspeakable and full of glory"* (1 Peter 1:8).

In declaring ourselves Christians, we affirm that we are righteous in the true sense in which men are called so in the Bible. We, of course, profess to have experienced the effects of righteousness upon the happiness of those who possess it and to be able as witnesses to testify to the world what those effects are. The Bible affirms, *"The work of righteousness shall be peace; and the effect of righteousness quietness and assurance forever"* (Isaiah 32:17), and in keeping the commandments of God *"there is great reward"* (Psalm 19:11). What God requires of us as Christians is to stand before the world and, from conscious experience and what the world see in us, to testify that these are the identical fruits which result from loving God's law, believing and trusting in Him, keeping his commandments, and practicing righteousness, as we profess to do. If we can thus testify for Christ, we are his true and faithful witnesses, and will be owned by Him as such at his coming and kingdom. Happy is that witness whom Christ will thus own. But if we cannot give such testimony, we are found false witnesses for Christ, and as such we shall stand in the judgment. Christian, where shall you and I then appear?

To be true and not false witnesses for Christ, we must have joy and peace in affliction. As Christians, we profess to have the faith by which sinners are justified. The Bible affirms that those who exercise this faith have joy in God, and consolation in Christ, in all the afflictions of life.

> *Being justified by faith, we have peace with God through our Lord Jesus Christ: by whom also we have access by faith into this grace wherein we stand, and rejoice in hope of the glory of God. And not only so, but we glory in tribulations also: knowing that tribulation worketh patience; and patience experience; and experience, hope: and hope maketh not ashamed; because the love of God is shed abroad in our hearts by the Holy Ghost which is given unto us.*
>
> (Romans 5:1–5)

This is declared to be the common experience of all true believers. "*In all these things we are more than conquerors through him that loved us*" (Romans 8:37). "*Our light affliction, which is but for a moment, worketh for us a far more exceeding and eternal weight of glory; while we look not at the things which are seen, but at the things which are not seen*" (2 Corinthians 4:17–18). Christ requires us to testify to the world from experience that such are the effects of believing in Him. Christian, are you able to give such testimony for your Lord? If so, He will own you as a faithful and true witness for Him. If not, will you not be ashamed before Him at His coming?

To be found faithful and true witnesses for Christ, we must have fellowship with God and His Son Jesus Christ and have great power in prayer. *"Truly our fellowship is with the Father, and with his Son Jesus Christ"* (1 John 1:3). This is declared to be true of all Christians. *"The effectual fervent prayer of a righteous man availeth much"* (James 5:16). Christian, is this true? What says your experience? You profess to be a righteous man. Have you power with God? Do you know what it is to prevail with Him in prayer?

Christ promises to every believer, *"Whatsoever ye shall ask of the Father in my name, he may give it you"* (John 15:16). He requires you to test the efficacy of His name so you can testify from experience that His declaration is true and, thus, recommend it to the world. Can you thus testify to the efficacy of that dear and venerable name at the throne of grace? Can you, for this reason, hope that Christ will at last own you as a true and faithful witness for Him?

To be found true and faithful witnesses for Christ, we must possess great and impartial love to all true believers. As Christians, we profess, as above remarked, to have the Spirit of Christ. What is that Spirit? What says the Spirit of inspiration? Hear it: *"Having loved his own which were in the world, he loved them unto the end"* (John 13:1). *"I lay down my life for the sheep"* (John 10:15). *"As the Father hath loved me, so have I loved you"* (John 15:9). Does the Spirit of Christ dwelling in you—as you profess to the world—induce in you the exercise and practice of similar love to Christ's brethren? Is this the testimony that, from personal experience, you can bear to the influence of that Spirit? If so, Christ will own you at last as a faithful and true witness for Him. But will He thus own you?

To be found faithful and true witnesses for Christ, His Spirit, which we as Christians affirm to be within us, must induce in us similar love toward the souls of men. The Bible affirms of those who have His Spirit,

> *The love of Christ constraineth us; because we thus judge, that if one died for all, then were all dead: and that he died for all, that they which live should not henceforth live unto themselves, but unto him which died for them, and rose again.*
> (2 Corinthians 5:14–15)

Can you say from experience as a witness for Christ that such is its constraining influence upon those in whom His Spirit dwells? If so, He will own you as a faithful and true witness when He comes to gather up His jewels. Permit me, however, to ask you the solemn question, *Will He thus own you?*

To be found true and faithful witnesses for Christ, there must be in our conscious experience a continued growth in the strength and power of our holy exercises and in the blessedness thence resulting. The Bible affirms that "*the path of the just is as the shining light, that shineth more and more unto the perfect day*" (Proverbs 4:18). Can you as a witness for Christ testify from experience that this declaration is true, and will Christ, as the faithful and true witness, testify to the universe at the great day that you have been thus faithful and true to Him? I might enlarge upon this part of the subject by an enumeration of a greater number of particulars, but these are sufficient.

The Need to Give Full Testimony for and Not Against Christ

All we need to qualify us to stand before the world as faithful and true witnesses for Christ is a fulfillment of our covenant vows to God and the church. When we stood up before God and the world to avouch the Lord Jehovah to be our God, we then pledged ourselves, under the solemnity of an oath, to test in our own experience the truth and faithfulness of God in every promise and declaration of His Word. And as a result, we pledged to be able to testify to the world, as the witnesses of Christ, regarding the truth and faithfulness of God in all such promises and declarations. Remember, then, Christian, that if you are not fully qualified to stand before the world as a witness for Christ, it is because of fearful unfaithfulness in respect to God's holy covenant. Let me also remind you of the fact that the first and great duty devolved upon you by your covenant vow is to qualify yourself, through the grace and Spirit of God, to testify as a witness for Christ.

You have only to avail yourself, Christian, of the revealed provisions of grace for your sanctification and blessedness, and you are, in all respects, a qualified witness for Christ. That you might be dead to sin and live to righteousness (see 1 Peter 2:24), *"that the righteousness of the law might be fulfilled in* [you]" (Romans 8:4), and that, consequently, the blissful fruits of righteousness might abound in you. Thus, you will be qualified as a witness for Him to testify that the fruit of righteousness is peace, and the effect of righteousness is quietness and assurance forever. (See Isaiah 32:17.) He has borne your sins in His own body on the tree. (See 1 Peter 2:24.) He has given you His Word and Spirit and all the ordinances of His grace. He has pledged Himself to you so that if you will avail yourself of these provisions by faith, He will render the truth of every promise and declaration of God's Word—which you are called to testify of—a conscious reality in your experience. What a fearful responsibility rests upon you to render yourself, in all respects, a qualified witness for Christ.

Christians themselves, and God through them, can demonstrate to the world the truth and faithfulness of the exceeding great and precious promises and declarations about the Christian experience *only* by the experience and testimony of His people to the reality of such experience. How, for example, can it be shown to the world that *"great peace have they which love thy law"* (Psalm 119:165) and that *"the work of righteousness shall be peace; and the effect of righteousness quietness and assurance for ever"* (Isaiah 32:17)? It is only through the experience and testimony of those who love the law and perform those works of righteousness. The same principle holds true in respect to all the promises and declarations of inspiration, like those above cited. The necessity and importance, then, of Christians being able to give this testimony for Christ is just as great as that the world should be convinced that God is true and faithful in the promises and declarations of His Word. How infinite are the obligations resting upon every Christian to stand before the world fully qualified to testify as a true and faithful witness for Christ.

People, in their convictions of the truth of the Bible, are more influenced by such experience and testimony than by all other considerations together. Array before them the external evidences of the truth of the Bible, and they can remain still in unbelief. Present them with any naked declaration of Scripture, and they are comparatively unmoved. Present now that same declaration, verified in the actual and manifest experience of a multitude of believers, and they are not only forced to acknowledge the declaration itself to be true but also the Bible that contains it to be from heaven. Thus it is that the church, by fully qualifying herself to testify for Christ, has the power to force infidelity and skepticism in every form from the earth and to bring the world back to God. The necessity and obligation resting upon all Christians to qualify themselves to testify for Christ is just as great as the importance of the redemption of the world, whose redemption is suspended, as far as instrumentalities are concerned, upon such testimony.

The main objections brought against Christianity everywhere rest upon its apparent effects in the visible experience of those who professedly embrace it; these effects, in a vast majority of instances, are so unlike the results the Bible affirms will follow a reception of the gospel. So long as this state of things continues, for that long unbelief will fill the earth and the great mass of men will remain estranged from God. If the light that is in the professed people of God is so comparatively dark, how great must be the darkness that covers the earth, how gross the darkness that covers the people! A church fully qualified to testify for Christ—and such a church only—can become the light of the world. Let the church become visibly adorned with all the blissful fruits of righteousness, and the cavils of the unbeliever are silenced, the vain excuses of the impenitent are wrested from them, and the gospel becomes omnipotent for the redemption of lost men. So great is the necessity and obligation resting upon Christians to be able to give full testimony for Christ.

Remarks

I will first point out a great mistake into which many have fallen in regard to the advantages the early Christians enjoyed for demonstrating to the world the truth of the gospel, as compared with the advantages possessed by Christians now for accomplishing the same object. On account of the power of miracles and the gift of tongues, it is thought that their advantages were altogether superior to those now enjoyed. It would be easy to show that through the record of these events that has been left us and the great facility of spreading these records before the world, such as through the press, we now enjoy almost, if not quite, as great advantages in this respect as they did.

There is another respect, however, in which our advantages are so much superior to theirs, as to render the balance altogether in our favor. Our advantages in acquiring a knowledge of the gospel and consequently of giving the world a full demonstration of its truth (the highest demonstration it admits) are indefinitely superior to theirs. For example, thousands of years ago, an inspired writer affirmed, "*Great peace have they which love thy law: and nothing shall offend them*" (Psalm 119:165). In that affirmation it is clearly implied that none have such peace who do not love this law. The experience of all sinners presents a full demonstration of the truth of this implication. If the experience of the church today presented a demonstration full of the truth of that affirmation, how could the world resist the conviction that that law is from heaven?

Again, thousands of years ago, an inspired prophet made the following affirmations: "*The wicked are like the troubled sea, when it cannot rest, whose waters cast up mire and dirt. There is no peace, saith my God, to the wicked*" (Isaiah 57:20–21). The unvarying experience of all sinners in all ages presents an undeniable demonstration of the truth of the above declarations. Again he says, "*The work of righteousness shall be peace; and the effect of righteousness quietness and assurance for ever*" (Isaiah 32:17). If at this distant age the church presented a demonstration, in her experience, of the truth that the effect of righteousness is quietness and assurance, would she not exhibit to the world a standing proof of the truth of the Bible?

Once more, eighteen hundred years ago, an inspired apostle affirmed that everyone who believes in Christ overcomes the world and that no one who does not believe in Him does overcome the world. (See 1 John 5:4–5.) The bondage under the power of sin that all who are destitute of faith in Christ experience fully proves the declaration last cited. Should the church, through faith in Christ, present to the world a glorious victory over the world, the flesh, and the devil, what need would there be of miracles to demonstrate the divine origin of the Bible? The church herself would then be, to all the world, a standing miracle, proving beyond all contradiction that the gospel is from heaven.

Suppose now that, while all the declarations of the Bible relating to the impenitent meet an unquestionable fulfillment in the conscious and manifest experience of sinners, so too all the exceeding great and precious promises and affirmations of that sacred book pertaining to believers are equally fulfilled in the experience of the church. Would it not be just as obvious to all mankind that the Bible is the sun and center of the moral world as it is that the natural sun is the great light and center of the natural world?

Are not the advantages of the church to give such demonstrations increased, just in proportion to her distance from the time when the Scriptures were written? For these reasons, together with the greater ability to understand and publish the gospel, may it not be safely affirmed that the church was never before placed in circumstances so favorable to show to the world the divine origin of that gospel as she is at the present time?

We may understand the true cause of all the infidelity that exists. Unbelievers, it should be stated, are without excuse before God. But when we inquire for the cause of the strange unbelief that, in various forms, pervades Christendom, may it not be safely affirmed that if the church had given the testimony for Christ that she might and ought to have given, such infidelity would never have existed? Is not the church, then, responsible for its existence and perpetuity? Can we reasonably hope that the condition of the world will be much changed for the better as long as the testimony of the church, "known and read of all men," in her own experience and example is so strongly against the Bible?

Suppose, reader, that the world could have no higher evidence than the church presents, in her common experience and example, of the truth of such promises and declarations as we have been considering. Would not the world be justified in the conclusion that the Bible is not from God? Blessed be God; other testimony does exist that vindicates the faithfulness and honor of God and leaves the sinner without excuse.

We may understand what the honor of God and the salvation of the world demand. It is the raising up of a witnessing church for Christ—a church who can, through her own experience, bear full testimony to the world of the truth and faithfulness of God in all the exceeding great and precious promises and declarations of His Word pertaining to believers in this life.

When Zion will thus arise and shine, her light having come and the glory of the Lord being risen upon her, then the Gentiles will come to her light and kings to the brightness of her rising, and all the earth will be full of the knowledge and glory of the Lord as the waters cover the sea. (See Isaiah 60:1–3; Habakkuk 2:14.)

The kind—almost the only kind—of testimony that the great mass of the church is able to give for Christ here claims our attention. Take a single passage in illustration: "*Thou wilt keep him in perfect peace, whose mind is stayed on thee: because he trusteth in thee*" (Isaiah 26:3). Few can testify from conscious experience that those who thus trust in God and stay themselves upon Him are in fact kept in perfect peace. This is their testimony: *If* we should thus trust in God and stay ourselves upon Him, He would thus keep us. What more is this than impenitent sinners can say? It is the mere expression of an opinion and is no testimony at all. And the worth of the opinion is destroyed by a course of life directly opposed to such declarations. The witness affirms his belief that if he would stay his mind upon God, He would keep him in perfect peace. He then, by withholding such confidence, demonstrates to the world that in that declaration he is not sincere, and thus he annihilates the force of his own affirmation.

The testimony of the church in favor of the gospel will never be received and ought never to be received as of any value until there is a manifest consistency between her professions and her conduct.

We see, from this subject, how far anyone can have evidence that he is a real Christian. "*In keeping of them* [God's commandments] *there is great reward*" (Psalm 19:11). "*Whom having not seen, ye love; in whom, though now ye see him not, yet believing, ye rejoice with joy unspeakable and full of glory*" (1 Peter 1:8). To the extent that anyone is conscious that these and similar declarations of the Bible are fulfilled in his experience, he has evidence that he is a Christian. To the extent that he lacks such experience, he is not only destitute of such evidence, but the probability is altogether against him.

What, then, in the light of this subject, must we think of the real condition of a large portion of professing Christians? Faithfulness to souls compels me to say that either the Bible is not the Word of God or they are not Christians. Their uniform experience is a continual affirmation that God is not true and faithful in the promises and declarations of His Word pertaining to believers in this life. Will Christ say to such at last, "Well done, true and faithful witnesses! You have been faithful over a few things, and I will make you rulers over many things. Enter into the joy of your Lord." (See Matthew 25:23.) *"Be not deceived; God is not mocked: for whatsoever a man soweth, that shall he also reap"* (Galatians 6:7).

In the light of this subject, we see why it is that preaching the most soul-stirring truths of the gospel has so little effect upon sinners. It is the testimony of the church, given in her experience and example before the world, that causes what the preacher says to not be regarded. When a minister warns sinners *"to flee from the wrath to come"* (Luke 3:7), does the church in her manifest concern for them, in her daily intercourse with them, affirm to sinners that such warnings are worthy to be regarded? When the preacher promises present and eternal blessedness on condition of *"repentance toward God, and faith toward the Lord Jesus Christ"* (Acts 20:21), does the testimony of the church, through her manifest experience, affirm to sinners that such promises are *yes* and *amen* in Christ Jesus? Nothing is further from the truth. No wonder, then, that the gospel of the blessed God does not prove *"mighty through God to the pulling down of strong holds"* (2 Corinthians 10:4). And Christian, it is a solemn inquiry how far you and I are responsible for this state of things. Is it not time for us to go upon our knees and put this solemn question to ourselves?

In the light of this subject, we can understand the prejudice that now extensively prevails against individuals speaking of their own experience or telling what the Lord has done for their souls. (See Mark 5:19.) Such a prejudice surely has no foundation in any precept or example recorded in the Bible. On what foundation then does it rest? I am constrained to express the conviction that it rests on a conscious want of any important experience about which to give testimony. Could a person, as he lay floating as a little speck in an ocean of bliss that knew no bounds but the extent of his capacities, have refrained from testifying of what the grace of Christ had wrought in him? By no means! In all instances, when *"the love of God is shed abroad in...hearts by the Holy Ghost"* (Romans 5:5), those who fear the Lord speak often to each other (see Malachi 3:16) and *"magnify the Lord"* (Luke 1:46) by testifying to the power of His grace in their own souls.

We may now understand one of the reasons for the hardness of heart and abandonment of the Spirit of God that a large portion of the church complains so much about. It is the gross hypocrisy that is practiced in many of our most sacred exercises. Take a single example in illustration. How often does the church in her hymns testify before the world to her own love and devotion to Christ in language like the following:

E'er since, by faith, I saw the stream
Thy flowing wounds supply,

...

Redeeming love has been my theme,
And shall be till I die.[5]

I ask if this declaration is true. Has redeeming love been the theme of the mass of the church "e'er since, by faith, she saw the stream"? What, then, must be the influence upon the world, and upon our own hearts, of testifying to such a fact when it is known to be untrue? Again,

---

5. William Cowper, "There Is a Fountain Filled with Blood," 1772.

Since from his bounty I receive
Such proofs of love divine,
Had I a thousand hearts to give,
Lord, they should all be Thine.[6]

How often does the professor of religion declare before God and the world that if he had a thousand hearts, he would give them *all* to Christ—and then openly take away *his one heart* from Him and bestow it upon the most trifling objects conceivable. Has not God said, *"Be ye not mockers, lest your bands be made strong"* (Isaiah 28:22)? Is He not *"a God of truth and without iniquity"* (Deuteronomy 32:4)? And has He not said that evil will not dwell with Him? (See Psalm 5:4). If, then, in His sacred presence, we in any form testify to what is untrue, will He not consider it and send leanness into our souls?

We see from this subject that if the doctrine of Christian perfection is not true and also if it is never actually to be realized in the experience of believers in this life, then Christ will never have a witness here *fully* qualified to testify to the world about His truth and faithfulness in many (and I may say *most*) of His exceeding great and precious promises. Take one as an illustration:

> *And the very God of peace sanctify you wholly; and I pray God your whole spirit and soul and body be preserved blameless unto the coming of our Lord Jesus Christ. Faithful is he that calleth you, who also will do it.*
>
> (1 Thessalonians 5:23–24)

Now it is here asserted that the God of peace is worthy of our confidence for not only *perfect* but *continued* sanctification. When we thus trust Him, He will thus sanctify and preserve us. No

6. Samuel Stennett, "Majestic Sweetness Sits Enthroned," 1787.

Christian, until he has so trusted God for this blessing—as to be brought into and preserved in a state of entire consecration to Christ—can testify that God is worthy to be trusted for such a blessing. And insofar as he withholds the confidence in God needed to receive the grace of entire sanctification, insofar does he in his conduct before the world testify that God is not worthy to be trusted in respect to any such promise. The same principle holds true in respect to a great portion of the promises of divine grace, since they directly proffer to our faith the same blessing. Should we suppose, as the doctrine of imperfection affirms, that Christ has by an express revelation required us to believe that He will never have a witness on earth fully qualified to testify to His own truth and faithfulness?

We may notice the unreasonableness of the sentiment so common in the church, that if an individual should attain to a state of perfection, he would not be permitted to live any longer upon earth. On this sentiment I remark:

1. It has not the shadow of a foundation in a solitary passage, hint, or principle of the Bible.
2. It is opposed to the positive teachings of inspiration. "*What man is he that desireth life, and loveth many days, that he may see good? Keep thy tongue from evil, and thy lips from speaking guile. Depart from evil, and do good; seek peace, and pursue it*" (Psalm 34:12–14).
3. The principle itself is intrinsically absurd. It affirms that when Christ has once fully qualified an individual to testify for Him, He will not allow him to give testimony at all. Such, reader, is the doctrine of imperfection.

We see when it is that a Christian witnesses a good confession for Christ. It is when he testifies that Christ has fulfilled in him any promise of His grace, whatever it may be, and when his life corresponds with that testimony. Such testimony is in the highest sense honorable to Christ. Suppose an individual professes to have received from Christ, as far as past and present experience goes, a fulfillment of the promise recorded in 1 Thessalonians 5:23–24, and his life corresponds with that profession. That testimony is most credible and most highly honorable to God. Such witnesses for Christ the church needs, and a great cloud of such witnesses, I doubt not, Christ will soon raise up for Himself.

We may judge of the propriety of the strange prejudice that exists in many minds against such testimony for Christ as this. To illustrate, permit me to state a fact. A brother in the ministry had for *years* been able to testify for Christ only that his first love had left an "aching void within," which neither the world nor any thing he could subsequently find in the gospel could fill. As long as he gave this gloomy testimony, it was received as honorable to Christ and as an evidence that he was a "faithful minister of the New Testament." Subsequently, however, he was permitted to behold with open face, as in a glass, the glory of the Lord and was changed into the same image, from glory to glory, even as by the Spirit of the Lord. (See 2 Corinthians 3:18.) He then came before his brethren as a witness for Christ and humbly testified that Christ, in conformity with His own exceeding great and precious promises, had circumcised his heart to love the Lord his God with all his heart and with all his soul—that He had sprinkled clean water upon him and made him clean—that He had sanctified him wholly and was preserving him with a conscience void of offense toward God and toward men.

In respect to the *blessedness* of the state to which the grace of Christ had brought him, he testified that, in conformity with the promises of God, the sun was no more his light by day. Neither for brightness did the moon give light unto him, but the Lord was unto him an everlasting light, and his God was his glory. His sun no more went down; neither did his moon withdraw itself; for the Lord was his everlasting light, and the days of his mourning were ended. As soon as he thus testified to the truth and faithfulness of Christ, in His acknowledged promises to His people, his associates, who had received his former testimony as honorable to Christ took measures to eject him from the ministry. They would not rest till, like Joseph, he was separated from his brethren. Truly may God say, *"The ox knoweth his owner, and the ass his master's crib: but Israel doth not know, my people doth not consider"* (Isaiah 1:3).

We see why it is that many Christians complain that they find very little to do for Christ and are able to exert but little influence as Christians in the world. A witness will not often be called to testify in court when it is known that he has little or nothing to say that would be of use. But when it is known that he has important facts to state, his testimony will certainly be sought. Is not this the reason, Christian, why Christ does so little through you—because you have nothing to testify to that would be honorable to Him or serviceable to His cause? If, on the other hand, you will so avail yourself of His grace as to qualify yourself to testify for Him, very soon will come to you the sweet message "The Master has come and calls for you." He will place you in circumstances where great results will turn upon the testimony that you will render for Him. *"He that abideth in me, and I in him, the same bringeth forth much fruit"* (John 15:5). And now, Christian, *"abide in him; that, when he shall appear, we may have confidence, and not be ashamed before him at his coming"* (1 John 2:28).

6

THE GLORY CONFERRED UPON THE BELIEVER

"And the glory which thou gavest me I have given them; that they may be one, even as we are one: I in them, and thou in me, that they may be made perfect in one; and that the world may know that thou hast sent me, and hast loved them, as thou hast loved me."
—John 17:22–23

I have read, with great interest and profit, your remarks upon John 17:20–23," said a beloved brother to me some years since. "It seems to me, however, that there is a richness and glory about the passage which you have hardly begun to develop."

"The glory which thou gavest me I have given them." What does this mean? What an inheritance of glory and blessedness is here devolved upon the Christian! And all this glory and blessedness are mine when I have faith to receive them. This is the legacy Jesus Christ has left to every believer. Who can express the *"breadth, and length, and depth, and height"* (Ephesians 3:18) of the love disclosed in these blessed words! Yet it is all a reality and may be such in my own experience. I may enjoy this inheritance, not merely in eternity, but in this life also. For it is given for the express purpose of rendering believers *"perfect in one; and that the world may know that thou hast sent me, and hast loved them, as thou hast loved me."*

It was this conversation, together with a discourse upon these words subsequently delivered by that brother that led to the train of thought to which the attention of the reader is now invited. Three facts presented in this passage deserve special attention in preparation for the train of thought I will pursue.

It is a fundamental design of Christ, in the arrangements of His grace, to identify His people in all possible respects with Himself, conferring upon them whatever the Father has conferred upon Him.

> *The glory which thou gavest me I have given them.*
> (John 17:22)

> *That the love wherewith thou hast loved me may be in them, and I in them.* (verse 26)

> *That they might have my joy fulfilled in themselves [that they might be filled with the blessedness I possess].*
> (verse 13)

> *That the world may know that thou hast sent me, and hast loved them, as thou hast loved me.* (John 17:23)

> *Because I live, ye shall live also.* (John 14:19)

> *As thou hast sent me into the world, even so have I also sent them into the world.* (John 17:18)

The glory referred to in the text is a legacy conferred by Christ upon every believer. It is, therefore, his privilege as well as duty to possess and enjoy it. This is evident from the context. "*Neither pray I for* [my disciples] *alone, but for them also which shall believe on me through their word*" (John 17:20). He then adds, "*The glory which thou gavest me I have given them*" (verse 22)—that is, all believers.

It is the privilege and duty of every Christian to possess this glory not only in eternity but in this life. It is given, as remarked above, for the express purpose of inducing the world to believe in Christ. It is, therefore, given as a good to be enjoyed by the believer in this life. In the further elucidation of the great truths presented in this passage, we will inquire:

1. The glory the Father conferred upon Christ
2. The glory Christ has conferred upon His people
3. The design of this arrangement
4. The state to which believers must attain to possess this glory
5. How they may attain this state
6. The consequences of making such attainments and possessing this glory

The Glory the Father Conferred upon Christ

It implies the glory of giving the world and the universe a representation, full and distinct, of the moral character of God. The highest holiness of intelligent beings, and the highest blessedness of all the holy, depend upon such a revelation of the perfections, character, and glory of God being made to their minds. In the creation of the world, the invisible things of God, even His eternal power and Godhead, are clearly seen. (See Romans 1:20.) In the same work, together with the dispensations of universal providence, the moral perfections of God are shadowed forth with somewhat similar distinctness. In all these, however, the reflections of the divine glory are comparatively feeble. The heart of God could not by such means be unveiled to the apprehension of the universe with such distinctness and fullness that with open faces they could behold the glory of the Lord. (See 2 Corinthians 3:18.)

The plan of redemption presented an opportunity for accomplishing this glorious consummation. Here God could make such a revelation of Himself, of His infinite and boundless love to intelligent beings, that the glory resulting from all His former works would *"not be remembered, nor come into mind"* (Isaiah 65:17). The glory of accomplishing this work, the highest honor in the power of the Godhead to bestow, the Father conferred upon Christ. In the accomplishment of this work, Christ appears—in all He did, said, and taught—as the *"the image of the invisible God"* (Colossians 1:15), *"the brightness of his glory, and the express image of his person"* (Hebrews 1:3). *"No man hath seen God at any time; the only begotten Son, which is in the bosom of the Father, he hath declared him"* (John 1:18). That is, He disclosed His glory with full and perfect distinctness to the apprehensions of the universe. All who have seen Christ and have apprehended His character have seen the Father. The honor of appearing before the universe as a pure and spotless mirror, reflecting the image and glory of God, is the glory that the Father conferred upon Christ.

Another element of this glory is the honor of carrying into accomplishment God's purposes of infinite love and mercy in the redemption of lost men. In the counsels of eternity, the plan was laid, making provisions that the lost sinner of our race might escape the endless consequences of his own guilt and folly and be recovered to holiness and the favor of God. Of all the works of God, this excelled in glory. The glory of carrying this work into accomplishment, the Father conferred upon Christ. It was in view of this fact that Christ declared, just before He left the world, *"I have glorified thee on the earth: I have finished the work which thou gavest me to do"* (John 17:4).

Another element of this glory is the honor of having the Father dwell in Him and render Him, even in his humiliation, the object of the divine love and favor. When the Father brought His first-begotten into the world, He required even the hosts of heaven to worship Him. When He commenced His public ministry, the Father, by a voice from heaven, proclaimed Him as His beloved Son, in whom He was well pleased. (See Matthew 3:17.) Christ was never alone. The Father was always with Him. The Father dwelt in Him, and He lived by the Father. The Father judged no man but committed all judgment to the Son. Thus, at all times and under all circumstances, Christ was not only the real but the visible object of the Father's love and delight. What higher glory could the Father confer upon Christ than this, while in His humiliation on earth?

The Father always heard Christ when He prayed and always granted His requests. He could say with truth, *"Father, I thank thee that thou hast heard me. And I knew that thou hearest me always*" (John 11:41–42). This is another element of the glory the Father conferred upon Christ.

When Christ finished the work the Father gave Him to do, as a reward of His obedience,

> *God also hath highly exalted him, and given him a name which is above every name: that at the name of Jesus every knee should bow, of things in heaven, and things in earth, and things under the earth; and that every tongue should confess that Jesus Christ is Lord, to the glory of God the Father.*
> (Philippians 2:9–11)

All power in heaven and on earth was given unto Him. He was exalted to the throne of the universe, and the scepter of the universe the Father put into His hands. To be thus exalted by the Father in the presence of the universe is the last and crowning element of the glory the Father conferred upon Christ.

The Glory Christ Has Conferred upon His People

In the text, it is declared to be identical with the glory the Father conferred upon Christ. In what, then, does this glory consist? In general, I would say that it consists in the believer being introduced into a relation with Christ and with God through Him similar to that which Christ sustains with the Father. For example, Christ has conferred upon believers the glory of representing Him to the world as He represented the Father. Christ appeared in the world as the image and glory of God. The believer is permitted to behold as in a glass the glory of the Lord and be changed into the same image from glory to glory, to reflect the image and glory of Christ upon the surrounding world.

"God, who commanded the light to shine out of darkness, hath shined in our hearts, to give the light of the knowledge of the glory of God in the face of Jesus Christ" (2 Corinthians 4:6). As the mirror, when placed in the light of the glorious luminary of day, gives a reflection that is full and distinct of the image and glory of the sun, so God is here declared to shine in the heart of the believer for the purpose of giving to the sons of men, through Him, a reflection *"of the glory of God in the face of Jesus Christ."* The privilege and the honor of sustaining such a relation to Christ, and to God through Him, is the glory Christ has conferred upon believers. Christian, will you not dwell upon this thought till you receive its full impression in your heart?

Christ has conferred upon believers the glory of carrying into accomplishment His purposes of love and mercy toward lost men, just as there was conferred upon Him the glory of accomplishing those of the Father. *"As thou hast sent me into the world, even so have I also sent them into the world"* (John 17:18). After laying the foundation for the salvation of sinners in the work of redemption, one thing further needed to be accomplished. This redemption must be made known to the sons of men. The accomplishment of this last work was as essential as the former to the salvation of our race. He has conferred upon His people the glory of proclaiming to lost men *"the unsearchable riches of Christ"* (Ephesians 3:8). In its accomplishment, they are *"the light of the world"* (John 8:12), as He was the light of the world.

This is the glory, Christian, Christ has conferred upon you—to be a worker together with God, to be employed by Christ as His ambassador, as His minister, as He was employed by the Father, in the accomplishment of the purposes of infinite love and mercy toward lost men.

Another element of the glory Christ has conferred upon His people is this—the honor of having Christ dwell in *them* as the Father dwelt in Him.

> *I in them, and thou in me.* (John 17:23)

> *We will come unto him, and make our abode with him.* (John 14:23)

> *Ye are the temple of the living God; as God hath said, I will dwell in them, and walk in them; and I will be their God, and* they shall be my people. (2 Corinthians 6:16)

> *Know ye not that your body is the temple of the Holy Ghost…?* (1 Corinthians 6:19)

As the Father dwelt in Christ, and as this was the highest honor the Father could confer upon Him, so He has conferred this glory upon His people, making—together with every person of the sacred Trinity—His abode in them. This glory, Christian, Christ has conferred upon you. Christ could ask or desire no higher glory from the Father than this, that the Father should make His abode with Him. What higher glory can you conceive or desire of Christ than that He should make His abode with you? When on earth, Christ was never alone. The Father was always with Him. So, Christian, you need never be alone. Christ and the Father and the Holy Spirit may always be with you and in you, as the Father was with Christ and in Christ. As Christ lived by the Father and, through the Father's presence and love, as His blessedness was always full, so you also may live by Christ; through His presence and love, "*your joy may be full*" (1 John 1:4).

Christ has conferred upon His people the glory of having the same power with God in prayer that He Himself had. What a source of inconceivable glory and blessedness it must have been to Christ to know in Himself, and to have it manifest to the world and to the universe, that the Father always heard Him and granted His requests when He prayed. This same glory and blessedness Christ has conferred upon His people. Into the same relation to God in prayer, which He himself sustained, He has introduced them.

> *If ye abide in me, and my words abide in you, ye shall ask what ye will, and it shall be done unto you.* (John 15:7)

> *Whatsoever ye shall ask the Father in my name, he will give it you.* (John 16:23)

> *Ye have not chosen me, but I have chosen you, and ordained you, that ye should go and bring forth fruit, and that your fruit should remain: that whatsoever you shall ask of the Father in my name, he may give it you.* (John 15:16)

It is your privilege, Christian, not only to sustain such a relation to God in prayer, but to have it manifest to the world and to the universe that you do sustain that relation. This is the glory Christ as conferred upon you.

Christ has conferred upon His people the honor of being exalted by Him to glory and blessedness when they have accomplished His work on earth, just as He was highly exalted by the Father when He had finished the work the Father gave Him to do. "*To him that overcometh will I grant to sit with me in my throne, even as I also overcame, and am set down with my Father in his throne*" (Revelation 3:21).

Such is the glory Christ has conferred upon His people. In all possible respects, He has identified them with Himself, conferring upon them what the Father has conferred upon Him.

The Design of This Arrangement

One fundamental design is to produce a perfect union and identity of feeling and object between God and His people. "*That they all may be one; as thou, Father, art in me, and I in thee, that they also may be one in us*" (John 17:21). The Father dwelling in Christ, and Christ in Him, produces a perfect identity of feeling and object between the Father and Christ. Christ dwelling in His people, and they in Him, secures a similar union between God and them. To secure this union is a fundamental design of this arrangement.

Another design, equally fundamental, is to produce a similar union among Christians, one toward another. "*And the glory which thou gavest me I have given them; that they may be one, even as we are one*" (John 17:22)—that is, that the same union of sentiment, feeling, and object may exist among them that exists between us. "*I in them, and thou in me, that they may be made perfect in one*" (verse 23)—that an absolutely perfect union may exist among believers. The Father dwelling in Christ and Christ in His people—how perfectly adapted is this, not only to produce a perfect harmony between every believer and God, but to render all believers one just as Christ and the Father are one.

Another design of this arrangement is to make Christians the objects of the same love of God that Christ was and to impress the world with the conviction that believers are thus loved by God. Christ knew perfectly the value of His Father's love. The desire of His heart was that all believers might become the objects of this love. Hence, His object was to render their character, their interests, and their relations to God identical with His own. God would then love them as He loved Him, and He would so manifest His love to them that the world would know that He thus loves the believer. This was a fundamental design of this arrangement.

> *The glory which thou gavest me I have given them; that they may be one, even as we are one: I in them, and thou in me, that they may be made perfect in one; and that the world may know that thou hast sent me, and hast loved them, as thou hast loved me.* (John 17:22–23)

The last great design of this arrangement that I mention is this—that under the convictions above referred to, the world might be converted to God. Christ saw that if the world could be convinced that He was sent of God and that all who believed in Him were loved of God, as He Himself was, all men would be drawn unto Him. (See John 12:32.) He also saw that if believers could all be rendered really and visibly one, as He and the Father were, and if all Christians could thus become the objects of the same love from God that He was, the world would believe in Him. Hence, to render believers one, as He and the Father are one, He conferred upon them the glory the Father had given Him. To render them perfect in one, He condescends to dwell in them as the Father dwelt in Him. Thus the Father would love them as He loved Christ, and the world, beholding such a glorious reflection of the beauty and value of holiness, all resulting from a union to Christ by faith, would also believe in Him.

The State Believers Must Attain to Possess This Glory

In general, I would say that they must possess a perfect identity of character, feeling, and object with Christ. They must, in all possible respects, be brought by Christ into the same relations to God that Christ sustained. Nothing but a perfect image of an object can fully represent that object. The believer—to represent Christ, to be loved of the Father as Christ was, and to convince the world that He is the object of that love—must be changed into the very image of Christ. For example, He must be entirely free from sin and become purely and perfectly holy. Such was Christ—He knew no sin. (See 2 Corinthians 5:21.) He was *"holy, harmless, undefiled, separate from sinners"* (Hebrews 7:26). To represent such a being, we must be free from sin as He was. We must be holy, harmless, and undefiled as He was. We must be separate from the world as Christ was separate from the world. In no other state can the Father love us as He loved Christ.

We must be supremely consecrated to the duties of our sacred calling—the glory of Christ in the salvation of men. All interests and all pursuits must be wholly subordinated to this one end. Christ, when on earth, had no honors to acquire, no treasures to amass, no unhallowed propensities to gratify. He came into the world, not to do His own will, but the will of Him who sent Him. He sought not His own glory but the glory of Him who sent Him. (See John 7:18.) From this great work, He was never for a moment drawn aside by the allurements of the world, the flesh, or the devil. How, Christian, can you give to the world a representation of the character, spirit, and life of such a being? Only by being in the world as He was in the world. Only by being as ardently, as constantly, and as supremely devoted to His work as He was to the work of the Father.

Believers, to possess the glory Christ has conferred upon them, must have great power in prayer. Christ, as we have seen, was always heard when He prayed. The believer, when he approaches the throne of grace, stands there and presents His petitions in the name of Christ. Under such circumstances, he really represents His Savior. He is bound, therefore, to appear there in such a spirit and to present his petitions in the exercise of such faith in the efficacy of Christ's name that God will hear him always, as He did Christ. As a prince, he must have power with God and with men. (See Genesis 32:28.) You have no right, Christian, to approach that sacred spot and go away empty. You are bound always to leave it with that fullness of joy that Christ received in the same circumstances. Otherwise, you misrepresent your Savior. You reject the glory Christ has conferred upon you.

Christians, to possess this glory, must be united among themselves in the bonds of pure love. The union they are called upon to represent in their mutual harmony and love toward one another is the union and love existing between the Father and the Son. How can believers, in their intercourse with one another, represent such a union as this? Only by becoming one as Christ and the Father are one.

Christians, to possess this glory, must manifest, in all their intercourse with each other and with the world, a spirit of condescension. They are to represent to the world the infinite condescension of God in the work of redemption. Christ has conferred upon them the glory of doing this. To accomplish this object, they must "*mind not high things, but condescend to men of low estate*" (Romans 12:16).

Instead of aiming to lift themselves above others, they must be imitators of God by descending to those beneath them for the purpose of elevating them to the light and blessedness that they enjoy. The Spirit of the Lord God must be upon them as it was upon Christ. Like Him, they must be anointed of God to preach good tidings to the meek, to bind up the brokenhearted, to proclaim liberty to the captives and the opening of the prison to those who are bound, to proclaim the acceptable year of the Lord, and to comfort all who mourn. (See Isaiah 61:1–2).

If we would possess this glory, all our interactions with our neighbor, and especially our business transactions with him, must be a pure exemplification of the great law of love. Such was Christ. Such must we be if we would enjoy the glory of representing Him.

Once more, to possess this glory, we must be so perfectly satisfied with the inheritance Christ has conferred upon us, and so blessed in it, that we will be perfectly contented and pleased with all the allotments of divine Providence. Christ, when on earth, could say, *"The foxes have holes, and the birds of the air have nests; but the Son of man hath not where to lay his head"* (Matthew 8:20). Yet He was perfectly satisfied with His condition and blessed in it, because in it He could manifest the glory and love of God to the world and to the universe.

To hang upon the cross was a joy to Him, because in so doing He could glorify His Father on the earth and finish the work He had given Him to do. Such must be your spirit, Christian, if you would possess the glory Christ has conferred upon you.

How to Possess the Glory Christ Has Conferred upon Us

Here let me request you, reader, as a condition of attaining this state, to stop a moment and consider what this glory is that Christ has conferred upon you. *"The glory which thou gavest me I have given them"* (John 17:22). Have you ever apprehended the real meaning of these words? Have you considered what it is to behold with open face, as in a glass, the glory of the Lord till you are changed into the same image from glory to glory, and then to reflect that image upon the surrounding world? Have you considered what it is to be sent forth as the minister of Christ, as the light of the world, to carry into accomplishment the purposes of infinite love and mercy in the plan of redemption? Have you considered what it is to have Christ dwell in you as the Father dwells in Him; to have the same power in prayer that He had; to be loved of God as He was and to sit down at last with Him on His throne, even as He is now seated with His Father on His throne? O that your mind might take full possession of the idea.

You must admit it as a reality to your own mind that all this glory and blessedness may be yours as soon as you have faith to receive it. Christ has purchased it for you and now proffers it to you as a free gift, without money and without price. Will you admit that the purchase is real and the offer sincere? Will you permit the truth to come home to your heart, that this glory may be yours and yours *now*?

In the sincerity of your heart, as under the eye of your God and Savior, you must *choose* this blessing as your great inheritance. Stop, reader, for a moment and ask yourself, "What do I now desire of the Lord?" Can you say, in the depth of your soul, "Lord, You know all things, and You know that I now prefer above all objects in existence and choose, as my great inheritance, the glory Christ proffers to me"?

Then in the sincerity of your heart, make a full and final and solemn relinquishment of all things else—of property, reputation, kindred, friends, and life itself—for this inheritance of glory. Reader, are you ready to make the sacrifice? With a fixed, strong, and unwavering faith, look directly to Christ to bestow upon you this glory. Hang upon Him till He responds, *"According to your faith be it unto you"* (Matthew 9:29).

In the exercise of the same faith, enter upon the diligent and prayerful study of the Bible, seek the baptism of the Holy Spirit, and commence the discharge of every duty for the single purpose of giving, in all the relations of life, a reflection of the light of the knowledge of the glory of God in the face of Jesus Christ. If you will do this, reader, as the Lord lives, the glory Christ has given to all His people will be yours. So also will He give you an entrance into the everlasting kingdom of our Lord and Savior Jesus Christ, where you will shine as the brightness of the firmament and as the stars forever and ever.

The Consequences of Possessing the Glory Christ Confers

The space proper for me to occupy will permit only a bare specification of the following.

1. The world would then obtain full and distinct apprehensions of the real character of God. Men will not now search for God and consequently will not find Him in His works or in His Word because they do not like to retain God in their knowledge. (See Romans 1:28.) But when *"the light of the knowledge of the glory of God in the face of Jesus Christ"* (2 Corinthians 4:6) is reflected upon them, through the character and life of believers, the world will and must know God as He is.

2. The world would then know what true religion is. People in general are as ignorant of the real nature of Christianity as they are of God—and for the same reason. In this state of darkness and ignorance, they will remain until

they learn what Christianity is through living epistles known and read of all men. (See 2 Corinthians 3:3.)

3. The world would then know and appreciate the beauty and value of religion. In the light of the purity of believers and the beauty of holiness as reflected in their lives, sinners will also clearly see their own deep depravity, guilt, and bondage under the power of sin. In the light of the believer's peace and blessedness, they will be rendered deeply sensible of their own wretchedness.
4. Hence, the last and great excuse of the sinner for continuance in sin—the life and example of professing Christians—will be wrested from him. Their actual holiness will be a reality to his mind. He will of course feel that he has no excuse for not being holy himself. All the motives of the gospel, the value of religion, the vanity and folly of all opposite pursuits, heaven, hell, Christ, God, the judgment, and eternity, will exert their full and appropriate influence upon his mind.
5. Consequently, the world would be converted to Christ. Christ would then be lifted up, and of course, He would draw all men unto Himself. (See John 12:32.)

> *Darkness shall cover the earth, and gross darkness the people: but the* Lord *shall rise upon thee, and his glory shall be seen upon thee. And the Gentiles shall come to thy light, and kings to the brightness of thy rising.* (Isaiah 60:2–3)

When God's people are one as Christ and the Father are one, the world will believe in Christ and will turn from dead works to serve the living God. (See Hebrews 9:14.)

Christian, the salvation of the world depends upon you taking possession of the glory Christ has given you.

Remarks

In view of this subject, we may understand in what sense real Christians *"are the light of the world"* (Matthew 5:14). They have no light in themselves. The light they shed upon the darkness around them is wholly a borrowed, reflected light. Suppose a company of individuals is shut up in a dark room, a room into which not a single ray of the sun's light can directly penetrate. Suppose a number of mirrors were so placed as to convey into that room the full image of the sun and, consequently, render all within perfectly luminous. These mirrors are the light of that room. Yet the light they convey is not from themselves. It is exclusively a reflected light. So the Christian is *"the light of the world"* only by receiving into his own heart the *"the light of the knowledge of the glory of God in the face of Jesus Christ"* (2 Corinthians 4:6) and then reflecting the image of Christ upon the surrounding world.

In the light of this subject, we have also an appropriate and decisive test of Christian character. Every real Christian has been, by the grace of God, changed into the image of Christ. That image he reflects upon the world around him, and in its reflection he conveys a real *"knowledge of the glory of God in the face of Jesus Christ."* Every person who beholds him and marks his spirit and manner of life will learn what the Spirit and character of Jesus Christ are and what the nature of true religion is. Now the great question with you, reader, is this: What impression does your spirit, character, and manner of life make upon the world around you? I do not ask you whether you ever sin but whether your deportment before the world is such a reflection of the image of Christ that all who know you know, through you, the Spirit and character of Christ and the nature of true religion. If so, you are a Christian. If not, you are not a Christian.

We have, in the light of this subject, a distinct apprehension of the relations Christians sustain to Christ in this world and in eternity. In this life, the Christian reflects the image of Christ as He appeared in His humiliation upon earth. In eternity he will, in a similar manner, reflect the image of Christ in His exaltation to glory and blessedness at the right hand of the Father. He now, to use the language of inspiration by way of accommodation, bears *"the image of the earthly"*; then he will bear *"the image of the heavenly"* (1 Corinthians 15:49). It is by bearing the image of the earthly that we are prepared to bear the image of the heavenly.

The nature of entire sanctification in this life may now be distinctly stated. It does not imply a likeness to Christ in His present exaltation to glory and blessedness. In this respect, no Christian attains or is perfect in this life. (See Philippians 3:12.) It implies, on the other hand, a perfect likeness to Christ, as His image is reflected in His humiliation on earth. In both states and in both senses, entire sanctification is obtained in the same way. In eternity the Christian sees Christ as He is (see 1 John 3:2)—that is, he beholds His glory as it is reflected from the eternal throne, and he is thus rendered like Him. In this life, he beholds with open face, as in a glass, the glory of the Lord—that is, the image of Christ as reflected in His humiliation on earth. And he is *"changed into the same image from glory to glory, even as by the Spirit of the Lord"* (2 Corinthians 3:18). To be in the world as Christ was in the world is entire present sanctification. To see Christ as He is and consequently be rendered like Him is the entire sanctification to which saints attain in eternity.

We are now prepared to answer the question, whether the believer may properly indulge the expectation of attaining to a state of entire sanctification in this life. If he may properly indulge the expectation of possessing the glory Christ has conferred upon him, he certainly may with equal propriety indulge the expectation of attaining this state. This is because the former, as we have seen, in the body of this discourse, cannot be without the latter. Now if we cannot properly indulge the expectation of enjoying the glory referred to, the declaration of Christ "*The glory which thou gavest me I have given them*" (John 17:22) is the most solemn mockery conceivable. To bestow a gift and then require us to believe we will not possess it or to proffer it upon conditions with which we are required to believe we will never comply—what is this but to mock our misery and to take the most effectual means conceivable to increase that misery? The individual who cherishes the sentiment that Christ has done this (and everyone who denies the doctrine of entire sanctification does so) does fearful wrong to his own soul. He draws such a veil over the divine glory as renders it impossible for him to love God with the deep and melting tenderness with which he is required to love Him.

The sentiment, if a Christian were entirely sanctified Christ would take him to heaven at once, here demands a passing notice. Christians remain here by Christ as the light of the world, as mirrors to illumine the darkness that covers the earth and the gross darkness that covers the people by reflecting all abroad His own image. According to this sentiment, the moment Christ has so sanctified one of His people so that he will give the world a perfect reflection of His image—that is, fully answer the end of his sacred calling and the wants of fallen humanity—He will remove him to another sphere. Christ then is unwilling to have His own image so reflected in this world as to draw all men unto Him. Reader, where did you learn the sentiment that perfect conformity to the will of God and, consequently, to the laws of your own being would kill you? Did you learn it from the Bible?

We see what it is that hinders the conversion of this world. It is the condition of the church. Instead of being one, as Christ and the Father are one, what fearful discord and strife reign throughout all her borders. Instead of being "*holy, harmless, undefiled, separate from sinners*" (Hebrews 7:26) and giving the world a pure and hallowed reflection of the image and glory of Christ and of the beauty of holiness, the character of Christ and the nature of His gospel, as exhibited in the church's example, are presented to the world in a deep and dark eclipse. As long as this state of things continues, alas for this sin-ruined world. The church will never become to the powers of darkness terrible as an enemy with banners till in the beauty of holiness she shines forth "*fair as the moon, clear as the sun*" (Song of Solomon 6:10). Holiness is the secret of her power. The want of it is the sole cause of her present weakness and inefficiency. This alone retards the progress of salvation upon earth.

We see why it is that Christ was so perfectly satisfied with all the pains, hardships, and self-denials attendant on His humiliation on earth. These things were contemplated by Him as a means indispensable to one end—the accomplishment of the work His Father gave Him to do. In no other way could He finish the work of redemption and give the world and the universe a representation of God as He is. Hence, the endurance of all these was a blessedness to Him.

We may also understand the grand secret of perfect contentment with all the allotments of divine Providence, even the most afflictive. Let our hearts be as perfectly set upon finishing the work Christ has sent us to accomplish (and why should they not be?) as His was upon finishing what the Father had given Him to do. Let us contemplate every allotment of Providence, and especially the most afflictive, as an important point of observation from which we are required to give the world a reflection of the image of Christ. Then, like Paul, we will *"take pleasure in infirmities, in reproaches, in necessities, in persecutions, in distresses for Christ's sake"* (2 Corinthians 12:10). We will learn, in whatever state we are, to be content, for our very contentment is a reflection of Christ. (See Philippians 4:11.)

We see also how to harmonize all divisions and discord among Christians. Let each of the parties sacredly aim to give to the other a pure reflection of the Spirit of Christ, to be just as forbearing, just as forgiving, and just as faithful in reproof as they think He would be under the same circumstances. Let this spirit pervade the church, and how soon would all sincere Christians become one. Every conceivable difficulty would be perfectly harmonized by the mutual application of this simple principle.

We also perceive the duty devolved upon each party under the circumstances supposed, whatever may be the conduct of the other. It is to be just as forbearing, just as forgiving, and just as stern in your reproof as, after seeking wisdom from above, you think Christ would be in your circumstances. Then, reader, you will render full obedience to the command *"As much as lieth in you, live peaceably with all men"* (Romans 12:18).

How many individuals, when they receive injuries, real or imaginary, seem to feel that they are now at liberty to indulge any spirit and to pursue any course of conduct they please in return? "Why, the man has greatly injured me in my person, property, or reputation. Admit it, my brother." But does this circumstance permit you to indulge unchristian feelings or to pursue an unchristian course of conduct toward the injurer? That dearest of books that excels every other tells me that Christ, "*when he was reviled, reviled not again; when he suffered, he threatened not*" (1 Peter 2:23). That same blessed book also tells me that in these, as well as in all other circumstances, we are to walk as Christ walked. (See Ephesians 5:2.) Reader, will you not carry this sweet thought everywhere with you and let it hallow all your feelings, control your whole conduct, and harmonize your entire character with the image of Christ?

In the light of this subject, we see how to determine our duty in every variety of condition in which we may be placed. We will seldom be at a loss, in any circumstance, to determine how Christ would feel and act in the same circumstance. Now, if our eye is single to the inquiry "How would Christ feel and act if He was in the same condition that I am?" duty will always be to us as visible objects are when the bright shining of a candle gives us light.

A passing remark in regard to the prospects and condition of the sinner is demanded before the discourse is closed. The alternative is now submitted to you to assimilate your character to that of Christ or to that of the world. Hitherto you have chosen to bear the image of the world. As a consequence, your character has been receiving a rapid assimilation to all that is impure and unholy in the universe. Soon, if you persevere, the image will be complete. The last touch will be given to it, and then God will take that soul of yours and place it amid the eternal horrors to which you have adapted its character. Now the dark image of earth may be erased from your heart and character and the image of Christ delineated in its stead. But remember, soon this blessed privilege will be withdrawn forever. For the universe, I would not bear the image of earth for a single hour. "*Behold, now is the accepted time; behold, now is the day of salvation*" (2 Corinthians 6:2).

7

TAKING THOUGHT FOR THE MORROW

"Take therefore no thought for the morrow:
for the morrow shall take thought for the things of itself.
Sufficient unto the day is the evil thereof."
—Matthew 6:34

In the preceding part of the Sermon on the Mount, the Savior advanced many new and, to His hearers, unheard-of principles of action—principles directly opposed to all the maxims by which they had been accustomed to supply their necessities and regulate their deportment before the world. Instead of hating, they were to love their enemies, even the most embittered. They were to do good not merely to the righteous and the grateful but to the evil and unthankful. To those who asked of them, they were to give, not merely what was asked but, if possible, even more. To those who would borrow of them, they were to lend, hoping for nothing in return. In short, they were to live not to themselves but for God and for humanity. To these ends, their whole being was to be devoted.

Under such circumstances, questions like these would naturally suggest themselves to the disciples: How can we live in conformity with such principles and acquire the necessaries of life? How can we make it our supreme object to lay up for ourselves treasures, not on the earth, but in heaven? How can we *"seek...**first** the kingdom of God, and his righteousness"* (Matthew 6:33)? How can we conform all our transactions with men to the law of love, regarding the rights and interests and desires of our neighbors more than our own, and still obtain food to nourish and raiment to clothe and adorn our bodies?

These and similar questions the Savior answers by requiring His disciples to dismiss, at once and forever, all anxiety about their future temporal necessities, all solicitude about the bearing of duty upon such subjects. The reasons He assigns for such requisitions are the following:

1. The concerns of the soul are of vastly greater importance, and such solicitude will jeopardize its immortal interests. *"Is not the life more than meat, and the body than raiment?"* (Matthew 6:25). *"Ye cannot serve God and mammon"* (verse 24).
2. God clothes the grass of the field and feeds the fowls of heaven without any anxiety about the future on

their part. (See Matthew 6:26, 30.) Why, then, should redeemed sinners distrust His paternal providence?

> *Behold the fowls of the air: for they sow not, neither do they reap, nor gather into barns; yet your heavenly Father feedeth them. Are ye not much better than they?* (Matthew 6:26)

> *And why take ye thought for raiment? Consider the lilies of the field, how they grow; they toil not, neither do they spin: and yet I say unto you, That even Solomon in all his glory was not arrayed like one of these. Wherefore, if God so clothe the grass of the field, which to day is, and to morrow is cast into the oven, shall he not much more clothe you, O ye of little faith?* (Verses 28–30)

3. Such solicitude is wholly useless. It is a total waste of thought and feeling. It can add not a particle to the strength, beauty, or height of our persons nor supply a solitary necessity of our nature. "*Which of you by taking thought can add one cubit unto his stature?*" (Matthew 6:27).
4. This is the spirit of worldly men, "*men…which have their portion in this life*" (Psalm 17:14). The indulgence of such a spirit will separate the soul from God. "*After all these things do the Gentiles seek*" (Matthew 6:32).
5. God, their Father in heaven, was fully aware that they needed all such things, not only as creatures, but in the great work to which He had called them. They might, therefore, quietly rest in the peaceful assurance that no real want of theirs would be left unsupplied.

6. God's Word has pledged that implicit obedience to His will should be followed, as a certain consequence, with a full supply of all their necessities. "*Seek ye first the kingdom of God, and his righteousness; and all these things shall be added unto you*" (Matthew 6:33).
7. They could always have free access to the throne of grace, where they could ask and receive till their joy was full. (See John 16:24.)

   > *Every one that asketh receiveth; and he that seeketh findeth; and to him that knocketh it shall be opened. Or what man is there of you, whom if his son ask bread, will he give him a stone?* (Matthew 7:8–9)

8. Finally, the cares and duties of the present moment are abundantly sufficient to occupy our entire solicitude without dividing it between the present and the future. "*Sufficient unto the day is the evil thereof*" (Matthew 6:34).

Such are the reasons upon which the Savior bases the command "*Take…no thought for the morrow*" (Matthew 6:34). The original word here rendered "take thought" designates a "doubting, anxious, fearful, and perturbed state of mind in regard to the future." Such also was the meaning of the phrase "take thought" when our Scriptures were translated. A contemporary historian says of a certain individual, "His heart was broken, and so for thought [anxious care, or intense mental perturbation] he died."

We are not, of course, prohibited from *thinking* about or making provision for the future. But all anxious solicitude about the *result* of our efforts to secure that end and about the dispensations of Providence bearing upon it is prohibited. To give the reader a distinct apprehension of the state of mind forbidden in the text, take a single example—the visit of Christ to the house of Martha in Luke 10:38–42. As soon as Christ entered, she set her heart upon providing a sumptuous entertainment for her divine guest. About the accomplishment of this object she "took thought," and her mind was soon filled with care, doubt, and perplexity. Her thoughts, we may suppose, first turned upon the guest chamber. Everything there must wear the aspect of perfect neatness and order. Yet, in her disquietude, everything appeared the reverse of what it ought to be. Such and such things were in disorder. Such and such articles were soiled. What would the Savior and His disciples think when they should see things thus? Then everything upon the table must be prepared in the best style and nothing be wanting to perfect the sumptuousness of the feast. But such and such articles, needful to render the entertainment what it should be, were wanting and could not be obtained. Then, of those that were provided, some were very imperfect in richness and flavor, others might be injured in preparation, and the remainder might not be got in readiness in time. Almost everything seemed to be going wrong, and all her efforts to do appropriate service to her divine guest appeared likely to prove abortive. Thus, *"Martha was cumbered about much serving"* (Luke 10:40), and while Mary was peacefully sitting at the Savior's feet, hearing His words (see Luke 10:39), Martha's feelings (the natural result of her perturbed state of mind) kindled into displeasure against her sister and even against Christ Himself for permitting her thus to neglect her domestic concerns.

With these feelings Martha came to Christ and said,

> *Lord, dost thou not care that my sister hath left me to serve alone? bid her therefore that she help me. And Jesus answered and said unto her, Martha, Martha, thou art careful and troubled about many things: but one thing is*

needful: and Mary hath chosen that good part, which shall not be taken away from her. (Luke 10:40–42)

How many persons are almost constantly in a state similar to that above described in respect to their property, their business transactions, their reputation, their health, the interests and prospects of their children or families, the arrangements and dispensations of Providence, and everything that deeply engrosses their feelings?

While on a journey some years ago, I fell in company with a Christian brother who was going to the same place I was. Providential occurrences, which we could neither foresee nor prevent, occasioned, at a particular point, a long and (to a worldly mind) painful delay. When we had again got under way, the question of whether we would meet another hindrance equally long and painful depended on us reaching a certain place at a given time. About this, that brother took thought. His mind, during the day, was in continual perturbation. His family was out of health, and he had promised to be at home at a given period. His business, too, required him to return at the earliest possible moment. "Will the boat have left before our arrival? Driver, can you push us forward with greater rapidity?"

My own concerns were probably as pressing as those of that brother. Having, however, done all that I could to secure an arrival at the proper time, I had found grace to resign the whole subject with entire quietness to the will of God, and my mind was floating as peacefully along the current of Providence as if conscious that all had been arranged in conformity to my will. So sweet and hallowed was the presence of Christ during the day that I often had to cover my face and weep for joy of heart.

We arrived some hours before the boat started. I then sat down with the brother and endeavored to convince him not only of the folly and uselessness of the state of mind above described but of its great wickedness in the sight of God.

A brother in the ministry had for some time experienced symptoms of declining health. On this subject he took thought. His countenance wore the aspect of deep pensiveness, anxiety, and gloom. The solicitude and agitation of his mind would be rendered agonizing if even a child should suggest to him that he seemed to be out of health. What a total stranger was that brother to the blessedness of the apostle who, through the grace of Christ, had learned *"in whatsoever state I am, therewith to be content"* (Philippians 4:11).

> *Blessed be God, even the Father of our Lord Jesus Christ, the Father of mercies, and the God of all comfort; who comforteth us in all our tribulation, that we may be able to comfort them which are in any trouble, by the comfort wherewith we ourselves are comforted of God.*
>
> (2 Corinthians 1:3–4)

The individual who does not find the gospel an unfailing source of consolation in every condition in life cannot, with the full assurance of faith and hope, present that gospel as a source of consolation to any person in any condition. Such an individual is totally disqualified for the discharge of the duties of the sacred office.

A mother, as she looked out at her window, saw a little child in the garden having hold of a small but valuable fruit tree, which she might injure or destroy. The injury, if done, would be consummated before it was practicable for the mother to caution her child. "There," exclaimed the agonized mother, "the child has got hold of that tree! She will very probably ruin it!" The child passed on, however, and left the tree, as the mother might reasonably have supposed, uninjured. Yet the mother suffered more from simple apprehension than she ought to have endured from the actual loss of a hundred such trees.

Soon after, the mother looked again and saw the same child returning from the house of a neighbor while the heavens were blackened with an approaching tempest, which had unexpectedly risen. Now, instead of peacefully commending the child to the divine protection, the apprehensions of the mother took a new direction. Certainly the storm would descend before the child could get home! Her constitution was so delicate that if she should be overtaken by the storm, her health would be impaired and her life endangered! Some time before the descent of the rain, the child was safe beneath the paternal roof, and the mother, after suffering incomparably more than she ought to have endured had the apprehended calamity actually occurred, found that she had been *"disquieted in vain"* (Psalm 39:6). In that disquietude, however, she had been wholly unfitted for prayer for her child or any other object and for the discharge of any duty in which the sustaining grace of the gospel would have been manifested.

Reader, have the facts above stated opened up an important page in your past history? If so, you are now prepared for a consideration of the great truth to be illustrated in this discourse, which is this: Obedience to God is the supreme business of life—all about which it is lawful for us to "take thought." In obeying God, it is our duty and privilege to dismiss wholly all anxiety about consequences, especially in regard to worldly, temporal objects.

The reader doubtless recollects the answer given by the shepherd of Salisbury Plain to the question of a traveler about what sort of weather he thought it would be on the morrow. "It will be such weather as pleases me," answered the shepherd.

Though the answer was delivered in the most mild and civil tone that could be imagined, the gentleman thought the words themselves rather rude and surly, and he asked him how that could be. "Because," replied the shepherd, "it will be such weather as pleases God, and whatever pleases Him always pleases me."

The principle that I maintain is that it is our duty and privilege to be continually in this resigned, confiding, and peaceful state of mind under all circumstances and in reference to all interests and events, especially such as have a bearing upon our worldly condition.

Our profession as Christians, together with our acknowledged relations to God, requires this of us and prohibits, as most unbecoming in us and most dishonorable to God, every other and opposite state of mind. What relations do we, as Christians, sustain to God, to all His works and attributes, and to all the resources of His infinity? *"Behold, what manner of love the Father hath bestowed upon us, that we should be called the sons of God"* (1 John 3:1). As children, we recognize ourselves as *"heirs of God, and joint-heirs with Christ"* (Romans 8:17). God is our shield and our exceeding great reward. (See Genesis 15:1.)

> *All things are yours; whether Paul, or Apollos, or Cephas, or the world, or life, or death, or things present, or things to come; all are yours; and ye are Christ's; and Christ is God's.*
> (1 Corinthians 3:21–23)

God has pledged His Word to us that no evil will befall us and no plague will come near our dwelling. (See Psalm 91:10.) We believe that all things are working together for our good (see Romans 8:29) and that these light afflictions, which are but for a moment, are working out for us a far more exceeding and eternal weight of glory (see 2 Corinthians 4:17).

Now, does it become individuals who are holding such truths, possessing such interests, and sustaining such relations to the perfections and heart of God to be careful and troubled about many things? Ought not our minds always to be as free from carefulness as heaven's atmosphere is from darkness and clouds? How unbecoming in us, how dishonorable to the sacred name by which we are called, is the opposite state of mind?

Our minds cannot possibly be harassed with doubt, care, and perplexity except from one cause—the absence of faith in God and the presence of unbelief in the heart. While our minds are stayed on God, He has pledged to will keep us in perfect peace. (See Isaiah 26:3.)

> *As the mountains are round about Jerusalem, so the* Lord *is round about his people, from henceforth even for ever.* (Psalm 125:2)

> *God is our refuge and strength, a* ***very present*** *help in trouble.* (Psalm 46:1)

> *When thou passest through the waters, I will be with thee; and through the rivers, they shall not overflow thee: when thou walkest through the fire, thou shalt not be burned; neither shall the flame kindle upon thee.* (Isaiah 43:2)

When we believe all this and rest in it as a reality, we cannot...

> *fear, though the earth be removed, and though the mountains be carried into the midst of the sea; though the waters thereof roar and be troubled, though the mountains shake with the swelling thereof.* (Psalm 46:2–3)

Nothing but unbelief can make room for fear in our hearts at any time and under any circumstances. What right have we to stagger at the promises of God through unbelief? (See Romans 4:20.)

Another consideration that demonstrates the sinfulness of almost every species of carefulness in respect to worldly prospects is this: Such solicitude very seldom if ever respects the *necessities* but instead what may be called the *luxuries* of life. Reader, were you ever in circumstances where you really felt apprehensive that you would perish or when you went very long or severely suffered from hunger, cold, or nakedness? You have food and raiment, with no fear of not possessing them while you live. With these, what right have you to *not* be content? How sinful it is when, having these, you are *"careful and troubled about many things"* (Luke 10:41). Where is your heart and, consequently, your treasure when in such a state?

But let us suppose a Christian is placed in circumstances where, by obeying one of the principles of the gospel—the least important, if you please—he is necessitated to sacrifice his entire prospects of worldly good. If he obeys, he must, like Paul, suffer the loss of all things. (See Philippians 3:8.) Three important questions here arise: Will he, by an adherence to truth and duty, make the sacrifice? If so, with what *spirit* will he make it? Will it be done reluctantly or with all joyfulness? I answer, he must not only make the sacrifice but regard it as a privilege that he is permitted thus to suffer for the name of Christ. Reader, you are not a Christian unless every individual principle and truth of the gospel is held in such estimation by you that you would readily part with all worldly goods and prospects in its reception, defense, and practical exemplification.

Let us now imagine a Christian placed in the circumstances supposed. The following considerations will show how and with what spirit it becomes him then to act. In the providence of God, a crisis has come in which it is necessary that one of his children should make that sacrifice in defense of that truth or principle. The glory of God and the interest of truth and righteousness require it at his hands. God and the gospel of His grace will be more highly honored by obedience here than by ten thousand similar acts under ordinary circumstances. Will a redeemed sinner, a man who calls himself a Christian, fail to meet such a crisis and to meet it joyfully? Will he be careful and troubled about the sacrifices obedience will cost him? God forbid. No, Christian, the pearl of great price, in the exigency in which God has placed you, is now before you. For joy thereof, go, sell all that you have, and buy it. (See Matthew 13:44.) Remember that whether you are called to make such sacrifices or not, such must be the esteem in which every truth and principle of the gospel is actually held by you, or you can never obtain that pearl.

An opportunity is now presented to disclose to the world the highest and brightest possible exhibition and evidence of Christian character. If he obeys, the world will see that he serves God from principle and not from interest. By prompt, decisive, and cheerful obedience at such a time, he may give the world a more distinct and impressive exhibition of what the spirit of true Christianity is than by a whole life of obedience in ordinary circumstances. What if he should fail at such a crisis? He can never repair the injury he has done to the cause of Christ. He can never make up the good he would have accomplished if he had stood faithful at that one moment. Christian, where duty manifestly jeopardizes your reputation, your property, your worldly prospects, then is the time, by prompt and peaceful obedience, to show the world what Christianity is.

The blessedness—direct and indirect, immediate and remote—that is consequent on obedience infinitely surpasses all the evils that may or can result from such obedience. In one scale, there are a few light afflictions which are but for a moment. (See 2 Corinthians 4:17.) In the other, there is much greater present blessedness than could result from disobedience and a far more exceeding and eternal weight of glory hereafter. With what feelings ought a Christian to make sacrifices for truth and righteousness under such circumstances?

The evils of disobedience infinitely surpass, under all circumstances, the advantages that can result from such disobedience. If, for any worldly considerations whatever, you trample upon the least of God's commandments, you deny Christ before men and consequently subject yourself to Christ's denunciation *"Him will I also deny before my Father which is in heaven"* (Matthew 10:33). What evil is as great as this? What temporary advantages can balance such evils?

Contemplate also the spirit of worldly men. When the King of Persia was pouring his armies upon the plains of Greece, the states assembled in council and resolved that, to arouse the patriotism of the nation by a public exhibition of the spirit that at such a crisis ought to animate every bosom, one of their most distinguished sovereigns, together with a small but chosen band of followers, must meet the enemy at a given place and there die. The present exigency was judged to be of such importance as to demand such a sacrifice. The King of Sparta was selected as the victim. At the straits of Thermopylae, with three hundred associates, he met the enemy and died accordingly. Nor did he and his chosen band do it reluctantly; they did it with all joyfulness. The very night on which they were to die, before they went forth to the sacrifice, they celebrated a joyful feast together and then met death as a privilege. Now, what was Thermopylae, what was all Greece, when weighed in the balance against a single principle or truth of the gospel? And will a Christian be less ready to sacrifice all that he has for infinite rewards than men of the world for finite objects?

"Take a company of grenadiers," said a French general to a subordinate officer, "and repel the approach of the enemy at such a pass. You will lose your life, but you will save the army thereby."

"Yes, sir," said the officer, and in the dreadful pass, he died accordingly. Such is the spirit with which worldly men, under the influence of worldly principles, labor for a corruptible crown. With what spirit should a Christian make sacrifices to gain an incorruptible crown? (See 1 Corinthians 9:25.)

Consider also the examples of self-sacrifice for truth and duty recorded in the Bible. First of all—

> *Ye know the grace of our Lord Jesus Christ, that, though he was rich, yet for your sakes he became poor, that ye through his poverty might be rich.* (2 Corinthians 8:9)

> *Being found in fashion as a man, he humbled himself, and became obedient unto death, even the death of the cross.* (Philippians 2:8)

Nor with reluctance did He make the sacrifice. It was "*for the joy that was set before him* [He] *endured the cross, despising the shame*" (Hebrews 12:2). What He requires of us is that we be just as prompt and cheerful in suffering the loss of all things for His honor and truth as He was in making such sacrifices for us. Are we worthy of the name of Christians if this spirit—in reference to every truth and principle of the glorious gospel of the blessed God—is not in us?

The early Christians were not wanting in respect to this spirit. They rejoiced that they were *"counted worthy to suffer shame for his name"* (Acts 5:41). Among their highest privileges, they enumerated this—unto us it has been given *"not only to believe on him, but also to suffer for his sake"* (Philippians 1:29).

> *And now* [says Paul], *behold, I go bound in the spirit unto Jerusalem, not knowing the things that shall befall me there: save that the Holy Ghost witnesseth in every city, saying that bonds and afflictions abide me. But none of these things move me, neither count I my life dear unto myself, so that I might finish my course with joy, and the ministry, which I have received of the Lord Jesus, to testify the gospel of the grace of God.* (Acts 20:22–24)

Again, *"If I be offered upon the sacrifice and service of your faith, I joy, and rejoice with you all. For the same cause also do ye joy, and rejoice with me"* (Philippians 2:17–18). Such was the estimate in which ancient believers held the truths and principles of the gospel. Such was the spirit with which they suffered the loss of all things for that gospel. Will we not, in the same spirit, offer ourselves on behalf of every truth and principle of the same gospel? Whenever a truth or principle of the gospel is before us, will we take thought about the consequences resulting from a reception of that truth or from obedience to that principle?

Let us now, for a few moments, contemplate the circumstances in which men are ordinarily placed and the objects in view of which solicitude is commonly called forth. The farmer, we will suppose, has planted and sown his fields and used all required instrumentalities to secure a harvest. Let him now simply do the following things, and carefulness about the result of his labors will have no place in his heart.

1. Let him repose implicit confidence in the following promises and render continued obedience to the following precepts. *"Trust in the* Lord, *and do good; so shalt thou dwell in the land, and verily thou shalt be fed"* (Psalm 37:3). *"He that walketh righteously, and speaketh uprightly...shall dwell on high: his place of defence shall be the munitions of rocks: bread shall be given him; his waters shall be sure"* (Isaiah 33:15–16). Who can take thought about the morrow in the presence of such promises?
2. Let him bear continually in mind that he will have just such a harvest as pleases God. Why should he not be satisfied? How can he fail to be satisfied with the dispensations of infinite wisdom and love?
3. If he continues to be obedient and trusts the Word of God, he will have just such a harvest as is best for him. *"No good thing will he withhold from them that walk uprightly"* (Psalm 84:11). Not one of his real necessities will be left unsupplied. Where is the place for carefulness in the presence of such hallowed truths as these?
4. Let him bear in mind that taking thought will not add a single grain to his harvest nor a blade of grass to his pastures. At the same time, it will forfeit all claims to the divine protection and blessing.

Who does not see that such an individual cannot take thought for the morrow, saying, "What will I eat, or what will I drink, or what will I wear, or what will be the result of my efforts for a harvest?" (see Matthew 6:25) without sinning against God and without distrusting the truthfulness and faithfulness of

God? The considerations above presented are equally applicable to our condition in all the relations and circumstances of life. If it is sinful for us to be careful and troubled in any one relation, the same state of mind is equally sinful in every other.

"But," says one, "I am under engagements to others. I have contracted debts I am bound to meet." Not if providential occurrences render it impossible for you to do it. Consider the following questions: Did you do right in contracting those debts? If not, repentance for the past and no anxiety for the consequences are demanded. Are you now using all lawful instrumentalities to meet those engagements? Are you willing and desirous to do all that duty requires of you to accomplish that object? If not, repentance for present sin and no thought for the morrow are required of you. But suppose that those debts were contracted without sin or that all past sin has been repented of, that you are now doing all that duty requires of you. Then you owe it to God, to yourself, and to the world, even to your creditors, to resign the future with the utmost peacefulness to Providence. If God calls you to exemplify the Christian character in a state of poverty or bankruptcy, it will be because precisely such exemplification is needed. You ought to be just as willing to glorify God in that relation as in any other. You cannot, by taking thought, pay a solitary debt. You will thereby only injure your own soul and disgrace the sacred name by which you are called.

But how will we make provision for our children? You have little fear, I presume, that they will not have food and raiment. This is not the ground of your anxiety. To take thought even about them is sin. For the promises of God cover all the real necessities, not only of yourselves but also of your children. What then must be the character of anxiety for anything beyond these! Even if your children should be left fatherless, you may leave them with the Lord, and your widows may trust in Him. You are not fearful that your children will not have, day by day, their daily food. You are solicitous lest they should not become wealthy and honorable among men. Do you desire this, let me ask, as a means of their salvation?

Do not the Scriptures teach us that individuals in such circumstances are least likely to become heirs of the grace of life? "*A rich man shall hardly enter into the kingdom of heaven*" (Matthew 19:23). "*They that will be rich fall into temptation and a snare, and into many foolish and hurtful lusts, which drown men in destruction and perdition*" (1 Timothy 6:9). Are you careful and troubled lest your children should not be placed in the midst of such temptations as these?

"But my health is poor. What if I should be laid aside entirely?" Yes, reader, what if you should? That, then, is the very condition in which God most needs your services. Ought you not to be as willing to glorify Him in sickness as in health, in death as in life? Permit me to ask three questions here. How was this state of your physical system brought about? Was it by a violation of the laws of life and health? If so, repentance for the past, not solicitude for the future, is called for. Are you now living in strict conformity to the laws of life and health and, consequently, the laws of God in respect to food, drink, and dress? If you are and are in all interests committed to your God and Savior, remember that you cannot have too much sickness. Nor can you die too soon. Fear not, for God is with you. (See Isaiah 41:10.) He will never leave you or forsake you. (See Hebrews 13:5.) He will help you and strengthen you. He will uphold you by the right hand of His righteousness. (See Isaiah 41:10.) He will place you in circumstances where you can do the most to glorify His name. "*Take therefore no thought for the morrow: for the morrow shall take thought for the things of itself. Sufficient unto the day is the evil thereof"* (Matthew 6:34).

Remarks

We are now prepared to contemplate the light in which taking thought for the morrow—carefulness in all its forms—should be regarded. These are states of mind about which the great mass of Christians take very little account. To indulge them is commonly regarded as indicating mental or physical weakness rather than sin. Yet there are doubtless few forms of sin more offensive to God or more disastrous in their influences. How often did Christ rebuke this sin in His disciples? Not until they were emancipated from its influence were they prepared for the great work to which He had called them. Reader, whenever you find yourself inclined to be careful and troubled about many things, will you not stop at once and inquire the cause? Will you not ask yourself, "Why do these thoughts and feelings arise in my mind?" You will find that they have their origin exclusively in unbelief. You have taken your affections from things above and set them on things on the earth. You have consequently ceased to rest with implicit confidence in the truth and faithfulness of God. The natural and necessary result is that your mind has become perturbed with doubt, fear, and perplexity about the very objects upon which your heart is set. How aggravated is the sinfulness of such a state of mind when indulged, as it always is, in the presence of infinite realities and the exceeding great and precious promises of God, which cover our entire necessities in time and eternity?

The appropriate remedy of this state of mind next demands our consideration. If we would be fully emancipated from its influence, we must admit to ourselves and confess to God its aggravated guilt. We must feel and acknowledge that we have no more right to be careful and troubled than we have to perpetrate the crimes of murder and adultery. The great mass of individuals cannot be emancipated from this state of mind for the simple reason that they cannot be brought to confess, to themselves and to God, its sinfulness.

We must set our affections on things above and not on things on the earth. (See Colossians 3:2.) When the heart is set upon objects, infinite and eternal, carefulness in respect to things finite and temporary will be excluded.

In the exercise of simple faith, we must commend our entire interests to God, as unto a faithful Creator. When our minds are thus staid upon Him, He will keep us in perfect peace. Not a wave of trouble will ever roll across our peaceful breasts. Our hearts will be strangers to fear, except in respect to one thing—fear of offending the object of infinite and boundless love upon which our affection is fixed.

We now perceive the objects about which, when we are engaged in any employment, especially in enterprises of great importance, it is proper for us to take thought. It is about the simple and exclusive inquiry, "What is right, what is duty, what is the will of God?" About this we are ever to be careful but not troubled. For our eye being single to this one object (see Matthew 6:22), God has promised, *"I will instruct thee and teach thee in the way which thou shalt go: I will guide thee with mine eye"* (Psalm 32:8). About everything else, all care is to be dismissed, for God has promised that while our wills are in harmony with His, not a demand of our beings will be left unsupplied. Reader, are you now ready to commit the keeping of your soul unto God in well-doing, as unto a faithful Creator?

Finally, we notice the exalted privilege of the Christian. The sacred writer thus expresses it: *"That we, being delivered out of the hand of our enemies"*—from everything which would destroy our peace or disturb the deep and permanent repose of the soul in God—*"might serve him without fear, in holiness and righteousness before him, all the days of our life"* (Luke 1:74–75). It is his privilege to be *"as sorrowful, yet alway rejoicing; as poor, yet making many rich; as having nothing, and yet possessing all things"* (2 Corinthians 6:10). God is his shield and his exceeding great reward (see Genesis 15:1), and it is his privilege to serve God at all times and under all circumstances with perfect fullness of joy, to be so independent of all finite objects that no vicissitudes of time or place can do him real injury or disturb the fixed contentedness of his soul in God and in the arrangements and dispensations of His providence and grace.

An English officer was in a storm at sea, where everyone was momentarily expecting to be swallowed up in the bosom of the deep. While terror and dismay sat upon every countenance around him, he was as calm as a summer evening. "My dear," exclaimed his wife, "how is it possible for you to be thus calm and peaceful amid such a scene as this?"

The officer arose and, placing his back against a pillar, so that he could stand with steadiness, drew his sword and, presenting its point to her breast, inquired, "Are you not afraid of that sword?"

"No," was her reply. "My husband holds it, and I know he loves me too well to injure me with it."

"So," said the officer, "I know in whom I have believed. He holds the winds in His fist and measures the sea in the hollow of His hand, and He has declared that no evil will befall those who put their trust in Him."

It is your privilege, Christian, at all times and under all circumstances, to be in the same state of mind in reference to all objects and events. The Bible declares, "*They that wait upon the* Lord *shall renew their strength; they shall mount up with wings as eagles; they shall run, and not be weary; and they shall walk, and not faint*" (Isaiah 40:31). It is said of the eagle that when soaring in his native heaven, as he sees the approaching tempest, he first surveys the scene; if he is equal to the storm, he sails on to meet it and rides triumphantly through it. If the storm appears too powerful for his strength, he raises his wings and, mounting above the warring elements, sails in the eternal sunshine of the upper skies. So it is for those who wait on the Lord. When their strength is equal to the approaching tempest, God will keep them in perfect peace while it beats around them. But if it is too strong for them, He gives them wings of faith and love, on which they rise above the storm and ride with God upon it.

Christian, have you attained to this blessed state? Have your feet been planted upon those everlasting hills where your sun goes not down and your moon does not withdraw itself, where the Lord is your everlasting light and the days of your mourning are ended? To attain this is not only your duty but your privilege. Till you have thus attained, you are not prepared for the great work to which God has called you.

Dear sinner, you are now careful and troubled about many things. You are "*afflicted, tossed with tempest, and not comforted*" (Isaiah 54:11). In your own experience, you fully realize the truth of the fearful declaration "*There is no peace, saith my God, to the wicked*" (Isaiah 57:21). What, then, will you do when the storms and tempests of eternity sweep over you?

8

GROWING IN GRACE

"Grow in grace, and in the knowledge of our Lord and Saviour Jesus Christ."
—2 Peter 3:18

In the context of this verse, Christians are exhorted, *"Be diligent that ye may be found of him in peace, without spot, and blameless"* (2 Peter 3:14) and, *"Beware lest ye also, being led away with the error of the wicked, fall from your own stedfastness"* (verse 17). As a means of securing this good and avoiding this evil, the apostle exhorts them to *"grow in grace, and in the knowledge of our Lord and Saviour Jesus Christ"* (verse 18). The real meaning of the text, as it stands in the original, may be thus expressed: "Grow in the grace and knowledge of our Lord and Savior Jesus Christ."

There are two things we are here required to grow in—the grace and knowledge of Christ. How frequently and peremptorily these duties are enjoined upon us in the Bible, the reader is doubtless aware. In love and every grace, we are required to "*abound yet more and more*" (Philippians 1:9). In knowledge, we are required to "*go on unto perfection*" (Hebrews 6:1). I will not discuss the two duties presented in the text separately since they mutually imply each other, and neither can be performed as here required without the other. The attention of the reader is, therefore, invited to an elucidation of the following propositions:

1. What is implied in growing in grace
2. The necessity and importance of growing in grace
3. The instrumentalities and influences we need to accomplish this object

What Is Implied in Growing in Grace

The primary signification of the term *grace* is favor. To grow in the grace of an individual is to increase in qualities in which he takes pleasure and, consequently, to become the object of his increasing favor and delight. The child, for example, whose powers are continually expanding and who is making constant progress in those things in which the parent takes pleasure, continually grows in the grace of the parent. In other words, such a child is constantly an object of greater and greater favor and delight with the parent. To grow in the grace of our Lord Jesus Christ implies:

1. A continued growth in that in which Christ takes the highest delight—that is, in holiness with all

its appropriate moral, intellectual, and physical accompaniments

2. A consequent continued growth in the love and favor of Christ
3. That we continually receive more and more manifest, decisive, and endearing tokens of His favor and delight

As the Christian constantly grows in holiness—as all his powers and susceptibilities, as a consequence, receive a continued, beautiful, and harmonious expansion under the light and teachings of the Word, Spirit, and providence of God—every Person of the sacred Trinity continually regards him with greater and greater favor and delight, and he continually receives more and more manifest, decisive, and endearing tokens of the divine favor. This is growing in grace. Reader, do you know what this is by blessed experience?

Growing in grace does not imply that our holiness is in the present moment imperfect. The fact that we are required to grow in the grace of Christ no more implies that our present holiness is mingled with sin than the fact that we are required to grow in the knowledge of Christ implies that our present knowledge of Him is mingled with error. If this command implies that our present holiness is mingled with sin, then the holiness of Christ was not perfect. For it is declared that He grew in grace. "*Jesus increased in wisdom and stature, and in favour* [the original word is the same as that rendered "grace" in the text] *with God and man*" (Luke 2:52).

On the other hand, the more constant and entire our sanctification or consecration to Christ, the more rapid will be the expansion of all our powers and susceptibilities under the light and teachings of the Word, Spirit, and providence of God, and consequently, the more rapid will be our growth in holiness and in the grace of our Lord Jesus Christ. No person renders full obedience to this precept according to its real spirit unless his holiness is both constant and entire.

Hence, I remark again that growing in grace does not, as is commonly supposed, imply progressive sanctification—that is, that we continually become less and less sinful and in corresponding degrees more and more holy. This I infer for the following reasons:

1. We have, according to this construction of the text, a positive command in the Bible to give up sin *gradually*, consequently prohibiting our giving up all sin at once. To become by degrees less and less sinful is to give up sin gradually. If this is the meaning of the command *"grow in grace,"* we have a positive precept requiring a gradual and, of course, prohibiting an immediate renunciation of all sin. Who can believe that the Bible contains such a requirement as that?
2. On this supposition, the precepts of the Bible are directly contradictory, the one to the other. For we have many precepts requiring us to renounce *all* sin, at once and forever. Who can suppose that we have other precepts requiring a gradual renunciation of sin and consequently prohibiting obedience to the former precepts?
3. The above construction of this text charges upon the apostle the greatest absurdity conceivable. In the context, as we have seen, he requires Christians to be diligent, that they may be found *"of him in peace, without spot, and blameless"* (2 Peter 3:14). As a means to this end, he requires them in the text to *"grow in grace, and in the knowledge of our Lord and Saviour Jesus Christ"* (verse 18). Who can suppose that an inspired apostle has been

guilty of the absurdity of requiring us to become less and less sinful—that is, to renounce sin gradually—which is the common idea of growing in grace, and this as a means of being found of Christ in peace, without spot and blameless?

4. Entire sanctification implies perfect obedience to all divine requirements. Among these we find the command *"Grow in grace."* If this command implies a gradual renunciation of sin, then perfect obedience to all divine requirements would imply imperfect holiness—the most palpable contradiction. It is only when our holiness, or consecration, to Christ is entire that the precept under consideration is really obeyed. Such, reader, is growing in grace.

The Necessity and Importance of Growing in Grace

This will appear from the following considerations:

1. He who does not continually* "grow in grace, and in knowledge of our Lord and Saviour Jesus Christ" *is living in the neglect of known and acknowledged duty and in the practice of known sin.

Reader, are you fully impressed with the fact that you are always acting in the presence of a known and positive command of God to *"grow in grace, and in the knowledge of our Lord and Saviour Jesus Christ"*? There is no command in the Bible more sacred than this. What respect have you to this commandment? Do you make it your aim to become more and more an object of God's favor and delight? If not, remember that sin lies upon your conscience.

2. We must continually grow in the grace and knowledge of Christ or lose the degree of grace already possessed.

"Whosoever shall keep the whole law, and yet offend in one point, he is guilty of all" (James 2:10). You cannot, reader, at any time cease to obey the command to *"grow in grace"* without, for that period, losing all the holiness and favor with God you have already acquired. Life with you is a continued growth in holiness, with all its appropriate accompaniments. When you cease to grow, you cease to live at all. In such a state, you are dead while you live. (See 1 Timothy 5:6.)

3. A necessity for continued growth in the grace and knowledge of Christ is laid in the constitution of our being.

In their nature, all our powers and susceptibilities are progressive. The desire not only to possess knowledge and to be pure in heart but also for a continued growth in knowledge and purity is a fundamental want of our nature. All our powers and susceptibilities stagnate as soon as we become stationary. To live at all—to enjoy what we have already acquired—we must *"go from strength to strength"* (Psalm 84:7). We must be *"changed... from glory to glory"* (2 Corinthians 3:18). We must rise to higher and higher elevations in holiness and to wider and wider prospects of the divine works and glory in the boundless field of wisdom and knowledge that God has spread out before us.

4. Growth in the grace and knowledge of Christ is indispensable to our continued usefulness.

A minister of the gospel, for example, whatever his present acquirements may be, will soon lose his influence if he remains stationary, and this is so for two important reasons:

1. The progress of the public mind is onward, and such an individual will soon be left far in the rear. He of course

ceases to command public attention and to influence public sentiment.

2. The moment the mind becomes stationary, it ceases to act with its wonted vigor even upon subjects already known. Such a man will continue to ring his changes upon old and hackneyed subjects, with less and less interest to himself and others.

Now the same remarks are equally applicable to us as Christians in all the relations of life. We cannot remain stationary and retain the influence for Christ that we now possess. Continued growth is as essential to usefulness as it is to life with us as Christians. It is only when we "*mount up with wings as eagles…run, and not be weary…walk, and not faint*" (Isaiah 40:31), and our path is shining with constantly increasing brightness (see Proverbs 4:18) that we are spreading abroad the savor of the name of Christ (see 1 Thessalonians 1:8).

The Instrumentalities and Influences Needed to Grow in Grace

In general I would say we must regard this as the great business of our lives, as one of the most important duties that we owe to God, to ourselves, and to the world. We should feel that that day is lost in which we have not made progress in the "*grace, and the knowledge of our Lord and Saviour Jesus Christ*" (2 Peter 3:18). To be particular, if we would grow in grace as required, we must make the character of God, as revealed in His works and Word and especially in the plan of redemption, the great and continued theme of thought and study. Our souls must thirst for God, the living God. (See Psalm 42:2.) To know Him, to understand His way, and to find grace in His sight must be the great end of our being. It is the privilege of the sons of God to behold with open face, as in a glass, the glory of the Lord and to be changed into the same image, "*from glory to glory*" (2 Corinthians 3:18), even as by the Spirit of the Lord. It is only by thus knowing God and being changed into His image and reflecting that image all abroad that we do or can grow in grace as required. Remember also, reader, that we can thus know God only on one condition, that we make His character the great theme of thought and study. "*Ye shall seek me, and find me, when ye shall search for me with all your heart*" (Jeremiah 29:13).

Similar attention must be given to the study of the divine requirements, both in respect to their nature and their application in all our circumstances and relations in life. "*I have more understanding,*" says the psalmist, "*than all my teachers: for thy testimonies are my meditation*" (Psalm 119:99). The individual who thus meditates upon the divine statutes will continually "*grow in grace, and in the knowledge of our Lord and Saviour Jesus Christ.*" He will receive such a sweet and hallowed influence from the truth and Spirit of God as will continually render him more and more an object of the divine approbation and favor. Permit me, reader, to ask you if, in all the varied conditions and relations in life in which you are called to move, this is your great inquiry— "What sentiments, what feelings, what course of conduct, does pure benevolence, the great law of love, require me to cherish and pursue in these circumstances?" In short, is the law of God your meditation, day and night?

As a means of special importance to growth in grace, reader, acquaint yourself fully with the provisions of grace revealed in the gospel to perfect you in your obedience to God's pure and holy law. In these provisions for our redemption, God has given us a revelation of His infinite and boundless love to us. In knowing and believing that love, our love to Him is made perfect. (See 1 John 4:16–17.) We thus *"grow in grace, and in the knowledge of our Lord and Saviour Jesus Christ."* The great reason why Christians generally grow so little in the grace of Christ is their strange and melancholy ignorance of *"the riches of the glory of* [Christ's] *inheritance in the saints"* (Ephesians 1:18). They know not the provisions that Christ has made for their full and complete redemption. They do not, therefore, avail themselves of these provisions for their growth in holiness and, consequently, in the grace of Christ.

Frequent, I may add, constant and devout intercourse and communion with God is an indispensable means of growing in grace. It is at the throne of grace that we receive the fullest, the most distinct, and the highest manifestations of the divine glory. Here it is that our growth in the grace and the knowledge of our Lord and Savior Jesus Christ is the most rapid. Enoch walked with God. (See Genesis 5:24.) How constant and rapid must have been his growth in the grace and knowledge of God consequent on such intimate and endearing intercourse with Him.

In the appropriate cultivation of all our powers and susceptibilities, while our eye is focused in doing it, we grow in the grace of Christ. These powers were given us to be developed. When we acquaint ourselves not only with God but with all His works and providence, with all truth that lies around us in the universe, these powers and susceptibilities receive their appropriate growth and development. He who is thus seeking to develop and strengthen the powers God has given him and is doing this for the purpose of glorifying Him in the widest sphere possible is continually growing in the grace of Christ. He is doing that which renders him the increasing object of the divine favor. As he increases in wisdom, he increases also in favor with God and man. Reader, are you thus growing in the grace of God?

Remarks

We see how it is that those who, at particular periods, have made high attainments in holiness lose the blessedness then enjoyed. They cease their efforts to grow in grace and increase in the knowledge of our Lord Jesus Christ. We must be more and more blessed in Christ, or we cannot continue to be blessed in Him at all. We must abound in love more and more or lose what we have already attained. The moment we become stationary, the love of God ceases to be *"shed abroad in our hearts by the Holy Ghost which is given unto us"* (Romans 5:5). Remember, Christian, you must go from strength to strength and be continually changed into the image of Christ from glory to glory, or you will dwell in a land of darkness and shadow of death. (See Luke 1:79.) It must be our daily study to know more and more of Christ and to enlarge our attainments in all that is pleasing in His sight, or we will cease to be blessed in what we now know of Him. How many at this period fall into the snare of the devil? They are tempted to think at some bright hour that the victory is won. Under the influence of this temptation, their progress ceases, and soon, to their astonishment, they find themselves in greater darkness than ever before.

One of the fundamental characteristics of holiness in creatures, in all finite beings, here presents itself to our contemplation. God's holiness and consequent blessedness are incapable of increase or diminution. Not so with finite beings. Holiness in them is a state of perpetual progress in knowledge, purity, and blessedness. In no other form can holiness exist at all in them except at intervals of sickness, sleep, etc., when, from the nature of their circumstances, they can make no immediate progress.

The condition and prospects of a large proportion of professing Christians here demand our serious consideration. With many, the brightest spot in their whole Christian experience is the period that transpired immediately subsequent to their professed conversion. Reader, if this is true of your experience, you have fearful reason to conclude that you have never been born of God. If you have truly known Christ, you have counted all things as loss for the excellency of the knowledge of Christ Jesus our Lord. (See Philippians 3:8.) You, of course, have sought to know more and more of Him. In your experience, you also have had an exemplification of the truth of the declaration of Christ: *"This is life eternal, that they might know thee the only true God, and Jesus Christ, whom thou hast sent"* (John 17:3). *"The water that I shall give him shall be in him a well of water springing up into everlasting life"* (John 4:14). Your path, if it is that of the just, has shined brighter and brighter as the perfect day is dawning on. (See Proverbs 4:18.) Reader, is this your experience?

The maxim "If Christians were entirely sanctified, they would cease to grow in grace" next demands our consideration. If growing in grace implies a gradual renunciation of sin, this maxim is true. If, on the other hand, it implies, as we have seen it does, implicit obedience to all the other commands of God, together with a constant increase in all that is pleasing to Him, nothing is more false and pernicious in its tendency than the maxim under consideration. What a strange maxim this is. If a Christian should have respect to all God's commandments (see Psalm 119:6), he would make no progress in holiness or in the grace or favor of God. If, on the other hand, he voluntarily withholds from God a part of his heart and gradually, instead of immediately, as he is commanded, yields up his spirit of disobedience, he is then making progress in the divine grace or favor. Now a state of entire sanctification, instead of being inconsistent with growth in grace, is (as we have seen in the progress of this discourse) the necessary condition of such growth as required in the Bible. No man makes that progress in holiness and in the grace of Christ, which he is required to make, who is not in a state of entire obedience to every command of God.

We have also, in the light of this discourse, another striking instance of the manner in which the doctrine of imperfection has perverted the conceptions of Christians in respect to the most important truths and principles of the gospel. An individual under the influence of this doctrine meets with the requirement of the text *"grow in grace."* He at once assumes that in this command we are required to become less and less sinful and, in this sense, more and more holy. That is, that a gradual instead of an immediate renunciation of sin is here required of us. From this construction of the text, he draws the obvious conclusion that no Christian ever did or ever will, in this life, attain to a state of entire sanctification. For, if any one should make such attainments, he would cease to live in conformity with a plain and positive command of God. But the influence of this doctrine does not stop here. The individual under consideration now attempts obedience to the command *"grow in grace,"* according to the above construction. That is, he aims to become less and less sinful—to give up sin gradually. What a snare of the devil this individual has fallen into will be seen by the following considerations:

1. In aiming to become less and less sinful, that is, to grow in grace according to the above construction of the text, he ceases even to aim at obedience to other and numberless requirements of the Bible, which demand an immediate renunciation of all sin. For it is an absolute impossibility for us to aim or intend to become less and less sinful *and* intend to give up all sin at one and the same time.

2. The thing at which this individual is now aiming is perfectly undefined and indefinable. A child is in a state of voluntary disobedience to parental authority. What should we think if that child should resolve to give up the spirit of disobedience by degrees? He could have no definite conception of the object at which he is aiming. So it is with everyone who aims at a gradual renunciation of a spirit of disobedience to God. Christian, you cannot intelligently aim at such an object. No one knows whereof he affirms when he speaks of doing it.

To aim to "*grow in grace*" in this sense would be sin against God. It would imply, as above shown, a disregard of all those precepts of the Bible that require an *immediate* renunciation of all sin. Remember, Christian, that to aim to grow in grace in any sense that implies a gradual renunciation of sin is nothing but a growth in sin itself. Thus it is that the doctrine of imperfection has perverted the conceptions of the church in respect to the most important truths and principles of the gospel and has left her in a snare of the devil.

Finally, the subject, reader, as it is presented in the Bible, is now before you. In the light of it, you may judge of your past character, present state, and future privileges and duties. In regard to the past, if your growth in the grace and knowledge of Christ has not been constant and rapid, you have reasons of infinite weight for the deepest humiliation before God. With the book of inspiration and providence open before you and the aid of the Spirit of God always available to guide you into all truth, how much might you now know and enjoy of God and do for Him had you cried after knowledge and lifted up your voice for understanding (see Proverbs 2:3); had you continually aimed to abound more and more in love (see Philippians 1:19) and in every grace and virtue? Remember, also, that whatever your present attainments may be, however enlarged your vision of truth and full and perfect your love, the irrevocable condition of the continuance of the blessedness now enjoyed is a continued progress from strength to strength, a constant changing into the image of Christ from glory to glory. Whatever the degree of holiness now possessed, it must increase with the increase of knowledge and capacity, or it will cease to exist at all.

In regard to the future, what blessed prospects are open before you? God has brought you into *"a place of broad rivers and streams"* (Isaiah 33:21). How justly does He require of you a rapid growth into *"the measure of the stature of the fulness of Christ"* (Ephesians 4:13)? He has spread out before you *"all the treasures of wisdom and knowledge"* (Colossians 2:3). With what propriety does He require you to cry after knowledge and lift up your voice for understanding until you *"understand the fear of the* L*ORD*, *and find the knowledge of God"* (Proverbs 2:5), until you *"understand righteousness, and judgment, and equity; yea, every good path"* (verse 9).

This, Christian, is your duty. It is also your high privilege. And when you have attained to the highest elevation of which you can now conceive, you have just commenced the alphabet of eternity. Your progress is eternally onward. To serve and glorify and enjoy God with powers and susceptibilities that are perpetually enlarging, to be always approaching a comprehension of the infinitude of God without attaining it, to be perpetually changing into brighter and brighter resemblances of the divine image, to be ever growing in grace and knowledge of our Lord and Savior Jesus Christ—this is to fill up the endless future of the believer. Reader, will this blessedness be yours?

9

A WORD FITLY SPOKEN

"A word fitly spoken is like apples of gold in pictures of silver."
—Proverbs 25:11

This passage has, by some, been thus rendered: "A word fitly spoken is like golden apples in baskets of silver." That is, a word spoken with propriety, opportunely, and that is suitable to the occasion is as much in its place and as conspicuously beautiful as the golden fruit that appears through the apertures of an exquisitely wrought silver basket. The real meaning of the sacred writer is no doubt this: Among the various objects of surpassing beauty that the universe around presents, nothing is more beautiful than *"a word fitly spoken."* The rose is beautiful. So is the lily of the valley. The rainbow is beautiful. So are the stars. Surpassingly beautiful is

> The silver moon,
> When out of sight the clouds are driven
> And she is left alone in heaven.[7]

But more beautiful than all is a beautiful thought clothed in appropriate language and *"fitly spoken."*

Thought is beautiful for various reasons. Sometimes it is on account of what is intrinsic in the thought itself. *"This then is the message which we have heard of him, and declare unto you, that God is light, and in him is no darkness at all"* (1 John 1:5). The mind may contemplate the thought here expressed throughout endless ages, and its surpassing beauty will be the same yesterday, today, and forever. Indeed, it requires long and deep meditation for one to fully appreciate its beauty at all. Its beauty, however, does not consist in the form of expression but in what is intrinsic in the thought itself. *"And Enoch walked with God: and he was not; for God took him"* (Genesis 5:24). We think nothing of the form of expression here. It is the surpassing beauty of the thought itself that charms us. *"But we all, with open face beholding as in a glass the glory of the Lord, are changed into the same image from glory to glory, even as by the Spirit of the Lord"* (2 Corinthians 3:18). Is there in the wide world a thought that is so beautiful?

Thought is sometimes beautiful, not on account of what is intrinsic in the thing itself, but the manner in which it is expressed. *"Saul and Jonathan were lovely and pleasant in their lives, and in their death they were not divided"* (2 Samuel 1:23). It is the form of expression that imparts the inconceivable beauty to the thought here.

Sometimes we find each of the above characteristics united in the same thought. For example, "The divine promise of a

7. William Wordsworth, "The White Doe of Rylstone."

Redeemer, like a rich and beautiful bud, at first enclosed in manifold covering, swells and unfolds itself from age to age, till in Jesus of Nazareth, it opens into bloom, and scatters its fragrance over the world."

There is another circumstance that imparts beauty to thought—its adaptation, on account of the manner and circumstances in which it is expressed, to answer an important end. "How great," said a scoffing infidel to a child who had remembered its Creator in the days of its youth, "how great is the God you worship?"

"So great," replied the child, "that He fills immensity, and yet so small that He dwells in every heart that is humble and contrite."

The infidel stood confounded and rebuked at his own presumption and audacity and awed in view of the surpassing wisdom of even a child when taught of God. The thought contained in the above reply is exceedingly beautiful. Its highest beauty, however, arises from another circumstance—its wonderful adaptation as an answer to the question of the scoffer. It was a word fitly spoken.

A thought thus expressed has not only an indescribable beauty but a value equally great. Some have supposed that this is the chief idea that the sacred writer designed to express in the text, the great value of a word fitly spoken. Hence they suppose that reference is here had to the custom of ancient sovereigns presenting their guests, on great occasions, with silver trays or baskets filled with precious jewels and gold molded into the form of fruit. I suppose that both ideas, the beauty and value of a word fitly spoken, are referred to by the sacred writer. The full meaning of the passage may be thus expressed: *"A word fitly spoken"* is, on account of its surpassing beauty and value, "like apples of gold in pictures of silver."

In listening to the conversation of certain individuals, one circumstance strikes us with special interest—the peculiar adaptation of their thoughts, on account of the time, manner, and circumstances in which they are uttered, to accomplish the benevolent purposes of their hearts. As you mark their intercourse, you are almost continually constrained to say, "That was a word fitly spoken. How proper, how timely was that thought!" Here, reader, is wisdom such as we all need. How will we attain it so that our conversation will always be *"with grace, seasoned with salt"* (Colossians 4:6)? My object will be to answer this inquiry. In doing it, we will:

1. Notice some of the characteristics of the sayings referred to in the text
2. Show how to attain to the wisdom needed for what we say to bear the character of a word fitly spoken

Characteristics of the Sayings in the Text

In noticing the characteristics of the sayings here referred to, I would remark that whenever the mind gives utterance to thought, it does so as a means to an end. Hence, the first characteristic that I notice of a word fitly spoken is this: The end to be accomplished will be an important one, an end the accomplishment of which is demanded by benevolence. Thought should never be uttered to secure any but a benevolent end. When expressed to accomplish any other end, and especially an opposite purpose, it is out of place. Its utterance cannot be characterized as a word fitly spoken. When uttered to accomplish the ends that benevolence demands, thought is in its place. This is its appropriate sphere.

When thought is employed to answer a great end demanded by benevolence and when the thought uttered is best adapted to secure that end, then its utterance may with eminent propriety bear the high appellation, a word fitly spoken. When important exigencies occur when crises arise in which the eternal weal or woe of an immortal mind is trembling upon a moment's tender point; a thought arising from some pure and benevolent heart appears, a thought that we at once recognize as of all others best adapted to meet the present exigency. Like the bright star that arose to guide the Eastern sages to the Babe of Bethlehem, it appears at the very time and in the circumstances in which it was most needed, when nothing else can supply its place. When such a thought appears, we at once exclaim, "That is a word fitly spoken!" Truly such a word is like apples of gold in pictures of silver. Nothing in the universe possesses such beauty and value.

As an illustration, notice the reply of the child to the scoffer above referred to. Is there any thought conceivable that could, without injury, be substituted for it in that particular place? Any that could so well answer the end that benevolence then demanded? This is what embalms it as a word fitly spoken.

Take another illustration. The daughter of an English nobleman was providentially brought under the influence of the followers of Wesley and thus came to a saving knowledge of the truth as it is in Jesus. The father was almost distracted at the event, and by threats, temptations to extravagance in dress, reading, and traveling in foreign countries and places of fashionable resort, he took every means in his power to divert her mind from things unseen and eternal. But her heart was fixed. The God of Abraham had become her shield and her exceeding great reward, and she was determined that nothing finite should deprive her of her infinite and eternal portion in Him or displace Him from the throne of her heart. At last, the father resolved upon a final and desperate expedient by which his end should be gained or his daughter ruined, so far as her prospects in this life were concerned. A large company of the nobility were invited to his house.

It was so arranged that during the festivities, the daughters of different noblemen, including his own daughter, were to be called on to entertain the company with singing and music on the piano. If she complied, she parted with heaven and returned to the world. If she refused compliance, she would be publicly disgraced and lose, past the possibility of recovery, her place in society. It was a dreadful crisis, and with peaceful confidence did she await it. As the crisis approached, different individuals, at the call of the company, performed their parts with the greatest applause. At last the name of this daughter was announced. In a moment, all were in fixed and silent suspense to see how the scale of destiny would turn. Without hesitation, she rose, and with a calm and dignified composure, she took her place at the instrument. After a moment spent in silent prayer, she ran her fingers along the keys and then sang with an unearthly sweetness, elevation, and solemnity—accompanying her voice with the notes of the instrument—the following stanzas:

> No room for mirth, or trifling here,
> For worldly hope, or worldly fear,
> If life so soon is gone;
> If now the judge is at the door,
> And all mankind must stand before
> The inexorable throne!
>
> No matter which my thoughts employ,
> A moment's misery or joy;
> But O! when both shall end,
> Where shall I find my destined place?

Shall I my everlasting days
With fiends or angels spend?

Nothing is worth a thought beneath,
But how I may escape the death
That never, never dies;
How make mine own election sure,
And when I fail on earth, secure
A mansion in the skies.

Jesus, vouchsafe a pitying ray;
Be thou my Guide, be thou my Way
To glorious happiness.
Ah! write the pardon on my heart,
And whensoe'er I hence depart,
Let me depart in peace.[8]

The minstrel ceased. The solemnity of eternity was upon that assembly. Without speaking, they dispersed. The father wept aloud, and when left alone, he sought the counsel and prayers of his daughter for the salvation of his soul. His soul was saved and his great estate consecrated to Christ. I would rather be the organ of communicating such thoughts in such circumstances and to the productions of such results—I would rather possess wisdom thus to speak as occasion requires—than to possess all that is finite, beside. What hymn, what thought in the universe, could be substituted for the one then uttered? The time, the occasion, the thought expressed, the hallowed and sweet manner of its utterance, present a full realization of all that is embraced in our idea of fitness. That surely was a word fitly spoken.

8. Charles Wesley, 1763.

A word fitly spoken is also often marked by a peculiar fitness to answer the end of benevolence on account of its special adaptation to the particular state of the hearer's mind. We see, at once, that any alteration in the manner or form of expression would mar its beauty and value by its manifest want of adaptation in this one respect. Take a single illustration. Mr. Wesley once met a southern planter in a fearful rage at a slave who stood before him trembling on account of a sentence, the execution of which was to him far more dreadful than death. Mr. Wesley entreated the man to forgive the wrong.

"Never," was his haughty reply. "When I receive an injury, I never forgive it."

"Then," said Mr. Wesley, with a tone and manner peculiar to himself, "I trust you yourself have never committed a sin."

The reply was like a sudden flash from the pyre of the last judgment upon the mind of the angry man. A sinner like himself to adopt the maxim never to forgive! Yet the mild, benevolent, and sweet manner of that reply melted his heart. The offender was pardoned with a humble request from the master, if I mistake not, for forgiveness from the slave.

Suppose now the reply to have been given in the form which most likely would have been adopted by most individuals. For example, "Remember, you are yourself a great sinner, and if you do not forgive, you will not be forgiven by God." (See Matthew 6:14.) Such a charge, under such circumstances, would no doubt have roused his pride, together with the combative principles of his nature. His fury would have been redoubled upon his slave, and his contempt and indignation burned upon the reprover. All this was prevented by the form and manner of the reply. For the same reason, the truth uttered, entering between the joints of the harness, pierced to the very depths of the heart and conscience. (See

Hebrews 4:12.) Without being told directly of his great guilt as a sinner, the truth was so presented that he could not possibly avoid the deepest conviction of the fact, together with a corresponding impression of the fearful truth that the one who forgives not will never be forgiven. It was a word fitly spoken.

The circumstances of time and place in which a thought is expressed, often in connection with those above stated, embalm it as a word fitly spoken. We see at once that if it had been uttered at any other time or place or in any other circumstances, it would have had no efficiency to produce the results that now arise from it. Its appearance just at this moment, at this place, and under these peculiar circumstances imparts to it the ineffable beauty and value that command our admiration. As an example and an illustration, I would refer the reader to the tract entitled *The Christian Traveler,* one of the most interesting and profitable tracts ever published. Take the following scene from the tract—a scene that transpired on board a vessel on one of the western lakes. The young man, a mechanic, the hero of the scene, had at the breakfast table, with almost inimitable wisdom and propriety, obtained leave of the captain to attempt to put an end to the profanity of the sailors—one of the best means to reprove the captain himself for his own sin in this respect. Mark the manner in which the attempt was executed:

> As soon as breakfast was over, the oldest and most profane of the sailors seated himself on the quarter-deck to smoke his pipe. The young man entered into conversation with him, and soon drew from him a history of the adventures of his life. From his boyhood he had followed the ocean. He had been tossed on the billows in many a tempest; had visited several missionary stations in different parts of the world, and gave his testimony to the

> good effects of missionary efforts among the natives of the Sandwich Islands. Proud of his nautical skill, he at length boasted that he could do any thing that could be done by a sailor.
>
> "I doubt it," said the young man.
>
> "I can," answered the hardy tar, "and will not be outdone, my word for it."
>
> "Well, when a sailor passes his word he ought to be believed. I know a sailor who resolved to stop swearing, and did so."
>
> "Ah," said the old sailor, "you've anchored me; I'm fast—but I can do it."
>
> "I know you can," said the young man, "and I hope you will anchor all your shipmates' oaths with yours."
>
> Not a word of profanity was afterwards heard on board the vessel. During the day, as opportunity presented itself, he conversed with each sailor singly on the subject of his soul's salvation, and gained the hearts of all.

Thus, by a few observations made just as time and circumstances called for them and in a form and manner adapted to give them efficacy, that vessel, in which little else but oaths and blasphemies was before heard, was soon turned into a "floating Bethel" in which prayers for mercy were ascending and tears of penitence flowing. The scene was afterward changed to a canal boat, where by a similar course of conduct, speaking just as time and occasion demanded and in a form and manner adapted to make the deepest impression, another "floating Bethel" was created. Everyone who reads that tract cannot fail to notice that it was not merely the truths uttered but the time, manner, and circumstances of their utterance that rendered everything said like apples of gold in pictures of silver.

Here are the characteristics of true wisdom. Adopting the maxim "There is a time to speak and a time to refrain from speaking" (see Ecclesiastes 3:7), wisdom carefully watches the time and occasion most fit for speaking and then says the exact things the time and occasion require.

I mention but one characteristic more. What is said is seen to possess a peculiar fitness and propriety when contemplated in the light of the character, age, and relations of the speaker himself. We all know that what would appear highly fit and proper when spoken by one individual would be wholly out of place if spoken by another in the same circumstances. The reason lies in the difference of their character. When an individual who is living in the habitual practice of any known sin exhorts a sinner to repent, when an individual who is known to be worldly minded exhorts a sinner to give up the world for Christ and to look not at things seen and temporal, but at things unseen and eternal, we are shocked at the absurdity. On the other hand, let an individual whose spirit and life are in visible harmony with the gospel exhort a sinner to do the same things, and all is in place. Such a person, everyone says, has a right to say such things.

It is said of a sister in Christ, who lived many years ago in western New York, that she had probably been instrumental in the conversion of more sinners than any minister in the same region of the country. She was once asked how it was that she, while in the habit of speaking to every class of individuals, always spoke with effect without giving offense. Her reply was this—

> Whenever such an individual comes within the circle of my influence, I at once set my heart upon saying and doing what I can to secure his salvation. As soon as a fit opportunity presents, my plan is to converse with him on the "things which concern his peace." As preparatory to such an event, my aim is to order my entire deportment in his presence, so that what I say shall be impressed upon his heart and conscience, by all that he had previously seen in me.

Here was the secret of her power. What was spoken was always in time and rendered like apples of gold in pictures of silver by its correspondence with her entire character. It is in place for the truly good to urge the practice of goodness upon all around them. Nor is it fitting in any others to engage in this hallowed employment.

How We Attain the Wisdom Needed so that What We Say Will Have the Characteristics of a Word Fitly Spoken

The first and most important requisite is this: a truly benevolent heart, the consecration of our entire being to doing good. Whenever the mind is supremely devoted to any end, it readily perceives and appropriates to use the means best adapted to secure that end. A mind purely benevolent will possess a divine vision to discern the time and occasion when and means by which its own hallowed purposes and aspirations can be best realized.

If we would speak the words of wisdom, we must seek an enlarged and accurate acquaintance with the truth of God. Truth is the instrument by which the ends of benevolence are to be realized. However sincere and strong our benevolence, if we are ignorant of the truth, we will be ignorant of the means of doing good when the occasion presents itself. The benevolent mind, on the other hand, that is well instructed in the things of the kingdom will seldom draw the bow at a venture, and even then its direction will be guided by wisdom unseen. Remember, reader, "*when wisdom entereth into thine heart, and knowledge is pleasant unto thy soul; discretion shall preserve thee, understanding shall keep thee*" (Proverbs 2:10–11).

> *If thou criest after knowledge, and liftest up thy voice for understanding; if thou seekest her as silver, and searchest for her as for hid treasures; then shalt thou understand the fear of the* Lord, *and find the knowledge of God. For the* Lord *giveth wisdom: out of his mouth cometh knowledge and understanding.* (Proverbs 2:3–6)

You will then open your mouth with wisdom, and on your tongue will be the law of kindness. (See Proverbs 31:26.) The words of wisdom, as they drop from your lips, will be like apples of gold in pictures of silver.

Another essential prerequisite is a deep personal experience of the power of the truth and grace of Christ upon our own hearts. The individual who has gone down into the depths of Christian experience has descended into fathomless mines of the richest thought in the universe, mines in which he will find numberless pearls of great price. The merchandise of these—in the mart of souls—he will find to be far better than the merchandise of silver, and the gain of them will be better than fine gold. (See Proverbs 3:14.) In the depths of Christian experience, when the soul enters into direct communication with the thoughts, feelings, and operations of the infinite and eternal mind, feelings the most expanded and beautiful in existence are generated. These feelings generate thoughts of corresponding value and beauty, and such thoughts as occasion requires naturally clothe themselves in such language as renders their utterance like apples of gold in pictures of silver. Reader, amid those depths and heights, have you been taught to speak for Christ?

Another essential prerequisite is wisdom to discern the peculiar attitude and state of the hearer's mind when we are about to speak for Christ. Under such circumstances, we should seldom speak at random. Our thoughts and words should be well selected. Especially should they be adapted to the peculiar state of the hearer's mind at the moment. The individual who is best acquainted, experimentally and theoretically, with the gospel and is of the most "quick understanding" to discern the state of the hearer's mind is best qualified to touch those chords of thought and feeling in the soul that vibrate for eternity. Let me also say that in those depths of Christian experience in which the soul not only communes with God but with itself is where this wisdom is most effectually gained.

Once more: He who would possess the tongue of the learned must seek special wisdom from above for this high qualification. Reader, you have consecrated your body and spirit to Christ, have you not? Have you ever made a particular and special consecration of your *tongue* to Him? Have you ever sought the special baptism of the Spirit in respect to the use of this one member? How else can you open your mouth with wisdom and have on your tongue the law of kindness? (See Proverbs 31:26.)

Remarks

We are now prepared for a distinct understanding of the precept, "*Let your speech be alway with grace, seasoned with salt*" (Colossians 4:6). Salt was anciently considered as an emblem of wisdom on account of its well-known effects in preventing corruption from taking place and on account of its communicating a pleasing relish to the various kinds of food with which it was mingled. So, when a thought is uttered that is recognized as best adapted to answer a great and benevolent end, it is embalmed in the memory as infinitely beautiful and valuable. Its beautiful fitness, on account of the time and circumstances of its appearance, impresses it indelibly on our minds. Thus it is preserved, just as salt preserves from corruption that to which it is applied. This, then, is the meaning of the apostle. Let your speech be the genuine language of true wisdom, purity, and love, and let it be characterized by such manifest fitness on account of its wise adaptation to circumstances of time, place, etc. that the truth uttered will be forever preserved fresh in the mind of the hearer, there to exert its hallowed and sanctifying influence. Does your speech, reader, bear this characteristic?

An indispensable qualification to preach the gospel of Christ next demands our attention. "*The* L*ORD* *God hath given me the tongue of the learned,* ***that I should know how to speak a word in season to him that is weary***" (Isaiah 50:4). I would rather possess this one qualification than have my name sound like a war trumpet to the ends of the earth. Without it, I know I have never been anointed of Christ to preach His gospel. When will He ever have such a ministry as this? When will His watchmen be able to say in truth, each one for himself,

> *The spirit of the Lord* G*OD* *is upon me; because the* L*ORD* *hath anointed me to preach good tidings unto the meek; he hath sent me to bind up the brokenhearted, to proclaim liberty to the captives, and the opening of the prison to them that are bound; to proclaim the acceptable year of the* L*ORD*, *and the*

day of vengeance of our God; to comfort all that mourn.
(Isaiah 61:1–2)

We have, in the light of this subject, a proper standard by which to judge of discourses from the pulpit. The great question is this: Are they, on account of a wise adaptation to the state of the public mind, fitted to meet the wants of the hearer? A discourse may contain nothing but truth; it may be well arranged, executed, and delivered and yet be utterly powerless for want of adaptation. On the other hand, a discourse wanting in many of the respects just named may possess great efficacy because it bears the characteristic of a word fitly spoken. The want of this wise adaptation is the great reason, as it appears to me, why a vast majority of discourses are as "*sounding brass, or a tinkling cymbal*" (1 Corinthians 13:1).

We may now give a correct explanation of the maxim "There is a time to keep silence and a time to speak." (See Ecclesiastes 3:7.) It is a time to keep silence when circumstances of time and place are such that the truth uttered would not have the characteristic of a word fitly spoken. It is a time to speak when the hearer's mind is in a state favorable to receive the impress of the truth and when attending circumstances conspire to open an avenue for the truth to his heart. True benevolence, guided by wisdom, is eagle-eyed to discern such opportunities and never suffers them to pass unimproved.

Many individuals have adopted the principle that they have done their duty if they have spoken to others on the subject of religion, and that they have sinned if they have refrained from speaking. This, as we see, is a great mistake. We have done our duty in this respect if we have, in the best manner possible to us, improved every fit opportunity for speaking. We have grievously sinned if we have let slip any such opportunity. Reader, how stands your account with God and with souls in this particular?

Individuals, as we now see, sometimes form very unwise resolutions in regard to speaking to others on the subject of religion. I have sometimes heard purposes of this kind avowed: "I will never suffer an impenitent person to come into my presence without speaking to him about his soul." A resolution more unwise than this could not possibly be formed. On the other hand, suppose every true Christian were to form such a purpose as this: "I will never suffer a fit opportunity to speak for Christ to pass unimproved and will, by fervent prayer, diligent use of means, and faith in Christ seek every qualification requisite to discover such opportunities and to improve them in the best possible manner." Let such purposes be universally formed and, by grace, steadily adhered to; then this world would soon become as the garden of the Lord. The desert of sin would bloom as Eden.

And now, reader, I have prepared this discourse for the single purpose of bringing this momentous subject distinctly before your mind and impressing it upon your heart. I ask not what you have done heretofore but what you will do in the future. Will Christ take full possession of every member of your body and mind? Will your heart and tongue now be His? Will you now receive of this Spirit, that the aspirations of your heart, to which your tongue will give utterance, will henceforth be like apples of gold in pictures of silver? *"By thy words thou shalt be justified, and by thy words thou shalt be condemned"* (Matthew 12:37).

10

CHRISTIAN ADMONITION

"But exhort one another daily, while it is called to day; lest any of you be hardened through the deceitfulness of sin."
—Hebrews 3:13

The proper meaning of the term *exhort* is "admonish." So it is rendered by Professor Stuart. It includes, among other things of a kindred nature, "reproof and exhortation to repentance for sin committed, admonition to the performance of duty, and warning against temptations to future disobedience." What I said in the last discourse has, I hope, prepared the way for a consideration of the subject I design to illustrate in this—the duty of Christian admonition. As introductory to what I purpose to say, I would desire the attention of the reader to the following preliminary observations:

1. The duty of Christian admonition is devolved upon us by a positive command of God. We can no more neglect this duty without sin than we can cease to love God with all our hearts and our neighbor as ourselves (see Matthew 22:37–39) without sin.

2. This duty is devolved upon us as the business of every day—*"Exhort one another **daily**."* The individual who lives from day to day in the neglect of this duty is as certainly living in the habitual practice of known sin as the individual who is in the constant commission of theft, adultery, or profane swearing.

3. The importance attached in the text to the faithful discharge of this duty is no less than the eternal salvation or destruction of the soul—*"Lest any of you be hardened through the deceitfulness of sin."*

4. The sacredness and importance of this duty will also be obvious from a contemplation of the various relations in life that people are called to sustain to one another. Why are we called to sustain the endearing relations of husband and wife, parent and child, and members of the household of faith? Why are people associated together as families and communities, and why are all the business transactions of life so ordered in providence that we are thrown into perpetual intercommunication with each other? It is so that we may discharge the duty of admonition as we are journeying home to eternity. In this perpetual intercommunication, the

> condition, necessities, and duties of each are disclosed to the other, and thus the sacred obligation of mutual admonition stands continually revealed.

In further discoursing on this subject, we will consider—

1. The state of mind necessary to a proper discharge of this duty
2. Some of the circumstances in which Christian admonition, in some form, is especially called for
3. The different modes in which, as circumstances require, the duty of admonition is to be performed
4. Circumstances that impart to Christian admonition the highest efficiency

The State of Mind Necessary to a Proper Discharge of This Duty

The first and indispensable condition is this—a heart set upon the sanctification of the church and the salvation of lost men. Every Christian should contemplate himself as set apart and anointed of God to secure this result by every effort in his power. For this end, he is to live, and move, and have his being. (See Acts 17:28.) Without this state of mind, no duty is acceptably discharged. Without it, no individual, especially, can admonish a brother, with acceptance to God or with any rational hope of success. Without it, no individual will discover the proper time, occasion, means, and manner in which a duty so sacred and yet so delicate will be discharged. The great question then with you, reader, is this: Are you in this hallowed state of mind? Have you set yourself apart for the work of the Lord to do all in your power to sanctify the church and save lost men? Has

Christ accepted the consecration and given you His Spirit for the accomplishment of the duties of your sacred calling?

With a heart set upon the sanctification of the church and the salvation of sinners, another condition indispensable to the discharge of the duty of Christian admonition is this—special wisdom must be sought from above in respect to the means of accomplishing this result. Under the influence of such wisdom, whenever Christian admonition is such a means, the mind will readily apprehend the fact, together with the time, manner, and circumstances in which it may most effectually be employed.

No individual is in a proper state of mind, in reference to the discharge of this duty, who does not contemplate it as the business of every day. Whenever you come into the presence of a believer in Christ, you are required, if opportunity presents, to say and do something to make him a more holy man. And if you are in the presence of a sinner, you must say and do something, if the opportunity presents itself, to bring him to repentance. With a sacred reference to this end, all our intercourse with our fellow men is to be ordered. *"Let your speech be alway with grace, seasoned with salt"* (Colossians 4:6), that is, let your entire interaction with men be so ordered that it will tend to their sanctification and salvation. In other words still, let it be so ordered that it will be a perpetual admonition to them of what they ought to know, to do, and to be.

We should always enter upon this duty with much and fervent prayer for divine influence, illumination, and direction. Who, without great care, should presume to touch those chords in the soul whose vibrations are for eternal weal or woe? This, reader, is holy ground. Yet we must tread it or lose our own souls. But when we do it, we should have the assurance that the spirit and influence under which we act is divine, and the wisdom by which we are guided is above our own. God knows perfectly the state of every mind that is to be the subject of our admonition. How important it is that we be guided by His unerring wisdom so that what we say will be a word in season, a word fitly spoken.

The individual who would effectually discharge the duty of Christian admonition must himself continually walk with God. There must be a direct and continued intercommunication between his spirit and the Spirit of Christ. He must fully understand in his own blessed experience what are *"the riches of the glory of this mystery...which is Christ in you, the hope of glory"* (Colossians 1:27). When an individual is in that state of mind, there is a sweetness in his severity, a hallowed beauty about his solemn reproofs and exhortations, and a kind of heaven even in his mirth that renders all his conversation with others a perpetual admonition to love, to faith, to repentance for past sin, and to future obedience. And it renders that admonition almost irresistibly attractive and influential. On the other hand, when he is not in this state, he is certain, almost, to mingle something of his own spirit with the admonition in such a manner as to turn the grace that would otherwise flow from his lips into bitterness.

Circumstances Where Christian Admonition Is Especially Called For

1. Whenever a brother or sister is about to enter upon any important enterprise in which great spiritual interests are involved

Under such circumstances, we should seek an opportunity to remind him of the vast interests pending, to admonish him of the infinite responsibilities thrown upon him to show himself a faithful servant of the cross in such a crisis, and to assure him that we will bear his case with special urgency at the throne of grace. Admonition should always, and especially here, be directed with a special reference to the character of the individual and the peculiar circumstances in which he is called to act. If, for example, he is naturally timid and the crisis is one that calls for great courage and decision, we should remind him that God expects His servants to be *"strong and very courageous"* (Joshua 1:7) and not to *"fear, though the earth be removed, and though the mountains be carried into the midst of the sea"* (Psalm 46:2). If his faith is likely to fail, we should remind him of the unique and infinite fullness of the grace of Christ, which was provided and is now proffered with special reference to this particular crisis. If strong temptations to pride will present themselves, we should remind him of the fact that we will with peculiar interest remember him in prayer that he may stand behind the cross and hold up only Christ and not himself. If circumstances are likely to arise that strongly tend to provoke his spirit, we should remind him that it will be a subject of special prayer with us that he may put on the meekness and gentleness of Christ.

2. *When an individual is about to enter into new and (to him) untried relations in life*

We should then remind him of the infinite importance of making a new and special consecration of himself to Christ in this new relation. We should put him in remembrance of the fact that as new duties arise, new and special grace is required—that the grace that sufficed under other circumstances will not suffice now. We should solemnly admonish him to appropriate by faith the special grace Christ now proffers, which, if he avails himself of it, will enable him in this new relation to *"serve God acceptably with reverence and godly fear"* (Hebrews 12:28).

3. *When any important work is to be done that requires the mutual cooperation of the friends of Christ*

Suppose, for example, that a church is about to make a united and special effort for the revival of God's work in the sanctification of His people and the salvation of sinners. How important now is the duty of mutual admonition, that every stumbling block may be removed and that the way of the Lord may be fully prepared in all hearts. Then the entire sacramental host may be brought to stand each in his proper place, waiting for the sudden coming to His temple of the messenger of the covenant, whom we delight in, and standing ready for every good word and work. (See 2 Thessalonians 2:17.) When the duty of mutual admonition is affectionately and faithfully discharged under such circumstances, the heavens will drop down righteousness (see Isaiah 45:8), and the salvation of Zion will go forth as a lamp that burns (see Isaiah 62:1). If this duty is not discharged, the work of God will be marred, and the people of God will be left as a "*heath in the desert, and shall not see when good cometh*" (Jeremiah 17:6).

4. *When an individual has come or is about to come into circumstances of strong temptation*

Then it is of infinite importance that he receive admonition in respect to the nature of the temptation, the importance of great watchfulness and prayer, and the special faith to appropriate the grace of Christ necessary to "*withstand in the evil day*" (Ephesians 6:13). A word in season, at such a crisis, "*shall save a soul from death, and shall hide a multitude of sins*" (James 5:20).

5. *When individuals are under influences particularly favorable to their sanctification or salvation*

Then a word of kind and earnest admonition should be given in respect to the interests involved in the present crisis and the great importance of its right improvement. The entire destiny of the immortal spirit may depend upon a word fitly spoken at such a time.

6. When an individual is known to be under the special strivings of the Spirit

A word of solemn and appropriate admonition, just as the crisis of the soul is quivering on the beam, often turns the scale of destiny, and a redeemed spirit, which would otherwise have wandered in the shades of eternal night, takes its place among the morning stars to "*shine as the brightness of the firmament… as the stars for ever and ever*" (Daniel 12:3). Reader, how can you meet a soul at the judgment whom you have, at such a crisis, failed to admonish?

7. When a brother has fallen into sin

At such a time, the solemn command "*Thou shalt in any wise rebuke thy neighbour, and not suffer sin upon him*" (Leviticus 19:17) should be held in special remembrance. Nor should the admonition be long delayed. Who would not prefer to have the artillery of the universe pointed at him rather than suffer a single sin, for a single minute, to lie upon his conscience unrepented of and unforgiven? Equally unwilling should we be to see the same fearful curse lie upon the conscience of a neighbor, especially a brother in Christ.

8. When a brother has come under an influence by which he is likely to be drawn into some delusion

Here everything depends upon the admonition being in time. There is a point in the progress of all fatal delusions beyond which all reasoning and admonition will, with infallible certainty, fail of their effect. The deluded soul is drowned in destruction and perdition. (See 1 Timothy 6:9.) None who go there return again; neither do they take hold of the paths of life. (See Proverbs 2:19.) But a word of affectionate exhortation, before the fatal step is taken, may prevent the endless train of evils that would otherwise ensue.

9. Once more: When an individual needs to be drawn under an influence that would be likely to result in his sanctification or salvation

The salvation of a soul often depends upon his hearing, at a given time, a particular truth. And whether he hears it or not may depend upon the kind admonition of a friend who knows its value. In a revival in an eastern city, more than twenty individuals joined one particular church. In the relation of their Christian experience, these individuals disclosed the fact that they were drawn to hear the truth, which by the Spirit caused their salvation, by the kind and earnest solicitation of a single sister in Christ. Except for her solicitations, they would not have attended to the word of hearing at all and would then have been in their sins.

Another sister called upon a friend who had been educated in error to ask her to attend for an evening at the house of God where the waters of life were flowing. The request was repelled with scorn. It was repeated again with the same result. Nine times, if I mistake not, she repeated her calls to renew her earnest invitation, with the same result. The tenth time she was successful, and the hearing of the truth in that one instance resulted in the conversion of that soul to God. *"In due season we shall reap, if we faint not"* (Galatians 6:9).

I have given the above as examples of the instances in which Christian admonition is imperiously demanded and as waymarks to guide the reader in the discharge of this solemn duty.

The way is now prepared to consider the ways in which admonition is to be performed.

Different Modes in Which the Duty of Admonition Is to Be Performed

Sometimes, and not infrequently, we do it simply and exclusively by the light of a correct example on our part. Many instances occur in which we are brought into such relations to others that our example, if conformed to the laws of God and of our own being, while theirs is not, will stand in visible and impressive contrast with the line of conduct they pursue. In such circumstances, it often happens that silent example placed in distinct visibility before the mind will be the most impressive and influential admonition that we can possibly render, much more influential than if accompanied with words.

I once, for example, met a very useful brother in the ministry who had adopted habits in respect to food and drink that, though common, were very injurious to his health and consequently to his usefulness. When we met at table, my example was in marked contrast with his. When questioned on the subject, I was careful to state the great benefits I had received in consequence of a change in my habits, especially in the particulars in which he was suffering. On account of the peculiar relations I sustained to him, nothing was said by way of direct admonition. A mutual friend, however, was earnestly solicited to speak with him on the subject, as opportunity should occur. A few weeks subsequent, I received the pleasing intelligence that the habits of that brother were in all respects corrected, as I desired.

This intelligence, however, was accompanied with a severe rebuke from him because I had, without uttering a syllable of admonition, repeatedly witnessed him in the indulgence of habits so injurious. I had given, as he thought, a poor exemplification of the principles I professed. I returned the reply that I had gained the end upon the attainment of which I had prayerfully set my heart. In this I would rejoice though the more I loved him, the less I was loved by him. Cases like the above not infrequently occur, and we should ask wisdom from above to discover "*the times and the seasons*" (1 Thessalonians 5:1).

Admonition may often be most effectually administered through the agency of a second person. If I find that another person has more influence than myself over the individual who needs admonition, especially in respect to the point where it is demanded, I should at once seek to avail myself of his agency while I carry the case to a throne of grace.

The best form of admonition is often this: the putting into the hand of the individual some book, tract, or publication that treats upon the subject upon which admonition is needed. This should be done with a kind request that he will give the subject an attentive, candid, and prayerful examination. How often is a soul saved from death by such simple means as this.

The last mode of admonition that I mention is this: kindly speaking ourselves as opportunities present themselves. This is the form of the duty especially referred to in the text. For its neglect we will stand without excuse at the judgment.

One inquiry more of great importance presents itself here.

Circumstances That Impart to Christian Admonition the Highest Efficiency

Among these I mention the following:

1. A character in visible and uniform conformity to the spirit and principles of the gospel

There are individuals (such is the beauty of holiness uniformly reflected in their example) into whose presence I never come without being, by their presence, even without anything being said on spiritual subjects, sensibly admonished to renewed love, faith, humility, purity, and purposes of obedience. Indeed, even the remembrance of them has about it a hallowed savor that sweetly draws the soul to the heart of Christ. When such persons address a word of admonition to us, who has power to resist it? If you, reader, would speak for Christ with effect, seek, and by grace, obtain the possession of such a character.

2. An established reputation for what may properly be called Christian prudence

An individual who is in the habit of speaking out of time and season and in improper circumstances soon acquires a character in the estimation of others that renders his words ineffective, whatever he may say on any particular occasion, even when they are well-ordered in respect to manner and place. On the other hand, an individual who uniformly speaks with a wise adaptation to character, state of mind, and circumstances of time and place soon establishes a reputation for Christian prudence that secures an attentive and candid hearing when he speaks, and consequently he imparts the greatest efficacy to all his admonitions. Now, reader, the truth I wish to impress upon your heart is this: You are bound to possess such a reputation. This reputation you cannot acquire by aiming to acquire it but by actually speaking for Christ through wisdom obtained from above, according to the dictates of Christian prudence.

3. A wise adaptation to circumstances of time, place, character, and state of mind in each particular instance

Captain C., while abroad upon the ocean and in a state of impenitency, read the little work on Christian perfection that I gave to the public some years since.[9] While reading, he said to himself, "This religion, if I possessed it, would be worth the universe to me." With these impressions, he returned to Boston and immediately attended upon the ministry of Brother Finney, where he soon obtained peace in believing. He went among his friends on shore and abroad upon the ocean, proclaiming everywhere the full salvation of Christ. In all the ports he has since visited, his vessel has been known as a "floating Bethel." He recently returned to Boston with his entire crew, I believe, hopefully converted to Christ. In a meeting for prayer, he requested the brethren of the church with which he was connected to unite with him in thanksgiving to God that every day, with two exceptions—when his vessel lay much of the time on her beam's end in a furious tempest, the morning and evening sacrifice had ascended to God on board his ship, and God had given him the hearts of all his crew.

At the same time, he would not have them suppose that in every instance he had fully exemplified, during his absence, the full salvation of Christ that was so dear to his and their hearts. In one instance, while in a state of great exhaustion during a tedious storm, he, for a moment, indulged and gave utterance to feelings of irritation. Soon after, the cook, a man recently converted I believe, came to him and with great simplicity and Christian sincerity said, "Captain, was that like Christ? I am very ignorant, but I want to know if Christ would have spoken just as you did then?" His heart was melted and subdued at once. He called the crew below, and there, with tears of penitence, he confessed his wrong. Then as they all kneeled together in prayer, the full salvation of Christ flooded the ship. All hearts

9. Asa Mahan, *Scripture Doctrine of Christian Perfection*, 1844.

were filled. It was the pretty and sweet manner of that admonition, together with its adaptation to circumstances of time and place, that gave it such a subduing efficacy. The same is true in all instances.

4. Deep-felt and humble confession of sins, on our part, if any are known that may serve as stumbling blocks

Without this, in such a case, all that we may say will be worse than useless.

Remarks

We notice the spirit with which admonition should be received when we ourselves are the subjects of it. Sometimes we may be admonished to repent of sins that we are conscious we are not guilty of. Whether this is so or not, kind admonition should be regarded by us as one of the strongest proofs of brotherly love. It should bind our hearts to him who administers it, as to that of a brother or sister or mother. He is doing the will of his Father in heaven in one of the most important departments of Christian duty.

We notice among the most sacred obligations that Christ has devolved upon His people a duty in the discharge of which the church is, of all others, most deficient. It is the duty of Christian admonition. For myself, I contemplate with horror the vows the church voluntarily, and most solemnly and sacredly, assumes in respect to every convert whom she receives into her bosom when I think of the manner in which these vows are fulfilled. In that solemn covenant, the entire church pledges to the convert the most kind and assiduous supervision of all his spiritual interests, that she will watch over and admonish him in the Lord and by all the means in her power seek his peace and edification.

But how is that covenant subsequently regarded? When the convert is in circumstances of temptation, who feels obligated particularly to caution him and stir him up to watchfulness and prayer? When he is weak, who strengthens him? When he is afflicted, who comforts him? When he errs from the truth, who corrects him? (See James 5:19–20.) When he is likely to forget, who stirs up his pure mind by way of remembrance? And when his reputation is assailed, who shares his reproach? Is not the church *"hardened against her young ones, as though they were not hers"* (Job 39:16)? How ready are her members to take up an evil report against a brother—to suspect him of wrong or question the purity of his motives? (See James 4:11.) But let us bring the subject home to our own hearts, reader. How stands the dread account with you and me in respect to this sacred department of Christian duty?

We now perceive one of the chief sources of discord and division in the churches of Christ. Where the duty of Christian admonition is faithfully discharged in the bonds of Christ, there the unity of the Spirit in the bonds of peace will be preserved in all hearts. But when this is neglected, there is discord and every evil work. The moment you cease to admonish a brother, as God gives you opportunity, that moment you will cease to love him as a brother. Continuance in this neglect will, before long, render him as a stranger and a foreigner to your heart.

It may be well for us now to stop a moment and contemplate an important test of Christian character. The proper test is practical obedience to all God's requirements. But when we contemplate the subject in a general point of view, our conclusion will be that it is probable, rather indefinite. It would be preferable, at times at least, to select some one specific command—plainly revealed and everywhere regarded as devolved upon us with peculiar sacredness in the Bible—and contemplate our character in the light of that one precept. The text furnishes us with such a precept. In the Word of God, it is revealed with special distinctness, and its peculiar sacredness is recognized in the covenants of every church, probably, on earth. In testing our character in the light of such a precept, two questions naturally present themselves. First, what is the influence of our example? Is it a standing and impressive admonition to all who feel its power to love, to faith, to purity, and to consecration to Christ? Second, what is the character of our direct and personal intercourse with our fellow men? Does it show a sacred respect to the precept *"Exhort one another daily"* (Hebrews 3:13)? I feel a strong desire, hearer, to sit down with you and, while none but God will hear, to present the solemn question to your heart and conscience—How stands the dread account with you in the light of this plain and positive command of God, which you acknowledge to be so sacredly binding?

We perceive the occasion of the decline of revivals of religion. Revivals commence with a faithful discharge of the duty of Christian admonition. *"They go from strength to strength"* (Psalm 84:7) while this duty is faithfully performed. With its neglect, they decline. This is a changeless arrangement of Divine Providence.

We notice the inquiry often practically raised by those who are living in disregard of their most solemn responsibilities to their fellow men. *"Am I my brother's keeper?"* (Genesis 4:9). Yes, reader, you are your brother's keeper. If you see evil coming upon your brother and you give him not warning, if he errs from the truth and you allow sin to come upon him, if temptations beset his path and you do not exhort him to watchfulness and prayer, if he becomes remiss in duty and you do not stir not up his pure mind by way of remembrance—in short, if you do not discharge to everyone around you the duty of Christian admonition, God will require His blood at your hands. (See Ezekiel 33:7–8.)

A word to the impenitent reader, and then I'll close. With what feelings do you receive the word of solemn admonition from those who seek your eternal peace? How do they now appear who admonish you? How can you meet in eternity those with whom you have lived in sin, before whom you have set the example of impenitence, and whom you have never admonished to repent? How will you then regard the voice of solemn admonition that you now despise?

When the harvest is past and the summer is gone;
And sermons and prayers shall be o'er;
When the beams cease to break on the sweet Sabbath morn,
And Jesus invites thee no more:
When the rich gales of mercy no longer shall blow,
The gospel no message declare;
Sinner, how canst thou bear the deep wailings of woe?
How suffer the night of despair?
When the holy have gone to the regions of peace,
To dwell in the mansions above;
When their harmony wakes in the fulness of bliss,
Their song to the Saviour they love:
Say, O sinner! that livest at rest and secure,
Who fearest no trouble to come,
Can thy spirit the wailings of sorrow endure,
Or bear the impenitent's doom?[10]

10. J. Harrison, "When the Harvest Is Past."

11

DIFFICULTIES CONNECTED WITH THE DOCTRINE OF IMPERFECTION

"Why should it be thought a thing incredible with you, that God should raise the dead?"
—Acts 26:8

Almost every truth with which men are not familiar encounters this one difficulty when first presented to their minds—it wears the appearance not only of strangeness but of incredibility. What is more familiar or reasonable and credible with us than the doctrine of the resurrection? In a very different light would it stand before our minds were we called to listen to it for the first time. The speaker might have the same occasion to put the question to us that Paul put to Agrippa: *"Why should it be thought a thing incredible with you, that God should raise the dead?"* How strange and incredible the doctrine of perfect love appears to individuals not familiar with it and who have not been taught of God to understand it! They seem inclined to say, "If God should make windows in heaven, then might these things be."

What if we should present it in the form in which the apostle presented the doctrine of the resurrection? "Why should it be thought a thing incredible with you that God should, by His grace and Spirit, sanctify a believer wholly and cause him to stand perfect and complete in all His holy will?" If God has provided grace and given His Holy Spirit to make that grace effectual to that result, why should it be thought incredible that a believer in Jesus should realize that result in his own experience? This doctrine, on that supposition, becomes most reasonable, most credible. The opposite doctrine becomes most unreasonable and incredible. The difficulties all lie on one side. This leads me to the subject to be illustrated in the present discourse.

The Difficulties Connected with the Doctrine of Imperfection

These difficulties, to a consideration of which special attention is invited, will be found to be such as to be entirely fatal to that doctrine.

The first that I notice is found in the covenants of the churches. The church covenant is an oath, voluntarily assumed, in the presence of God, angels, and men. So it is universally regarded. But what, Christian, does your covenant pledge you, in a manner so fearfully solemn, to do? Turn to Exodus 34:27–28, and you will see.

> *And the LORD said unto Moses, Write thou these words: for after the tenor of these words I have made a covenant with thee and with Israel. And he was there with the LORD forty days and forty nights; he did neither eat bread, nor drink water. And he wrote upon the tables the words of the covenant, the ten commandments.*

This is God's covenant, a covenant to do our entire duty, or to be in a state of entire sanctification or in the continued exercise of perfect love. And this covenant is embraced in all its fullness in the covenant of every evangelical church on earth. If any church should lower her covenant so as not to embrace all this, as a few are said to have done of late, she would cease to be in covenant with God. For this is the covenant He has prescribed.

Now there are two positions that have been taken by the different schools in theology on this subject.

The brethren of the old school maintain that it is a natural impossibility, even from any grace received in this life, to keep the covenant. According to this view of the subject, the convert takes a solemn oath in the presence of God, angels, and men to perform an acknowledged impossibility! Reader, what do you think of that? What would you think if a witness in a court of justice should take an oath to perform what he and all the court knew and acknowledged to be an impossibility? Would not that be perjury? This is what all the churches do according to the doctrine of the old school. This is the difficulty in which the doctrine of imperfection is involved, according to the teaching of that school. How can that difficulty be evaded? How can a doctrine stand when it is seen to be involved in such a difficulty as this?

The brethren of the new school, on the other hand, maintain that this covenant may be kept, that grace fully adequate is proffered to us in the gospel to keep it and that it is better not to vow than to vow and not pay. They then pledge the convert, under oath, to keep that covenant. At the same time, they require him to hold it as a revealed truth of God that he will not keep it and that it is a dangerous error to expect to do it himself or to believe that any Christian ever did or ever will in this life keep it. In other words, they require the convert to take an oath in the presence of God, angels, and men to keep the covenant with the avowed expectation of not keeping it. What is perjury if this is not? Where, too, will we look for the perfection of absurdity if not here? And what must be the influence upon the convert's mind of such an oath in connection with such an expectation? Is he not thereby prepared to violate that covenant almost without compunction? Can we conceive of a more fatal snare for his soul? The very first act he performs, in connection with the church, is an act of perjury, an act performed with the expectation of ever after daily repeating it in thought, word, and deed.

Another difficulty is found in the prayers of the church. All Christians admit that the Bible authorizes and requires us to pray for grace to exercise perfect love, that it assures us when we thus pray that God is able to bestow that grace upon us and authorizes us to expect *"exceeding abundantly above all that we ask or think"* (Ephesians 3:20). With all these facts before us, the advocates of the doctrine of imperfection maintain that we are required to pray for grace to *"stand perfect and complete in all the will of God"* (Colossians 4:12), expecting not to receive the grace for which we pray. Now here the following difficulties look us directly in the face, and it does appear to me they would look at any man strangely who should, in their presence, attempt to maintain this doctrine.

1. *The absurdity that praying under such circumstances with such expectations involves*

A western synod was about to pass some strong resolutions against the doctrine of perfect love. A member of the body, an elder of leading influence, arose and remarked that before passing resolutions so solemn and important, they ought, as it appeared to him, to spend a season in prayer. He then proposed that the brother who had introduced the resolutions should lead in the exercise. The brother rose and prayed, *"The very God of peace sanctify you wholly; and I pray God your whole spirit and soul and body be preserved blameless unto the coming of our Lord Jesus Christ"* (1 Thessalonians 5:23). At the close of the solemn appeal to the throne of grace, the elder rose again and remarked that he now, as he believed, understood the real difference between the synod and the brethren they were about to condemn. Those brethren maintained they are bound to pray for grace to exercise perfect love, expecting to receive the grace for which they pray. The synod was now about to pronounce this expectation to be a dangerous delusion. They were about to resolve that we are required to pray for such grace expecting *not* to receive the blessing. He asked the synod if it became them as the standard-bearers of the sacramental host to pass such resolutions. After a short pause, the resolutions were laid on the table, never, it is hoped, to be taken up again. The difficulties presented looked them all out of countenance; such is the absurdity that looks every man in the face who prays, as all are required to do, for entire sanctification and yet holds the doctrine of imperfection.

2. The moral tendency of thus praying

Suppose a parent requires a child to present daily a special request for a particular blessing, and he distinctly informs the child he is *able* to grant his request and to do "*exceeding abundantly above all that* [he asks or thinks]" (Ephesians 3:20), but then he informs the child that he is changelessly determined not to grant his request. Could a child possibly continue to love a parent under such circumstances? This is the same position we hold with our Father in heaven if, as the doctrine of imperfection affirms, God requires us to pray for grace to exercise perfect love while expecting not to receive that grace. Reader, can you believe that God has done any such thing? If so, has He not rendered it necessary that we should all be mockers when we pray, and thus our "*bands be made strong*" (Isaiah 28:22)?

3. The illogical reasoning involved in praying thus

If God has revealed the fact that grace to exercise perfect love is never, in this life, to be given in answer to prayer, such grace as is expressly taught in such passages as Jeremiah 7:16 and 1 John 5:16 is not an object of prayer. The fact, then, that we are required to pray for such grace is demonstration of the fact that it lies within the circle of rational hope. But it is said by the advocates of the doctrine of imperfection, "We do pray for entire sanctification, expecting to receive it when we die." Then pray for entire sanctification in the article of death. The absurdity consists in praying for present sanctification and expecting, not as the Bible requires, which is even more than we ask or think (see Ephesians 3:20), but expecting less than we ask or think.

Another difficulty is suggested by the revealed provisions and promises of grace for the sanctification of Christians in this life. Here also, two positions have been taken by the two schools in theology above referred to. The brethren of the old school deny that provisions and promises for the entire sanctification of Christians in this life are revealed in the gospel. The brethren of the new school admit and affirm the full adequacy of the revealed provisions and promises, and yet they deny (a denial that the brethren of the old school affirm involves the highest absurdity) that a state of entire sanctification in this life is an object of rational hope.

Now the difficulty that the position of the old school involves is a palpable contradiction of the plainest possible teachings of inspiration. I will cite a few passages as examples.

"Who his own self bare our sins in his own body on the tree, that we, being dead to sins, should live unto righteousness" (1 Peter 2:24). To be dead in sin, all evangelical denominations admit, implies total depravity. To be dead to sin, then, must imply perfection in holiness. That we might become thus dead is the revealed object of Christ's death. He has, then, made provision for our entire sanctification, or he has failed to finish the work the Father gave Him to do. Contemplate also the following command: *"Likewise reckon ye also yourselves to be dead indeed unto sin, but alive unto God through Jesus Christ our Lord"* (Romans 6:11). How absurd is the command to reckon ourselves dead indeed unto sin but alive unto God through Jesus Christ if provisions do not exist in Him for our becoming thus dead and alive—that is, for our entire sanctification.

As a specimen of the promises pertaining to our sanctification, take this one:

> *The Lord thy God will circumcise thine heart, and the heart of thy seed,* ***to love the Lord thy God with all thine heart, and with all thy soul,*** *that thou mayest live.*
>
> (Deuteronomy 30:6)

The Bible affirms that *"love is the fulfilling of the law"* (Romans 13:10) and that all the law requires is that we love God with all our heart and with all our soul. We have, then, the same evidence that perfect love is proffered to our faith in the promises, that we have that it is required in the moral law. This, then, is the difficulty in which the position of the brethren of the old school involves us. In taking their position, we join issue directly and openly with the Bible. The doctrine of imperfection cannot find a resting place here.

The position of the brethren of the new school involves us, if possible, in a difficulty still greater—that the revealed provisions and promises of grace are not a foundation for rational hope. Reader, what do you think of that? Was ever a position presented to your contemplation that is more abhorrent to all the hallowed convictions and impressions *"the glorious gospel of the blessed God"* (1 Timothy 1:11) has raised in your mind?

But this position is condemned by these brethren themselves in their preaching and instruction in respect to all other subjects except this one. The revealed provisions and promises of grace are presented as a foundation sure and steadfast for the hope of pardon, salvation, and every blessing they proffer to our faith—except entire sanctification in this life. Now, why are they affirmed as an adequate foundation of hope in respect to all other blessings and denied in respect to this one? No advocate of the doctrine of imperfection has yet been able to answer this question. I hesitate not to affirm that no one ever will be able to answer it.

But another difficulty that this position involves here presents itself. What must be the effect upon the moral sensibilities of cherishing the impression that the revealed provisions and promises of grace are not an adequate foundation of hope? Can anything be more fatal? I would as soon entertain the thought that God can lie. I cannot conceive that the latter can be more fatal in its influence than the former. Now, reader, one of these alternatives you must take. With the old school, you must deny the adequacy of the provisions and promises of grace to our sanctification in this life, and thus place yourself at open issue with the Bible. Or with the new school, you must maintain that the revealed provisions and promises of grace are not an adequate foundation of hope. Or else you must admit the blessed doctrine of perfect love. Which of these positions do the Bible and reason require you to take?

We now come to another fatal difficulty in which the doctrine of imperfection is involved—the nature of faith according to that doctrine. The Bible affirms that *"without faith it is impossible to please* [God]" (Hebrews 11:6). When we pray, we are told to *"ask in faith, nothing wavering"* (James 1:6); otherwise, we should not expect to *"receive any thing of the Lord"* (verse 7). What, then, is faith, and what is unbelief according to the doctrine of imperfection? Suppose an individual bows the knee unto the Father of our Lord Jesus Christ and that this is the burden of his prayer: "May the very God of peace sanctify me wholly and preserve my whole spirit, soul, and body blameless unto the coming of our Lord Jesus Christ." (See 1 Thessalonians 5:23.) What would be faith, and what unbelief, in putting up such a prayer according to the doctrine of imperfection? If we put up that prayer, expecting to receive the blessing for which we pray, that is unbelief, according to this doctrine. We are, then, forbidden by God to expect to receive anything from the Lord. If, on the other hand, we put up such a prayer, expecting *not* to receive the blessing for which we pray, we *"ask in faith, nothing wavering"* (James 1:6). If this doctrine is true, this is faith, and this is unbelief in prayer.

The nature of faith in the promises pertaining to sanctification in this life is equally singular according to this doctrine. An individual, we will suppose, appears before God to plead such promises as the following, which God says He will do for us. *"Then will I sprinkle clean water upon you, and ye shall be clean: from all your filthiness, and from all your idols, will I cleanse you"* (Ezekiel 36:25). Now, according to the doctrine of imperfection, if we plead such promises and expect to realize their present fulfillment in our experience, that is unbelief. We then stagger at the promise of God through unbelief. If, on the other hand, we plead such promises and expect *not* to realize their fulfillment in our experience, that is faith. We are then *"strong in faith, giving glory to God"* (Romans 4:20).

The same principles hold true in respect to the provisions of grace for our entire sanctification in this life. To rely upon these provisions, expecting to realize in our experience the end for which they were made, is unbelief. Relying upon them, expecting not to realize that end, is faith, according to the doctrine of imperfection. Reader, is not this faith and unbelief, according to this doctrine? Do not the advocates of this doctrine maintain, for example, that we are bound to pray, and pray in faith, for our entire sanctification in this life? Do they not also maintain that it is not proper to expect to attain to that state? So Dr. Woods expressly affirms. To pray, then, for entire sanctification, expecting to receive that blessing, is unbelief. To pray for it, expecting not to receive it, is faith. But is this the nature of faith and unbelief according to the Bible? Have we not here an inexplicable difficulty—a difficulty from which the doctrine of imperfection cannot be extricated?

Another difficulty is found in the nature of the argument for the truth of the Bible from internal evidence. This argument may be thus stated: That system of religion must be true, and the only true one, which is most favorable to moral rectitude and best adapted to meet the entire necessities of man as a creature and as a sinner. The gospel is better adapted to produce these results than any other and all other systems. It, therefore, must be true. Now this principle, if legitimate (and its legitimacy is universally admitted), is equally applicable and decisive as a practical test of all the particular truths and principles of Christianity. Of two conflicting doctrines or principles—each professedly founded on the Bible and only one of which can be true—the one that is most favorable to holiness and best adapted to meet our entire necessities as creatures and as sinners must be true. Let us test the doctrines of imperfection and of perfect love by this principle.

Only one of these doctrines can be true. The other must be false, and that must be true which is most favorable to holiness and best adapted to our wants as creatures and as sinners. In one particular, all admit that the doctrine of perfect love has the most decisive advantage, its superior adaptation to our necessities. Every Christian, in every prayer, prays in all sincerity that this doctrine may be true and the opposite doctrine false. He is fully conscious that if the doctrine of perfect love is true, his "*joy may be full*" (John 16:24). If the opposite doctrine is true, it is impossible that his "*joy may be full.*" In this respect, we fitly say, "*Their rock is not as our Rock, even our enemies themselves being judges*" (Deuteronomy 32:31). In the universally acknowledged ability of the doctrine of perfect love to meet the fundamental and changeless wants of the church, we have the same evidence that this doctrine is true and the opposite one is false as we have that the gospel is true and every other system of religion false.

But how stands the case so far as tendency to holiness is concerned? That we are bound to pray for entire sanctification and to aim at that state, all admit. Which is most favorable to effectual, fervent prayer—the expectation of obtaining the object for which we pray or the certain expectation of not obtaining it? Which is most favorable to energetic effort—the expectation of obtaining the object at which we aim or the certain expectation of not obtaining it? What is the verdict of the reason and common sense of the human race? Everyone knows. Nor is the Bible silent on this point. It affirms that believers are saved by hope. To extinguish hope is to annihilate faith and paralyze effort. This is what the doctrine of imperfection does. When we bow the knee to the Father of our Lord Jesus Christ to ask for the blessing Christ has required us to pray for, that doctrine comes in and annihilates the possibility of faith by extinguishing hope. When we would aim at the standard the Spirit of God has elevated, that doctrine comes in and paralyzes effort by extinguishing hope. In its fundamental elements, it is a great incubus upon the faith and moral energies of the church.

Another difficulty is found in the manifest unsuitability of the doctrine to the laws of mind, as universally acknowledged in all other departments of human action. There is not a department of human action in the wide world in which the expectation of success is not universally acknowledged to be indispensable to permanent energy of effort. A writer in a late political paper thus expresses the difference between *can* and *can't*:

> I do not know a word in the vocabulary of language that sounds so forbidding to the feelings, so stagnant in its effects as the word *can't*. It is irreconcilable to any thing in morals or philosophy. It checks the current of life, and brings all the energies of body and mind into

a state of lethargy; makes the present a cold winter's waste and desert of despair—the future, an inextricable wilderness, the entrance of which is an interminable labyrinth of darkness and woe; while upon "can" Faith shines with bright, diffusive, benign rays of the meridian sun—wakens and cheers every thing into active light and energy; removes mountains; crosses trackless oceans and continents into unexplored regions; makes the desert teem with life and beauty; builds States and Empires; turns the current of mighty streams; opens canals and builds railroads; erects temples, the spiritual guide posts, whose spires point to Heaven.

The truth of all this is fully and universally acknowledged in every department of human action, with the exception of religion. What is the doctrine of imperfection here? It is a sacred consecration upon the altar of our faith, of *can't* as a permanent and essential motive to energetic action. The *can't* of the old school is natural; that of the new is moral; but yet, as one of its advocates expressed it, it is "a powerless power." Both are equally paralyzing within the circle of their influence. What right, I ask, has *can't* to a place upon the altar of our faith, relative to the commands of God and in the presence of the proffered grace of the gospel? No more, I answer, than swine's flesh or the broth of abominable things. (See Isaiah 65:4.) Can anyone tell us why it is that the extinguishment of hope annihilates faith and paralyzes effort in all departments of human activity but religion, while here it is an essential element of such activity? Till this mystery is explained, it must be regarded as a fatal difficulty in the way of the doctrine of imperfection.

As another difficulty, I notice the unintended testimony that the advocates of this doctrine, when speaking upon other subjects, are almost constantly giving in favor of the doctrine of perfect love and in condemnation of the opposite doctrine. I will give a few examples in illustration of the manner in which this testimony is given. At a great national convention held some years ago, on the subject of temperance, a convention attended by a host of ministers and laymen of leading influence, a resolution embracing this affirmation was unanimously passed—that all hope of reformation to the drunkard is suspended upon this one principle, that he may set his heart upon subduing his appetite for strong drink with the expectation of success.

At an annual meeting of the American Board held in Philadelphia, they affirmed that all their efforts for the evangelizing of the natives of this country were paralyzed by the impression so general and strong through the churches that they are doomed as a race to annihilation from the earth. The impression weakens the efforts of the missionaries themselves by extinguishing hope, and if not erased from the public mind, it will prevent the salvation of that people. One of the most distinguished professors of theology in this country has laid this down as a self-evident proposition—the belief on the part of the sinner that he will not repent renders all efforts to induce him to repent as absolutely powerless as the belief that it is impossible for him to repent. Now who does not see that if the principles affirmed in all the above instances are true, the doctrine of perfect love must be true and of most hallowed tendency, while the opposite doctrine must be false and of most pernicious tendency? What the hope of success is to the drunkard aiming at reformation, the doctrine of perfect love is to the believer struggling after entire conformity to the will of God. What the extinguishment of hope would be to the drunkard, the doctrine of imperfection is to the believer in respect to the holiness that God requires. So, also, it is in the other instances above named.

But one of the most striking and decisive instances of the kind of testimony under consideration that I have met with is found in a paragraph from an article originally published in the *Boston Recorder* and republished in the *New York Evangelist*. The following is one of the reasons here given in answer to the inquiry as to why one's prayers are not answered:

> Perhaps you pray without *expecting*. Such prayer cannot be in earnest. What a man has no expectation of receiving, he can only ask for in a faint and feeble manner. And this not expecting, is a want of confidence in God. His promises are made for the very purpose of awakening expectation in our hearts. It is ill treatment of God, not to expect Him to fulfill His own promises. An unexpecting appeal of prayer ought to be expecting a denial.

Now what testimony more strong and explicit could possibly be given against the doctrine of imperfection than is here indirectly and undesignedly given—testimony the more to the purpose because it is undesigned? How inconsistent and absurd is the opposition of such men to the doctrine of perfect love, after giving such testimony in its favor. Thus it is that the advocates of the doctrine of imperfection are, without intending it, continually throwing insuperable difficulties in the way of that doctrine, difficulties that are daily becoming more and more palpable to the church and to the world and that render its speedy destruction absolutely certain.

Another difficulty in which the doctrine of imperfection is involved is found in the attitude in which the investigations of the most distinguished commentators, in this country and in Europe, placed the doctrine before its truth or falsity became a great question with the church. Prior to this event, the proof-texts on which, as admitted by its advocates, the doctrine rests were in the light of the universally admitted laws of interpretation, examined by learned commentators on both sides of the Atlantic—commentators holding this very doctrine. What was the result of these investigations? That most of these passages, to say the least, have no reference to the doctrine whatever.

In respect to Romans 7, for example, it has been found that the entire early church, for the first four or five centuries of the Christian era, understood the apostle in this passage to be describing the experience of the convicted legalist and not at all of the true Christian. This same construction is now considered as demanded by all the correct laws of interpretation, by the entire body of evangelical commentators on the continent of Europe, by a majority, I believe, of those in Great Britain, and by such men as Professors Stuart and Robinson of this country. Nor have the arguments adduced by them in favor of this construction yet been refuted.

The declaration of Paul "*Not as though I had already attained, either were already perfect*" (Philippians 3:12) was found to refer, as the context shows, not at all to perfection in *holiness* but in *glory,* and consequently it has no bearing upon the doctrine of Christian perfection whatever. In a conversation I had with the former president of the Union Theological Seminary regarding 1 John 1:8, "*If we say that we have no sin, we deceive ourselves,*" he replied at once, "I have long since given up that passage as having no bearing whatever upon the subject." The term *sin* is sometimes used in the sense of "ill-desert or desert of punishment." This is its meaning, as the context shows, in this passage.

Thus, in the preceding verse, the apostle says, "*If we walk in the light, as he is in the light, we have fellowship one with another, and the blood of Jesus Christ his Son cleanseth us from all sin*" (1 John 1:7)—that is, condemnation. In other words, through Christ our sins are fully pardoned. He then adds, "*If we say that we have no sin* [to be pardoned, that is, if we affirm the thought repeated in verse 10 that we have never sinned and consequently do not need the grace of pardon through Christ], *we deceive ourselves, and the truth is not in us*" (verse 8). The apostle simply asserts, then, that all men are sinners and need pardon through Christ and that those who deny this truth, as the proud Jews did, are self-deceived. The passage has not the most remote reference to the doctrine of the perfection or imperfection of believers in Christ.

The same meaning attaches to the declaration of Job, "*If I say, I am perfect, it shall also prove me perverse*" (Job 9:20). He is there speaking not of his present character as a sanctified man but in reference to his past life. If I should assert my perfect freedom from deserving punishment based on having, in my former life, sinned, that—he intends to say—would prove me a perverse man. Thus the "seven pillars" on which this doctrine has been supposed to rest have been, one after another, swept away and in most instances by its own advocates, so that it has now not even a foundation of sand on which to rest. What must be the destiny of a doctrine sustaining such a relation as that to the Scriptures interpreted according to the universally admitted laws of interpretation?

I mention but one difficulty more. It is the manifest absurdity involved in most of the arguments in favor of the doctrine of imperfection. I will cite a few as examples.

First, examine the command to *"grow in grace"* (2 Peter 3:18). To grow in grace implies, it is said, not present perfection in holiness but a gradual approach to it. Hence the precept to *"grow in grace,"* requiring such approach, implies present imperfection. On this supposition we have a positive command of God, requiring us to give up sin gradually and consequently forbidding the renunciation of all sin at once. Entire obedience to God, then, would imply disobedience to a positive command of the gospel. Reader, do you believe that? Can this be the real meaning of the command *"grow in grace"*?

The Christian warfare, as described in the Bible, implies (it is said) present imperfection. If so, the command *"Fight the good fight of faith"* (1 Timothy 6:12) requires us, as in the instance above named, to be in a state of partial disobedience to God. The Christian warfare, as described in the Bible, is war with temptation and not with sin, and it implies that not yielding to the temptation, as is often supposed, is a glorious victory over it. So far as we yield to the temptation, we are not fighting at all as required. We are in *"captivity to the law of sin"* (Romans 7:23). *"For of whom a man is overcome, of the same is he brought in bondage"* (2 Peter 2:19). Our warfare is then not with sin but with conscience and with God. How melancholy is the fact that what many give themselves credit for as the fight of faith is in reality a war with conscience and with God.

If the Christian were to attain to the exercise of perfect love, he would be taken instantly to heaven. Hence, existence in the body is assumed as present imperfection in holiness. This makes sin an essential element of Christian character as a life preserver. Sin, indeed, is the great life preserver of the church. Without it, she could not exist at all as *"the salt of the earth"* and *"the light of the world"* (Matthew 5:13–14). Reader, do you believe that? Yet the advocates of the doctrine of imperfection present it as one of the first truths of the gospel. It is one of the main arguments on which that doctrine rests.

All Christians are entirely sanctified at death and not before. Now entire sanctification in the article of death is held without a shadow of testimony, direct or indirect, by the Bible. Indeed, the only passage that can be supposed to have any bearing upon this point proves, if it proves anything in respect to it, that entire sanctification takes place, not at death, but—as a leader of some distinction in the Presbyterian church maintains—at the judgment. "*We know that, when he shall appear, we shall be like him; for we shall see him as he is*" (1 John 3:2). This passage, it is said, implies we will attain to a perfect likeness to Christ, that is, to a state of entire holiness, when Christ appears and not before. But the appearing here referred to is evidently at the final judgment, and consequently, it affirms, if it affirms anything on this subject, entire sanctification at the judgment and not before. The likeness here referred to, the reader should understand, is a likeness in glory. The moral likeness, which is preparatory to that, takes place, as the apostle informs us, in this life. "*But we all, with open face beholding as in a glass the glory of the Lord, are changed into the same image from glory to glory, even as by the Spirit of the Lord*" (2 Corinthians 3:18). I have noticed but a few of the difficulties in which the doctrine of imperfection is involved. These are sufficient, however, to show clearly that that doctrine is not founded upon a rock.

Remarks

We have, in the progress of this discourse, a striking illustration of the strange inconsistency of error. Suppose an advocate of the doctrine of imperfection was asked whether it is proper to pray for *any* real blessing, a blessing proffered to us in the divine promises, without expecting to receive the blessing for which we pray. His answer would be, "Such prayer cannot be in earnest. What a man has no expectation of receiving he can ask for only in a faint and feeble manner. And this not expecting is a want of confidence in God. His promises are made for the very purpose of awakening expectation in our hearts. It is ill treatment of God not to expect Him to fulfill His promises. An unexpecting appeal of prayer ought to be expecting a denial."

Ask him, whether we are not required to pray for entire sanctification and whether grace to attain that state is not proffered to our faith in the provisions and promises of the gospel. His answer, in the language of Dr. Woods, would be, "I believe it and always have believed it. The gospel is no gospel without it"—that is, without such provisions and promises. Ask him, still further, if it is proper for us to pray for entire sanctification in this life, expecting to receive the blessing for which we pray. In the language of Dr. Woods, he would reply again, "It is not proper to indulge such expectation." Ask him if he has not involved himself in a most palpable inconsistency in what he has just said. Very likely he will deny that there is any inconsistency at all in what he has affirmed!

We can understand why the gospel, which is *"mighty through God to the pulling down of strong holds"* (2 Corinthians 10:4), has apparently so little power. The true and only reason is this: Its influence has been neutralized by the intermingling of error with the truth. The doctrine of imperfection has been one of the great neutralizing elements that the enemy of all righteousness has thrown in to prevent the full efficacy of the truth upon the sanctified heart. But blessed be God; brighter scenes are in prospect.

The time is not distant when error in all its naked deformity and truth in all its native simplicity and power will be made visible to all minds. Then will the "*righteousness* [of the church] *go forth as brightness, and the salvation thereof as a lamp that burneth*" (Isaiah 62:1).

A reply often made to two of the arguments above adduced demands a passing notice here. In respect to what is objected against praying for entire sanctification without expecting to receive the blessing for which we pray, it is said, in reply, that we often pray for blessings we do not expect to receive. We pray that all men may be converted while we do not expect such a result. The cases, I would remark, are by no means parallel. God has never promised, in answer to prayer, to convert every sinner on earth. He has positively promised, however, to "*sanctify* [us] *wholly*" (1 Thessalonians 5:23) on condition that He be asked to do it. Suppose God had given us a positive promise that if we would ask it in faith, He would, in answer to our prayers, convert the whole world at once? Could we pray acceptably for that blessing *then* without expecting to receive it? For the same reason, prayer for entire sanctification, while expecting the promises proffering this specific blessing to our faith not to be fulfilled in us, is solemn mockery.

In reply, also, to what has been here argued respecting *aiming* to do our entire duty while expecting not to do it, it is said that men often aim at what they know they never will nor can accomplish. A painter, for example, aims to produce a perfect picture while he knows that he never will produce such a result. It might be readily shown that the painter does not aim, that is, intend, to produce a perfect picture but one as near perfect as possible to him. This is what he really aims at. Granting, however, that he is really aiming at the result under consideration and does this not expecting to realize the end aimed at, it by no means follows from such an admission that a man can honestly aim at doing what God requires, expecting not to do it. In the former case, a man aims to do what he knows he cannot possibly accomplish. In the latter, he aims only at what is and is known to be practicable to him. Now, if it should be granted (which is in fact denied) that a man may aim to perform a known impossibility, expecting not to do it, it does not follow from this that he can aim to do what he knows well that he may and ought to do (as is the case with full obedience to God), expecting not to do it. Suppose I know it practicable for me to walk twenty miles in a day. Can I honestly aim to walk that entire distance, expecting all the while to travel but fifteen miles? How perfectly absurd and contradictory the supposition. Equally absurd, and for the same identical reason, is the dogma that a man may honestly aim to do his entire duty, expecting all the while not to do it.

We are now fully prepared, finally, to meet the question whether the sacred writers did design to teach the doctrine that no believer ever has or ever will attain to a state of entire sanctification in this life. The following considerations render it, to my mind, demonstrably evident that they never did design to express any such sentiment.

If they have taught this fact, they have most palpably contradicted themselves. They have, on that supposition, in some parts of the Bible, affirmed that no individual ever did or ever will walk in all God's commandments and ordinances blameless. And in another part, they have taught that two individuals did this very thing. In other words, they have said that no man ever has or will become dead unto sin and alive unto God through Jesus Christ our Lord, yet that one individual has come into this very state. Do you suppose, reader, that the sacred writers have ever contradicted themselves in this manner?

On the supposition that the Bible requires us to believe that no Christian attains to the exercise of perfect love in this life, it requires us to believe something that is directly and irreconcilably at war with the main design of the gospel. A fundamental and revealed design of Christ in the provisions and promises of grace, in the gift of the Spirit and in the organization of the church is the entire sanctification of believers in this life. Can any fact be conceived of that is more perfectly adapted to defeat that design than the idea that this end will never be realized in the experience of a solitary saint on earth? Could such a revelation answer any other end than to hang weights upon the faith of the church and drag her down under the influence of unbelief? The apostle has declared:

> *Christ also loved the church, and gave himself for it; that he might sanctify and cleanse it with the washing of water by the word, that he might present it to himself a glorious church, not having spot, or wrinkle, or any such thing; but that it should be holy and without blemish.*
>
> (Ephesians 5:25–27)

God has authorized us, by "*exceeding great and precious promises*" (2 Peter 1:4), to look to Him by faith in order to be sanctified wholly and preserved blameless unto the coming of our Lord Jesus Christ. (See 1 Thessalonians 5:23.) Can anything be more perfectly adapted to prevent us from exercising the faith requisite to a realization of such promises in our experience than the belief of the fact, as a revealed truth, that we will never in this life exercise that faith? Is the Bible thus at war with itself? Has it required us to believe a fact that is at war with the main design of inspiration? Reader, can you believe it?

The manner in which the sacred writers invariably speak on this subject shows clearly that they never intended to teach any such thing. They everywhere required the exercise of perfect love, prayed for grace to exercise it, and spoke of it as if they not only intended, but expected, that it would be exercised. Take two or three examples:

> *Be ye therefore perfect, even as your Father which is in heaven is perfect.* (Matthew 5:48)

> *Whosoever heareth these sayings of mine, and doeth them, I will liken him unto a wise man, which built his house upon a rock.* (Matthew 7:24)

What if Christ, after uttering that command and saying that whoever will hear and obey it is like a wise man who builds his house upon a rock, had added, "Whosoever hears that command and avows the expectation of obeying it or the belief that any man ever has obeyed or will, in this life, obey it, I will liken him to a foolish man who built his house upon the sand"? This is just what He would have said had He taught the doctrine of imperfection.

"*Let patience have her perfect work, that ye may be perfect and entire, wanting nothing*" (James 1:4). What if the apostle had added, "Brethren, if any of you indulge the expectation of letting patience have her perfect work, so that you will become perfect and entire, or if you believe any saint ever has done or will do this, you will fall into a most dangerous delusion"?

"*Walk before me, and be thou perfect*" (Genesis 17:1). What if God had added, "Now, Abraham, if you indulge the expectation of obeying this command or believe that any individuals ever have obeyed or will obey it, you will no longer be called the father of the faithful"? What a strange farce the sacred writers have acted if we suppose they have placed together such absurdities as these!

Reader, God has provided better things for His people than this doctrine proffers to our faith. And now, I pray that you may attain to a full understanding and experience of the *"riches of the glory of this mystery among the Gentiles; which is Christ in you, the hope of glory"* (Colossians 1:27).

> *For this cause I bow my knees unto the Father of our Lord Jesus Christ, of whom the whole family in heaven and earth is named, that he would grant you, according to the riches of his glory, to be strengthened with might by his Spirit in the inner man; that Christ may dwell in your hearts by faith; that ye, being rooted and grounded in love, may be able to comprehend with all saints what is the breadth, and length, and depth, and height; and to know the love of Christ, which passeth knowledge, that ye might be filled with all the fulness of God. Now unto him that is able to do exceeding abundantly above all that we ask or think, according to the power that worketh in us, unto him be glory in the church by Christ Jesus throughout all ages, world without end. Amen.* (Ephesians 3:14–21)

12

TEACHINGS OF THE SPIRIT

"And all thy children shall be taught of the Lord; and great shall be the peace of thy children."
—Isaiah 54:13

"When he, the Spirit of truth, is come, he will guide you into all truth: for he shall not speak of himself; but whatsoever he shall hear, that shall he speak: and he will show you things to come."
—John 16:13

Everyone who has correctly informed himself in respect to the history of the Spirit is aware that all the forms of dark fanaticism that have, in any age, attended her existence have taken their rise, mainly, in false and perverted conceptions of the nature, extent, and conditions of the teachings and illuminations of the Holy Spirit. On the other hand, all eminent attainments in holiness have been accompanied by and had their chief basis in clear, well-defined, and correct views on this important subject. A full and true elucidation of this subject is, at the present time, one of the great wants of the church. Special attention is, therefore, invited to the following train of thought, which is designed, as far as practicable, to accomplish this important end. As preliminary to the attainment of this result, I note the following.

We read in the Scriptures that man is made in the image of God. (See Genesis 1:27.) "*Therewith* [that is, with the tongue] *bless we God, even the Father; and therewith curse we men, which are made after the similitude of God*" (James 3:9). "*He* [the husband] *is the image and glory of God*" (1 Corinthians 11:7). Whatever else is implied in such passages, one thing we must understand from them—the laws and susceptibilities of the human are copied after the divine mind so that man is capable of knowing the things God knows and of resembling Him in character.

While man can thus know the objects of God's knowledge and feel and act in view of his knowledge as God does, yet in one important way the human mind differs essentially from the divine. God's mind, all His powers, are incapable both of increase or diminution—His knowledge, His power, His wisdom, His goodness remain forever the same. To eternity, they can never be either greater or less than they have been from eternity. They are all infinite. On the other hand, man is capable of endless progression in the development of all his faculties. This is the law governing all the powers of the soul. Our intellect is capable of endless growth. Our knowledge can forever increase. Our susceptibilities are capable of eternal expansion.

Progress is a fundamental and perpetual demand of human nature. We are so made that if our powers do not advance in constant growth, we are wretched of necessity. A given amount is not enough. We may be satisfied with that now, but when that point is gained, our being cries out for higher and more perfect views. We must continue to enlarge our sphere, to expand our powers through everlasting duration. If, at any stage of its progress, the mind should cease to grow, it would cease to be blessed, based on the very nature of its constitution.

But further, the mind grows only by exercise. This is a universal law of life, a principle operating everywhere. How does the physical system become strong and vigorous? By exercise. In what manner does a parent develop the physical capabilities of his child? By placing him where he must exert the strength he does possess, put forth vigorous efforts in the use of his limbs, grapple with weights as heavy as his arms can support—perhaps often by having him attempt what at present his strength is partially unequal to. Thus the physical powers are strengthened and perfected. So it is with the mind. The intellect must grapple with the great questions of truth. In this way only can it gain the strength that is its privilege to wield. If the mind was placed in circumstances where it should gain its knowledge without exertion, it would never grow. Its condition would be like that of a child, as to his physical powers, whose wants should be supplied without any movement on his part. Such a child could never acquire bodily strength. So with the mind. If knowledge should be communicated to it with no exertion on its part, if no great problems were submitted to it to be solved, and if there were no grand demonstrations to be elaborated, it could not grow.

But while it is true that strong and vigorous effort is necessary to perfect the mind, it is equally true that the mind, at every stage of its progress, needs to know some things with infallible certainty without the possibility of mistake. Those truths that pertain to duty, the great rule that governs it in all its actions, must be known with infallible certainty. Its eternal destiny is suspended here. Will the mind not know what duty is? Will a line be marked and the man required, on pain of death eternal, to pursue it without the possibility of knowing the line, without the ability to know it with infallible certainty? Surely not. It must know the rule of duty, and that without the possibility of mistake. It is needful, also, to possess all knowledge requisite to one's highest well-being and greatest usefulness. These, too, must be known with infallible certainty.

We are now prepared to contemplate the most perfect system of divine administration that the mind can conceive—that best adapted to secure the perfection and highest blessedness of created intelligences. Three different and opposite systems present themselves to our contemplation.

Under the first, all knowledge, a thing certainly possible with God, would be communicated to the mind without any effort on our part and communicated with no mixture of error. This system, as you perceive, is wholly unadapted to the growth, maturing, and to the perfection and blessedness of the mind.

The second is that in which the mind would be necessitated to labor somewhat for the acquisition of knowledge, but when this one condition is fulfilled, all knowledge would be communicated without the possibility of mistake on any subject. While this system possesses certain advantages, it labors under the most manifest and fatal defects. Under its influence, the mind would be freed entirely from the necessity of reviewing the ground already passed over for the purpose of discovering and correcting errors, an exercise that is most favorable to mental development and that, above all others, tends most effectually to impress deeply and indelibly the truth upon the heart. This system, also, is unadapted to our social nature. It renders each mind independent of all others. All comparison of opinions, everything in the form of discussion, is entirely superseded. It is when (I almost said "only when") mind grapples with mind on the arena of thought in the discussion of the great problems of universal, eternal, and immutable truth that the mental powers grow up into vigorous manhood.

The third system is that in which everything pertaining to duty, everything necessary to our highest usefulness and well-being, will be taught with infallible certainty while, in reference to all other things, we will be left to search out the truth and required to do it in the exercise of our own powers and faculties. It is not indeed without any help at all, but we are left in such circumstances that, in respect to things not absolutely essential, we will be always liable to error.

Now I suppose we will be always liable to error. Now I suppose this to be the most perfect system possible for the perfection of intelligent natures. All the true interests are perfectly secured; all principles and knowledge that are fundamental to the action of the mind and to the perfection of an enduring blessedness are revealed to the soul with a certainty that cannot be shaken. Then for the strengthening and maturing of faculties, enlarging the sphere of usefulness and enjoyment and the capability of exertion and of happiness, great problems are thrown out to be grappled with—problems, in the solution, or attempted solution of which, a constant and perpetual growth will be secured of all the capabilities of our being. Such a system we should judge, knowing what we do of the nature of the human constitution, to be best adapted to its necessities and development, to its most perfect and permanent blessedness.

Now suppose that God were to send His enlightening Spirit to dwell in the hearts of men for the purpose of teaching them; what might He be expected to do? Under the first two systems, He would be required to bring all knowledge to the mind with no effort whatever on its part, or when the mind had made certain efforts, to enlighten it to such a degree as to render it, on all subjects alike, infallible. While each of these systems has its advantages, they are, as we have seen, most unfavorable to the growth, maturity, and perfection of the mind.

Under the third system, upon the question of duty and in respect to all truths—a knowledge of which is indispensable to our highest usefulness and well-being—the teachings of the Spirit, when His divine illumination is sought in the manner and with the state of mind required, would be unequivocally clear and infallibly certain. On these questions, no possibility of delusion would be left to the honest and trustful heart. In other directions, great problems would be thrown upon the mind to be solved without the promise of such infallible guidance. In their solution, He would consent to us more or less, as infinite wisdom should see to be best, but He would yet leave us to find them out ourselves in the appropriate exercise of our own powers.

On this system, God would give us His pledge that if we will only be honest-hearted, confiding, and active, we will never be deceived on any subject, so as to injure our happiness or endanger our safety. Then He will point out great problems in ourselves, in the Bible, in His providence, and in the universe upon which to exercise our faculties to their utmost stretch, problems so great and extensive as to continually open and unfold before our minds and forever occupy our expanding powers, keeping up an endless increase in knowledge, holiness, and bliss.

In the first two systems, we would be infallibly taught on *all* subjects, but we could never grow. Our minds would never be duly exercised and would never increase in strength. In the one last named, we would be taught infallibly as to our duty and so much as to secure complete and perfect blessedness and the highest usefulness. But as to the great problems of matter and mind, these would be left always, to a greater or less extent, liable to error. Now the question I wish to present to your minds is this: Under which of these supposed systems are we actually placed? In conformity to which system are we to expect the teachings of the Spirit? This brings me to the main topic of this discourse and opens the way for a statement of the position I will endeavor to establish, which is this:

> In all subjects necessary to salvation, our highest usefulness, holiness, and peace, we can have absolutely infallible guidance. In all other subjects, great problems are thrown upon our minds that we are required to attempt to solve without the promise of such infallible guidance.

This I will prove to be the actual condition of man by a reference to undeniable facts.

Contemplate the heavens above, the movements and the splendor of the celestial orbs. We turn to the Psalms and find that thousands of years ago, in the youth of mankind, a man under the influence and teaching of God's Spirit looked upon the heavens with this sentiment: "*The heavens declare the glory of God; and the firmament showeth his handywork. Day unto day uttereth speech, and night unto night showeth knowledge*" (Psalm 19:1–2). It was indispensable to his highest blessedness and holiness, that he should be brought into such a relation to the heavens as this, that he should know, that the fact should be visible and should be an ever present reality to his soul, that in the heavens the glory of God shines forth. Thus far, then, he was taught. In this knowledge, he could not be mistaken. Of this fact he was absolutely certain.

Every person may be taught, as David was instructed, to behold God in the heavens, His wisdom in every part of the expanse, His goodness and love in every star. But there are great and intricate problems about the heavens that God has thrown upon the mind without the promise of supernatural and infallible guidance in their solution. What are these stars? What laws govern their movements? What is the mechanism of the heavens? At these we must labor with a continual liability to err. Good men, in all ages, have wrought in the solution of these problems and have always, to a greater or less extent, failed. It is scarcely two centuries since the true mechanism of the heavenly bodies was found out, since the great chain that binds the universe of worlds, in one harmonious round, was brought forth from the mystery of all former ages since the creation. Now, why did not God reveal it at first? Or why was not the revelation made at some time with infallible certainty? Because it was better for men to labor at it, try it over and over and over, continue to fail, be in error thousands of years, but by and by work it out. He saw it best, and He left man so, left him without infallible guidance here yet necessitated him to work at the celestial problems, to attempt them over and over, to continue to toil at them for long ages above his strength.

Look next at the earth. God made the psalmist sensible, thousands of years ago, that the earth is full of the goodness of God—full of it. He showed him that in all the changes thereof, everything that exists manifests the goodness of God. He could be sensible of that—he *knew* it. It was a reality to his soul. And the Holy Spirit can and will make that a living omnipresent reality to every honest mind so that God will be present as infinitely good in everything.

> *Though the earth be removed, and thought the mountains be carried into the midst of the sea; though the waters thereof roar and be troubled, though the mountains shake with the swelling thereof.* (Psalm 46:2–3)

> *Although the fig tree shall not blossom, neither shall fruit be in the vines; the labour of the olive shall fail, the fields shall yield no meat; the flock shall be cut off from the fold, and there shall be no herd in the stalls.* (Habakkuk 3:17)

Yet the Spirit of God in the soul will make every such man, as He did the prophets of old, *"and my soul shall be joyful in the Lord: it shall rejoice in his salvation"* (Psalm 35:9). He will make the heart of the trustful perpetually sensible that the earth is full of His goodness, full of God's wisdom and love. This God will do because this sense of His love is absolutely essential to happiness. But suppose a man should ask, "*How* can all this work out the great ends of benevolence?" God says, "Find that out yourself. They will infallibly do it. I can make you sensible of that fact, can give you a certain assurance of that truth. But you must work out the problem yourself. Search the laws of My universe, the tendencies, the results of things on the whole, and by and by you will see. The problem will open and burst upon you in all its glory."

There are many mysteries in the providence of God, in the arrangement of things on the earth. Volcanoes heave their mighty fires. Hurricanes and earthquakes desolate the earth. Animals devour one another. Misery meets us everywhere. Now how is it that from all this the love and glory of God is to come forth? God says, "That is the problem I give you to solve. I will not reveal that to you. If you will look to Me, I will give you such a manifestation of My presence and love that it will be a living reality to you that I am good in all things. So you will rest in the fullest peace upon My bosom with the most absolute assurance of My eternal and boundless love." God is ready by His Spirit to bring every honest mind into that state.

In the moral world, too, the same darkness hangs over the divine administration. Voltaire appears and begins to spread his poisonous influence through the earth. Myriads are ruined by his teachings. He lives on, and eighty years alone suffice to measure his life and send him to the grave. Spencer is born. He begins to speak as if his lips were touched with seraphic fire. He utters forth a few strains, sweet as the music of the angels, and dies. Oh, why did Voltaire live so long and Spencer die so soon? Does God rule the world in love? Yes, and God's Spirit will make us, if we are honest and trustful, sensible of it in the fullest degree. But if we ask *how*—if we go and ask God, bearing even on our lips the promise, *"If any of you lack wisdom, let him ask of God, that giveth to all men liberally, and upbraideth not; and it shall be given him"* (James 1:5)—our heavenly Father will reply, "You must search that out yourselves. I will not reveal it. I will show Myself to your heart and ravish it and assure you of all My benevolence. But it is not best for Me to tell you how." Watch the movements of Providence and see how these things work and result, and by and by you will be able to cry, "Ah, now I see it! I see how God brings good out of evil." God has thrown these mysteries before us because it is wisest and best that we should exercise our powers in the solution of the glorious problems of His universe.

Look, now, at the human mind. Contemplate some things we all know—that we are free agents, accountable, immortal, and created; these we need to know at all times and in every stage, and these we may know and know infallibly. But there are, far down in the depths of the mind, mysteries unrevealed. Unfathomed distance lies beneath every plummet's sounding. These secrets need to be read. These jewels need to be brought up from the deep ocean. And God has kept the mind laboring incessantly for ages upon the great mental problems, for their solution, but thus far, even, with only partial success.

Why did not God bring them out to the light at first or make them infallibly sure at some time in man's progress? Suppose He had thus revealed them. It might have been good, perhaps, for knowledge is good. But it would not have been as good as the very labor itself of the solution would be to the maturing of the mind and the perfection of its faculties. There is the good—the good resulting from labor, just as labor is good to a child. God bids the mind to go down to those depths, to descend and fathom those wells, to dig down to the profound deep of those precious mines and bring up those invaluable gems, to dive into those ocean caves and raise to the surface the pearls hidden there. He says, "I will help you by giving you opportunity and advantage but not infallible guidance; you will be liable to mistakes. Exercise your powers with diligence, yet with great candor and caution."

Once more, the Word of God presents a most striking illustration of the great truth I am endeavoring to establish.

In the first place, when we contemplate its general features, the fact strikes us at once that its great practical truths lie on the surface. There is a highway cast up through the Bible on which *"the wayfaring men, though fools, shall not err"* (Isaiah 35:8). In the rule of duty, the truths necessary to the perfect and highest blessedness of the soul, and its entire holiness, no man need err, and no honest mind does err. A little child can find the path. But suppose a man asks, "Have we not a system of divinity in the Bible? Would it not be well to have a thoroughly digested system of the doctrines and duties of religion?" Yes, it would be well. But God has given us the Bible, His providence, and our own reason, and He has thus left us to find out the system. "But we are liable to be deceived." Yes. "Give us infallible guidance." No. God says, "Work it out; dig, labor, toil, and, in the very labor and toil, you will grow. Your minds will expand and be prepared to apprehend the higher mysteries of My kingdom. I give you no infallible guidance here. I throw upon you the responsibility of attempting the solution, of finding out and arranging the grand system of truth." God looks on our work and sees the mistakes into which we fall. He looks on with a parent's eye, and He would like to correct our errors. But He sees that to secure us against error by removing the necessity of labor and thus preventing the continued growth of the mind would be far worse than to permit our falling into numberless mistakes in the prosecution of our work.

Again, the revelation of the coming of Christ to the prophets was only partial. The Spirit told them of a glorious consummation: *"Unto us a child is born, unto us a son is given: and the government shall be upon his shoulder: and his name shall be Wonderful, Counsellor, The mighty God, The Everlasting Father, The Prince of Peace"* (Isaiah 9:6). A glorious Messiah! And then His kingdom, *"of the increase of his government and peace there shall be no end"* (verse 7). A blissful prospect! Their minds inquire, *What will He be? What is the form, manner, and character of His kingdom? When will be the grand consummation?*

The Spirit tells them, "That, I do not, with perfect distinctness, reveal. Go, search, inquire. It is the will of God that you try to discover the time and the manner of the coming of the Messiah. Be diligent. But I will not tell you. It is a mystery for you to work at and attempt to solve. The sufferings of Christ and the glory to follow must be a mystery till the glorious day appears. I will give you opportunity, throw around you certain indications. You will be liable to mistakes. But search and exercise your powers."

In this state, God kept the ancient prophets. What did those sublime prophecies mean? The Spirit was stirring up their souls to pair forth great predictions—glorious scenes were passing before their view. They asked, "What do they mean? And when are they to be?"

God told them, "Let your minds range the fields of glory. Go, rapt in vision, through the regions of celestial blessedness. Put your minds to the utmost stretch. The best I can do is to let you work at the problem, and you may know, for your own consolation, that the angels are engaged in the work, too."

The particular doctrines of the Bible also furnish appropriate illustrations of the truth of my position. For instance, we see this in the doctrine of the atonement. How plain it is from the sacred volume that Christ died to atone for our sins and that by faith in His blood, repentance, and forsaking our sins, we may be freely forgiven all our transgressions. Every mind can find that out from the Bible. No one need mistake, and no honest mind does mistake here. The fact of reconciliation and forgiveness, on repentance and faith, lies out as in the clear sunlight. And that is all that is necessary to our perfect peace and highest blessedness. So much is taught with infallible certainty. *"Believe…and thou shalt be saved"* (Acts 16:31) is adapted to even the lowest comprehension. But when the question "*How* does the death of Christ make atonement for sin and open the way for reconciliation?" is asked, here we are met with differing opinions.

Edwards, the younger, said, "I have been engaged for many years in studying that question. It is the Gordian knot in theology." He had tried at the solution. Good men for eighteen hundred years have exerted their utmost power with attempts, but partially successful, to untie this Gordian knot. Why was it not revealed at once in a clear and well-digested scheme of divinity? Because all knowledge that is indispensable has been revealed, that practical view of the atonement that is essential to sanctification is given without a liability to mistake, with the aid of the Holy Spirit sent down from heaven; it is better that the mind should use its power in unfolding the mysteries of Jehovah's government and the deep principles of His administration. It is better that the mind should mature its strength by grappling with the tremendous problems and trying to elaborate the sublime demonstrations from the great universe of truth as it passes in solemn grandeur before our astonished gaze. Here our faculties are aroused to their utmost stretch in attempts repeated again and again, and yet again, and ever partially unsuccessful to comprehend the glories of the infinite Lawgiver and King.

Every great doctrine of our holy religion would furnish a similar illustration. The child can know all that is essential to forgiveness and sanctification and perfect and perpetual blessedness. But it is needful that we grow, and for this we must toil and labor, and for this, these great problems are thrown upon us to task our utmost powers and draw out the inborn capabilities of our beings. I have now said enough to show the true relation we sustain to the Bible, the object of the Spirit's teaching, the department of His infallible guidance, and the department in which we are left, to a great extent, to our own labor to solve for ourselves.

Remarks

This subject lays open to us the real differences between honest inquirers. It is important to know in what department of inquiry honest minds differ. Now in everything pertaining to salvation and blessedness, in the perception of the rule of duty and the apprehension of the glory of God, in His works and His Word, they do not differ. All agree here. These things the Holy Spirit has taught to all God's spiritual children with infallible certainty. But step out of this field into a region in which men are left to study and conclude for themselves with a liability to error, and there you find good men differ widely. There they are, trying to get at the truth, and God looks down upon them as a parent does upon his child when he is attempting to do something he is unacquainted with, not in anger but in love. Does the parent, because of the mistakes of his child, apply the chastising rod? No, surely. The child tries and tries, does the best he can, and fails, and then tries again. The parent looks on with complacency, and says, "That is well, my son. You are not quite right, but try again. You will see how by and by. By and by, you will be able to use your limbs with skill. I will not take your tools and do the work for you, for I wish *your* arms to be strong and *your* head to possess skill."

One child works on one plan and another on a different one. The parent says, "Go on. Let each see how the other does and improve as fast as he can; I will instruct you as much as it is wise for me to do, but it is best for you to exercise your own powers."

So it is with our heavenly Father. He leaves good men to differ in those great problems of the gospel that lie within the field of human research and without the department of knowledge indispensable to holiness and happiness. Each one brings up his view. They differ much; most likely all are at least partially, if not wholly, wrong. But they never differ on the things indispensable to joy in God and perfect salvation. Why does God permit them thus to differ? Not because differences are not an evil in themselves but because the system in which there will be the necessity of mental exertion and, of course, an incidental liability to error is incalculably better on the whole than that in which there should be perfect infallibility and, therefore, no increase and no growth of the mental faculties (and, consequently, of bliss). God leaves men to search, lets them seek diligently, indicates the truth so far as He can, and yet leaves the mind to labor with all its might.

We learn the uses of such errors in judgment, to good men, together with a consciousness of their own fallibility. The Bible says, *"All things work together for good to them that love God"* (Romans 8:28). I will express an opinion warranted by this passage—that the errors of good men work to their good. You may think that mysterious, but I believe it, and these are my reasons.

First, it affords continual opportunity for the exercise of candor in reexamining opinions and humility in confessing and retracting errors. A mind launches out into the ocean of inquiry and, after sounding and sounding, and after a long and careful search, forms and expresses an opinion. This opinion is met and rebutted. He sets to it again, searches, studies, and casts his plummet, and finds something wrong. He acknowledges his error, takes to pieces his whole system, constructed with so much labor and painstaking, removes the mischievous portion, reexamines the whole range of the subject, and reconstructs his system—or waits with it unfinished till more complete knowledge enables him to go on and perfect it with less likelihood of being again obliged to demolish and build his fabric anew. Is all this an *evil?* No, the labor is a good, and a greater good than all the rest is the candor continually exercised through the whole in weighing opposing evidence and giving up dearly cherished opinions and the humility in acknowledging errors and retracting them.

Second, it tests candor in listening to another's opinion. "Brother, have you been into that field?"

"Yes."

"What did you find?"

"Such and such things."

"But my conclusions are totally different."

"How so? What were your reasons?"

"Such and such were my reasons."

"But to my mind it appears so, and these are my grounds."

What an opportunity is here for candor in listening to others and in calm and dispassionate weighing of the arguments of others. Without differences of opinion, without liability thereto, and without a department wherein men will be left to their own judgment, no such opportunity would be presented. Would it be well, would it be wise in God, to relieve us from the exercise of such Christian virtue? It would not be wise, for God has thrown us into exactly that position. Perhaps in comparing views we will find that we are both wrong. Well, we try it over, and when we think we have really found the right, again we compare, again we detect error, and again we go back to our investigations with a most useful lesson—to be cautious in framing opinions, to be certain of the ground we stand upon, and to be disposed to weigh well the opinions of a brother. Would it be wise for our heavenly Father to relieve us from this, to take from us all possibility of learning such lessons? No. It is best that children should use their own limbs, though at the danger of falling, and falling on the stones even, sometimes. It is best that the Spirit should teach infallibly only in certain cases and leave us, in others, to labor and grow. If we die without having solved our problems—no matter. *Growth* is still secured, which is the most important object after sanctification.

> The more our spirits are enlarged on earth,
> The deeper draught shall they receive of heaven.[11]

Third, another important benefit we should never forget is this: In tracing any error in an honest mind to its origin, we will, in the search, find somewhere a glorious truth to which the error has clung, but upon which truth, in reality, the mind leaned. In this way, the most important discoveries are often made. This shows the infinite wisdom and benevolence of God's plan in fitting the mind for eternity.

We now have a correct principle to guide us in the interpretation of the promises of the Bible in respect to divine teaching. For example, *"He* [the Spirit] *will guide you into all truth"* (John 16:13). *"If any of you lack wisdom, let him ask of God...and it shall be given him"* (James 1:5). The question is, will such promises be understood in an unlimited or restricted sense? And if in the last sense, what is the true principle to be applied in their interpretation?

A man commences the study of astronomy. Here, certainly, is truth, glorious truth. What if, in view of the promise *"He will guide you into all truth,"* he should avow the expectation of being

11. Edward Young, *Night-Thoughts*, 1742.

guided by the Spirit to a complete knowledge of that science in its most perfect form? What if he should take upon himself to denounce all who should question the truth of his theory thus formed as "*having not the Spirit*" (Jude 1:19)?

Take another case. Dr. Scott affirms that in writing his commentary, he never attempted the interpretation of a single passage of Scripture without an earnest and special prayer for divine illumination. What if he, on the ground that wisdom is promised to those who ask, and he had asked it, because the Spirit is promised to "*guide* [us] *into all truth,*" and he had sought its illumination, should claim to be an infallible interpreter? Who would grant that claim? If such promises authorize him to set up such a claim, they authorize every other man to set up a claim to absolute omniscience. For omniscience only embraces "*all truth*" according to the literal meaning of the phrase.

What, then, is the true principle to be applied in the interpretation of such promises? What degree of knowledge and illumination do they proffer to our faith? All of every kind and degree necessary to our highest holiness and peace. Thus far we are to expect a cloudless vision of truth, the infallible guidance of the Spirit of God.

We are now prepared to understand the true doctrine of the witness of the Spirit. This subject is thus presented in the Bible: "*Before his translation,* [Enoch] *had this testimony, that he pleased God*" (Hebrews 11:5). "*The Spirit itself beareth witness with our spirit, that we are the children of God*" (Romans 8:16). When an individual professes the witness of the Spirit in respect to any subject so indispensable to his holiness and peace as this conscious acceptance with God, his profession is altogether credible, a profession that all are bound to make in truth. But suppose he professes the witness of the Spirit to the truth of his exposition of the "days" of Daniel and John; of the beasts, horns, and other symbols of prophecy; of the *time* and *manner* of the second advent of Christ—indeed, of his own peculiar views of any one doctrine or systems of doctrines of the Bible; views in which he differs from his brethren. I would no more believe him than I would if he should profess the witness of the Spirit to his own omniscience. He has no more authority from the Bible for such a profession in the one case than in the other.

I notice a grand and, I may add, an almost universal error of the church, an error in which she cannot be morally innocent. She can, to a fearful extent, *"bear them which are evil"* (Revelation 2:2), morally evil, while she cannot endure a difference of opinion even in those obscure regions of thought and inquiry where she acknowledges men may be perfectly honest and yet fallible. Who does not know that a man may indulge in pride, luxury, covetousness, and worldly mindedness; that he may grind the faces of the poor, take from immortal minds the key of knowledge, and traffic in the bodies and souls of men; and yet he may sleep unreproved upon the bosom of the church.

But let an individual with a heart as honest as Paul's, and acknowledged to be so, range in search for truth just beyond the line of rigid orthodoxy and there profess to have found some priceless jewel. What is his reputation now worth? How totally opposite this is to the entire spirit of the gospel as set forth in the Bible. There we are required, by all means, to rebuke our neighbor and not allow *sin* upon him (see Leviticus 19:17) while we are required, with equal positiveness, never to separate from a brother, love him less, or in the least withhold our fellowship from him on account of sentiments that do not imply a dishonest, unsanctified heart. What a melancholy spectacle do religious controversies almost everywhere present. How commonly do they degenerate into personalities.

I will here express an opinion the reader is requested to ponder with solemn interest. He, above almost all others, has made the highest attainments in holiness and most perfectly represents the spirit of the gospel who can differ with a brother on all subjects not essential to salvation, discuss such differences with earnestness, reprobate his errors, and yet maintain his confidence in him as an honest man and his love for him as a holy man undiminished. A revival of this spirit in the church will be a revival of religion that is pure and undefiled before God. (See James 1:27.)

The account God will ask us to render at His judgment seat will not be regarding whether I was infallible on earth. No. He sent me here to solve great problems. He knew they were deep, intricate, and far reaching; He knew my powers were weak and infantlike. And He did not expect me to dive to the deep foundations of eternity, to soar to the heights of the infinite intelligence. But He threw them before me in all their solemn import to let me try my strength upon them and thus develop and mature my nature. But He will ask me, "Had you an honest heart? Did you toil to get up the hill? Did you climb and struggle to gain the summit? Were you open to conviction, to receive the light on all subjects?" If I can answer "Yes," He will reply, "*Well done, good and faithful servant*" (Matthew 25:23). I have no fear to meet my Lord in such a state of mind. Though I should be mistaken as to the time and manner of His coming, yet let Him say that I am honest-hearted, and I can hail Him with joy at His coming, no matter how and when it may be.

Here is the citadel of the soul. Here is the bulwark to be defended. Upon this salvation turns. It is more important to be honest than to be exactly correct in our opinions in all respects; to be honest inquirers than to know the exact forms of truth not essential to salvation.

I notice also a very common mistake in respect to a state of perfect moral purity. Very many seem to attach to such a state the idea of infallibility in judgment. An influential brother in the ministry thought he had discovered a wrong exposition of a single passage of Scripture in a work on entire holiness in this life. He immediately wrote us a very kind but earnest letter saying that if we expected him to believe our doctrine, we must not be detected in such an error as that. He had practically adopted the idea that perfect moral purity and infallibility in the interpretation of the Bible are inseparable. For myself, I have no such conception of that state. I have no idea that He who charges His angels with folly (see Job 4:18) without imputing sin to them requires, as a condition of perfect moral purity, infallibility in His children on earth. No; error in judgment on subjects not fundamental, not falling within the range of the infallible teachings of the Spirit, is perfectly compatible with a heart as pure as heaven itself.

Notice the great temptation to which those who have been taught much of the Spirit are liable. Satan, it should be remembered, shapes his temptations to the state of mind in which he finds the subject of his attacks. To one, therefore, who has enjoyed much of the Spirit's teachings, he will say, "It is time for you to *teach* theology. Ministers and others know nothing. You have the Spirit. You, therefore, know all things." (See 1 John 2:20.) Reader, beware of that fatal rock. All may have the Spirit without measure. But the Spirit is not given to all to render them theologians.

We notice the use we should make of those who have a deep and rich experience. If you wish to know how to get into those depths yourself, go to them. They can lead you, for they know the road. They are equal to that. But if you wish to get the solution of a difficult problem in theology, you will not go to them unless they are also theologians. Their experience in the Holy Spirit does not teach them the mysteries of philosophy or the facts of history. A rich experience they have, and that you can get from them, and by that you do well to profit. And let me say here—the most perfect teacher is the one who has drunk the deepest at the fountain of life in the Spirit and who has also taken the widest range among the sublime mysteries of God's kingdom that lie everywhere around us. When both are united, when one accompanies the other in a high degree, then have we a teacher indeed.

We may understand, finally, the meaning of that glorious passage describing the blessedness in store for the children of Zion: "*The sun shall be* ***no*** *more thy light by day; neither for brightness shall the moon give light to thee…for the* Lord *shall be thine everlasting light, and the days of thy mourning shall be ended*" (Isaiah 60:19–20). Into what a state has that soul come who has reached that place! To bring the soul into this state is the department of the Spirit's infallible teaching. He can bring a soul into such a relation to Christ, into such a relation to God, and to all that is finite that whatever may happen in the universe, naught can disturb its deep rest in God. That is the idea in the passage.

The individual who has attained this state, this divine illumination, has ceased to be dependent for his blessedness upon any changes in the sun or moon, upon any revolutions in the heavens above or in the earth beneath or in the universe around him. God is his everlasting light, and the days of his mourning are ended. Nothing that can happen can at all ruffle the strong, deep current that, flowing from the infinite heart of Jehovah, pours a full and overflowing tide of unceasing bliss into his. The sun may go out in darkness, the moon be turned to blood, the universe be wrapped in one general conflagration, and all created things pass away, yet not a particle of the glory and bliss of his soul will be taken away.

That mind opens its eye upon the revelations of the infinite. Its eternal home is the bosom of God. God is seen in everything—the darkness and the light, the visible and the invisible. God shines forth everywhere as the everlasting light of the soul. Brethren, it is our privilege even now to have our home in the skies. Through the enlightening Spirit, we may be led up those everlasting hills, plant our feet on those delectable mountains, and stand in ecstasy amid the revelations of eternity while we sojourn in the vales of our native earth. Will we be among the number who are reckoned "taught of God"? (See John 6:45.) O blessed, blessed, thrice blessed, is that soul who is thus taught.

13

INQUIRER DIRECTED

"For every one that asketh receiveth; and he that seeketh findeth; and to him that knocketh it shall be opened."
—Matthew 7:8

One truth of infinite importance is manifestly taught in this passage, that every individual of our race now on probation may set his heart upon attaining, in all its fullness, the salvation revealed in the gospel with the absolute certainty of attaining it.

For the sake of two classes of readers—the sinner wishing to know what he must do to be saved and the Christian inquiring after full redemption—I will now proceed in as short a space as practicable and, *"according to the grace of God which is given unto me"* (1 Corinthians 3:10), elucidate this great truth.

Let us, then, in the first place, consider this question:

Does Salvation Exist Alike for All in Infinite Fullness and for Every Need?

It would be strange indeed if it were otherwise. Why should God render salvation practicable to one individual and not to another? All alike are His creatures. All sustain the same relations to the law, on the one hand, and to the redemption of Christ, on the other. All have together violated the law and, consequently, fallen under the same penalty. For all alike, Christ has poured out his soul unto death. Toward each and every individual of fallen humanity, God has expressed the same kind regards, the same unwillingness that one should perish as another. He opens His infinite heart to the greatest as well as to the least sinner of the race, and He declares He is desirous that all should together partake of that eternal life His infinite grace has provided for and proffers alike to all. You do your own soul, and your God and Savior, infinite wrong, reader, if for a moment you entertain the withering thought that salvation, in all its fullness, is not as accessible to you as to any individual of the race.

The source, also, from which this salvation originates would lead us to suppose that we should find its provisions just as full and adequate for one necessity as for another. We cannot, without manifest unbelief, suppose a salvation characterized by anything less than an infinite and perfect fullness for every real necessity of the creature whose necessities it was designed to meet would, or could, proceed from the heart of God. Who could suppose he would find himself anything less than complete in the Son of God?

The provisions of grace also stand revealed in the gospel as just as full and adequate for the necessities of one individual as for those of another—and for any one necessity of that individual as for any other. The grace existing in Christ for each individual is absolutely infinite. All necessities are alike overshadowed by such grace as that. Never despair, reader, when inclined to seek the redemption of Christ, till you find your necessities surpassing infinity. Remember also the greater the necessity to be met, the greater the grace manifested in meeting it, and, consequently, the greater the glory that will thereby redound to Christ. "*Wherefore he is able also to save them to the uttermost that come unto God by him*" (Hebrews 7:25). What does the term "*uttermost*" here mean if it does not imply that the salvation of Christ is perfectly adequate to every solitary necessity of ours as creatures and sinners? This is the language of inspiration everywhere in respect to this great salvation. "*Ye are complete in him*" (Colossians 2:10). Such a declaration can imply nothing less than that every necessity of the believer is fully provided for in Christ. Whenever you find, reader, that any real want of yours cannot be met in Christ, then you may proclaim it to the universe that He is not able to "*save them to the uttermost that come unto God by him*" and that believers are not "*complete in Him.*"

It is absolutely certain that if you set your heart upon attaining this salvation and attaining it in all its fullness, and if God combines His agency with yours to secure that result, you will attain the end you are seeking. Nothing under such circumstances can surpass the power of Omnipotence. Is anything too hard for God? (See Jeremiah 32:27.) Suppose, now, that you really and truly commit your case into the hands of this everlasting God and that He undertakes on your behalf. Will your case, or any element or feature of it, be found to be too hard for Him? Will He fail to accomplish, to its fullest extent, what He has set His heart to attain? Oh, that you would test to the uttermost the power and resources of His grace. *"Eye hath not seen, nor ear heard, neither have entered into the heart of man, the things which God hath prepared for them that love him"* (1 Corinthians 2:9). Of the perfect practicability of attaining any good or any degree of good provided for us, no one can doubt based on the supposition that we are authorized to expect that God will actually combine His agency with ours to secure such a result. The great question with us then is this: Are we authorized to expect such divine cooperation?

This leads me to remark that God has pledged His Word and every attribute of His infinity, together with all the resources of His infinite grace, that everyone who, in compliance with the conditions of life, seeks the full redemption provided alike for all will not fail to attain it. *"They that seek the LORD shall not want any good thing"* (Psalm 34:10). Every real necessity of ours is certainly covered by such a promise as that. Whenever we set our whole hearts upon attaining full redemption from sin, we find ourselves in the direct presence of the promises: *"Faithful is he that calleth you, who also will do it"* (1 Thessalonians 5:24); *"And the LORD thy God will circumcise thine heart, and the heart of thy seed, to love the LORD thy God with all thine heart, and with all thy soul, that thou mayest live"* (Deuteronomy 30:6). In view of the infinite fullness of grace revealed for us in Christ and the promised cooperation of God with our own efforts to secure such a result, we are positively commanded to *"reckon ye also yourselves to be dead indeed unto sin, but alive unto God through Jesus Christ our Lord"* (Romans 6:11). Reader, will you heed that command? One other question remains to be answered:

How May We Attain This Great Salvation Ourselves?

To this question, special attention is now invited, as this is the great burden of the present discourse. If you would attain this salvation, reader, permit me to say, in the first place, that you must not place unbelief as a barrier between yourself and the infinite good that, through Christ, is proffered to your faith. You must not doubt or deny God's power or willingness to meet your case fully, however hard it may be. You must not limit the grace of God. You must not place your own case out of the circle of the provisions of His grace or the sympathies of His heart. On the other hand, you must admit that what God has promised, He is able also to perform (see Romans 4:21)—and as willing as able. As you bring your case to Christ, the first question He proposes to you is this: "Do you believe I am able to do this thing that you require?" Reader, what answer can you give to such a question?

You must also carefully discriminate between what you are required to do and what belongs exclusively to God in respect to the case. For example, we are not required, nor is it possible for us, to remedy any of the necessary or penal consequences of our sins. We have incurred infinite guilt and cannot remove it. We have destroyed our own peace of mind and cannot restore that peace again. We have rendered our feelings fearfully callous to the truth and cannot remedy the terrible evil. We have generated habits of wrongdoing and cannot prevent the tendencies of our nature to evil as the necessary consequence. None of these things can we do. But we can confess our guilt. We can, at once, cease the present doing of evil. We can also trust our Savior to remedy all these evils. We have destroyed ourselves, but in Him our help is found. We can trust Him for the help that exists in Him on our behalf. Now, this is just what we are required to do. Let us do our part, trusting the Savior to do His. This do, reader, and you will live.

It belongs to God, also, and not to us, to excite particular emotions in us by presenting, through the Spirit, the particular truths adapted to excite such feelings. We may struggle as long and as hard as we please to produce such feelings, and we will only thereby weary ourselves to no profit. The more intense the struggle in that direction on our part, the more profound will our insensibility become. All this belongs to the Spirit of God. We should never attempt to take the work out of His hands. There is one thing, however, that we can do. We can yield our whole being into the hands of Christ so that He, through the Spirit, may work in us all that is well-pleasing in His sight. This is what we can do, and this is all that we are required to do in the matter. It is His task, when we thus commit ourselves to Him as unto a faithful creator, to beautify us with salvation (see Psalm 149:4) by exciting in us all those emotions and sentiments that will render us most pleasing in His sight. How many almost fatally err here. Instead of yielding their whole being to Christ at once, trusting Him to move and mold and melt their feelings and stir up from their profoundest depths the great deep of emotion within them, they weary themselves in worse than useless efforts to induce particular feelings in their own minds. In other words, they waste time in vain attempts to do God's work instead of their own.

Nor does it belong to us, but to God exclusively, to do anything to make us willing to yield to Him prior to the act of surrender itself. God says, *"Seek ye my face"* (Psalm 27:8). The only thing required of us is the instant response, *"Thy face, Lord, will I seek"* (verse 8). We are to put forth no efforts at all before this response to induce a willingness in ourselves to make it. This is exclusively the work of the Spirit. It is rebellion against God to attempt to take the work out of His hands. The thing for us to do is to yield our whole being to God at once. The preparatory work, all that is needful, has already been performed on God's part. *"Look unto me,"* says Christ, *"and be ye saved"* (Isaiah 45:22). Make no efforts at all to render yourself willing to obey that command; on the other hand, obey it instantly by actually looking to Christ as directed. This is your part. Wherever you go, the duty of compliance attends you as the duty of the present moment.

If you would be a partaker of this great salvation, reader, you must not make any circumstances connected with your present state a reason for not doing, at once, all that God now requires of you.

No present want of deep conviction of sin, for example, must be made a reason for not instantly yielding yourself as the servant of Christ and commending yourself to His mercy. It is for you to follow, at once, all the light you have, to meet fully all the convictions of duty of every kind now lying upon your mind. It belongs to God, when you have done this, to roll that degree of conviction upon your mind that your highest good demands, and this, you may rest assured, He will not, in that case, fail to do. You know that you are a sinner. Confess the fact. You know that you need redemption. Commend yourself, at once, to the mercy of God in Christ. This is the duty that sacredly binds you at the present moment, whatever the degree of conviction resting upon your mind may be. The want of present intense conviction is no excuse for even a momentary continuance in impenitency and rejection of offered mercy, and it need be no hindrance to an immediate reception of proffered grace. Whatever your present state may be, the voice of Christ to you is, *"Look unto me, and be ye saved"* (Isaiah 45:22). Fasten the eye of faith instantly upon Him for the salvation proffered. All else that you need, His mercy will then provide for.

Nor must any want of present emotion be made such a reason. What excuse is this, reader, for the voluntary neglect of known duty? This very want of feeling, this profound insensibility to things unseen and eternal that sin has induced in your mind, is one of the highest conceivable reasons why you should, at once, commend yourself to the grace of Christ. As you thus, in deep humiliation for the wrong you have done your own soul, commend yourself to Him; it belongs to Him to dissolve all the sensibilities of your nature in love and tenderness by the revelation, through the Spirit, of His own unsearchable love and grace to your mind. "*We all, with open face beholding as in a glass the glory of the Lord, are changed into the same image from glory to glory, even as by the Spirit of the Lord*" (2 Corinthians 3:18). It is for you to commend yourself to the grace of Christ. It then belongs to Him to make this transforming manifestation of His own glory and love to your mind. Then will the great deep of emotion within you be moved to its deepest depths. Make, then, the want of feeling a reason for instantaneous trust in Christ to remedy the evil that presses upon you and not a reason, as many to their infinite loss make it, for remaining in unbelief.

Neither must you permit any fears of being deceived or of not holding out unto the end or of having passed already the line of mercy—or any other consideration whatever—to be a reason for not commending yourself at once, in faith and hope, to the grace of Christ or for the neglect of any other present duty. Do you, as you should, fear being deceived? Then, instead of rejecting mercy and rendering your eternal death thereby an absolute certainty, cry out with the psalmist, "*Search me, O God, and know my heart: try me, and know my thoughts: and see if there be any wicked way in me, and lead me in the way everlasting*" (Psalm 139:23–24).

Do you fear, as you are bound to do, that you will not hold out to the end? Will you make that a reason for turning your back upon the cross and seeking the gates of death? Rather seek the Lord with all your heart and with all your soul, that He may render you *"stedfast, unmoveable, always abounding in the work of the Lord"* (1 Corinthians 15:58). The peril of falling, which is real, should never be a reason for rejecting proffered grace but for the most fixed and earnest trust in Him that is able to uphold us by the right hand of His righteousness (see Isaiah 41:10) and to preserve us unto His everlasting kingdom (see 2 Peter 1:11).

Do you fear that you have passed the line of mercy? Test the ground of that fear, at once, by throwing wide open the door of your heart to Christ. If He has not taken His final departure, He will then come to you and dine with you, and you with Him. (See Revelation 3:20.) Remember, reader, we will never be deceived in regard to the ground of our hope or fail to hold out unto the end unless we ourselves consent to our own death. Instead, then, of making such considerations reasons for continued unbelief, *"give diligence to make your calling and election sure: for if ye do these things, ye shall never fall: for so an entrance shall be ministered unto you abundantly into the everlasting kingdom of our Lord and Saviour Jesus Christ"* (2 Peter 1:10–11).

If you would attain this salvation, reader, you must also set your whole being, with undivided heart, upon the infinite good therein proffered to your faith and upon nothing else; for example, the full and entire reconciliation and peace with God, together with a state of entire emancipation from the power of sin into the *"glorious liberty of the children of God"* (Romans 8:21) and a hope that is sure and steadfast, entering to that which is within the veil. (See Hebrews 6:19.) You must make up your mind at once to shrink at no sacrifices requisite to the attainment of this good but to meet fully all the convictions of duty the Spirit may impress upon your mind. An entrance into the everlasting kingdom of our Lord Jesus Christ is now, reader, open before you. (See 2 Peter 1:11.) Are you ready for the sacrifices and efforts requisite to admission to the treasures infinite that are there in store for you?

Finally, if you would attain this great salvation, reader, you must aim at it, not by attempting to do God's part of the work, but by actually doing your own. Break off, at once, from all forms of sin, and by the grace of Christ, meet fully all your convictions of duty. Devote your entire powers and interest, at once, to your God and Savior. In that consecration, open your whole heart to Christ in all the offices and relations He sustains to redeemed sinners. By an act of simple, unwavering trust, commit all your interests and necessities to Him, counting Him faithful who has promised (see Hebrews 10:23), faithful to save you even unto the uttermost (see Hebrews 7:25). When you have thus committed *all* to Him, wait in patient hope and earnest expectation till He gives you the witness of the Spirit that you are His; till He, through that Spirit, pours His full salvation into your heart; and till He comes with *"the Father of mercies, and the God of all comfort"* (2 Corinthians 1:3) and makes His abode with you (see John 14:23).

His manifested love may not, and probably will not, be granted to you the moment you trust Him. It may be necessary, before that blessing is given, that a preparatory process of heart searching, of emptying the soul of all that is unhallowed and finite, and of earnest and intense seeking after God be gone through with. During this process, very strong temptations to doubt and unbelief may present themselves. Yield not to them for a moment. Above all, take not back the full consecration you have made or entertain a doubt of your acceptance in it. If the Spirit leads you to search your heart or to empty yourself wholly, that Christ may be all to you, seek to have the work, in both respects, perfected. If the vision tarries, wait for it (see Habakkuk 2:3); wait in submission, in consecration, in obedience to all convictions of duty, in patience and in hope.

Do this, reader, and soon Christ will bring all His glory into your soul. One thing, permit me to urge, as of special importance here. Whatever your feelings at any time may be, do not, on that account, hesitate a moment about meeting fully and promptly all your convictions of duty. In short, reader, say of the Lord, "*He is my refuge and my fortress: my God; in him will I trust*" (Psalm 91:2). Having done this, then, hold fast your confidence till He manifests His salvation to you; then, through the endless future before, follow on to know the Lord. Do this, reader, and God will be your everlasting light, and the days of your mourning will be ended. (See Isaiah 60:20.) I conclude this discourse with three remarks.

Remarks

In the light of this subject, the meaning of the declaration of the inspired prophet, "*It is good that a man should both* ***hope*** *and* ***quietly wait*** *for the salvation of the Lord*" (Lamentations 3:26) becomes plain to our minds. The salvation here referred to is the love of God manifested to the soul and the great deliverance from darkness and the power of sinful habits and propensities thereby wrought for us. When the soul has made the consecration above described and, in patient (quiet) hope, is waiting for this deliverance, it is not commonly, as has been said, granted, as soon as faith is exercised in the promises. On the either hand, there is a longer or shorter period of patient waiting for God and of earnest hope and expectation of His appearing. No period through which the mind ever passes is of greater benefit to it than this, if its faith fails not. Every one who can look back upon such a period in his own experience has occasion to exclaim, "*It is good that a man should both hope and quietly wait for the salvation of the Lord.*"

Great injury is often done to inquirers after full redemption when they are told that the moment they exercise faith they will obtain the blessing, together with the witness of the Spirit to the fact. They exercise genuine faith, and the blessing does not come. They conclude, of course, that the act referred to was an act of sin. If they attempt again to believe, they can but repeat this act, now regarded as sinful. They are perplexed and know not what to do. The sealing of the Spirit, we should keep in mind, is *after* we have believed, and often, it is not till we have waited patiently for it.

How manifest is the fact from the plainest testimony of the Bible that full redemption through faith in Christ has been realized in actual experience. Look for a moment at the case of Paul. Throughout his writings, we find no intimations whatever that he was conscious of coming short of what Christ required of him. Not a solitary confession of sin drops from his pen. The only passages in which such confession has ever been supposed to have been made by him, have, as we have seen in a preceding discourse, no relation whatever to the subject.

We find him also, in one place, asserting that his aim was "*to have* ***always*** *a conscience void of offence toward God, and toward men*" (Acts 24:16). In another, we have his unqualified assertion that with just such a conscience, he actually served his God and Savior, "*whom I serve from my forefathers with pure conscience*" (2 Timothy 1:3). In other words, his conscience did not convict him of any sin. A pure conscience and a conscience void of offense must mean the same thing.

The often reiterated declarations he makes of himself can imply nothing less. Take a single passage as an example: "*I am crucified with Christ: nevertheless I live; yet not I, but Christ liveth in me: and the life which I now live in the flesh I live by the faith of the Son of God, who loved me, and gave himself for me*" (Galatians 2:20). No individual, in the light of the universally admitted laws of interpretation, can make such declarations mean anything less than a state of perfect love. The following remarks of Mr. Barnes fully express the meaning of this remarkable passage:

> *I am crucified with Christ.* In the previous verse, Paul had said that he was dead. In this verse he states what he meant by it, and shows that he did not wish to be understood as saying that he was inactive, or that he was literally insensible to the appeals made to him by other beings and objects. In respect to one thing he was dead; to all that was truly great and noble he was alive. To understand the remarkable phrase, "I am crucified with Christ," we may remark,
>
> (1.) that this was the way in which Christ was put to death. He suffered on a cross, and thus became literally dead.
>
> (2.) In a sense *similar* to this, Paul became dead to the law, to the world, and to sin. The Redeemer, by the death of the cross, became insensible to all surrounding objects, as the dead always are. He ceased to see and hear, and was as though they were not. He was laid in the cold grave, and they did not affect or influence him. So Paul says that he became insensible to the law as a means of justification; to the world; to ambition and the love of money; to the pride and pomp of life; and to the dominion of evil and hateful passions. They lost their power over him; they ceased to influence him.
>
> (3.) This was *with* Christ, or by Christ. It cannot mean *literally* that he was put to death with him, for that is not

true; but it means that the effect of the death of Christ on the cross was to make him dead to these things, in like manner as he, when he died, became insensible to the things of this busy world.

The individual who has been thus crucified with Christ and, by the power of Christ, has risen to the full enjoyment of the new and glorious life here spoken of has certainly attained to all that is meant by the phrase "perfect holiness" or "entire sanctification."

Without any qualifications whatever, the apostle also commands Christians to copy his example and promises them the favor of God in so doing. "*Those things, which ye have both learned, and received, and heard, and seen in me, do: and the God of peace shall be with you*" (Philippians 4:9). Would the apostle ever have given such directions as that if he was conscious in himself of anything less than full redemption? Here is the spot where every honest mind would have been careful, if in any other state, to have asserted the fact. Paul, reader, served Christ with a pure conscience. So, by grace, may you and I.

This leads me to notice, finally, what appears to me as one of the great secrets of high attainments in the divine life. It is this: the admission to our own hearts that what Christ did for the sanctification and blessedness of such an individual as Paul, in the particular sphere in which he was called of God to move, the Savior is actually able and ready to do for us in ours. With what inconceivable sweetness did this question come home to my mind, years ago, when my heart had been for some time turned upon the blessing of full redemption: Why cannot Christ do as much for my holiness and blessedness as He did for those of Paul? The deep response of my heart was, "Yes, He may, and He will do it if I will only receive Him by faith as Paul did." And, reader, should I tell you what the result has been of thus receiving the Savior? If I have any acquaintance with my own heart, I may say, with truth, that I have no other motive in making the disclosure than that you may know, and yourself experience, what the Savior of sinners does for those who trust him to do for them all He has promised. The following letter, written to my own family some years since, at the request of the partner of my joys and labors, will present the subject as fully and distinctly as any language that I could now adopt. I will, therefore, give the letter to the reader just as it was then written.

> My Dear Wife:
>
> I now sit down to complete a design which I have long contemplated, but the accomplishment of which the providence of God has seemed hitherto to prevent. It is to give you and the children, as far as I am able, some account of the dealings of God with my own soul during the several winters in which I have been separated from you—blessed seasons, in which God has led me into green pastures and beside the still waters, in which my dwelling place has been in a land of broad rivers and streams along the banks of the river of life and on those everlasting hills where my sun goes not down and neither does my moon withdraw itself, where the Lord is my everlasting light, and the days of my mourning are ended. As I commence writing, the waters of life rise and swell in my heart and bear my soul upward and onward into an ocean of such calm and serene and peaceful blessedness that language fails when I attempt to describe what I see and feel and enjoy. Inspiration only furnishes language that approaches the reality—"*Whom having not seen, ye love; in whom, though now ye see him not, yet believing, ye rejoice with joy unspeakable and full of glory*" (1 Peter 1:8).

Perhaps I cannot better succeed in giving you an apprehension of the state of my mind than by presenting some of the elements and sources of that blessedness with which I have served God and my generation these years that are passed.

The first source of blessedness is conscious peace with God. To look up into our Father's face with the full and sweet assurance that every controversy is fully and perfectly settled, that like Enoch we can now walk with God, and God Himself will walk with us and dwell in us and be our God, and we will be His sons and His daughters—we then know the blessedness Moses felt when God said to him, *"I know thee by name, and thou hast also found grace in my sight"* (Exodus 33:12). To have God thus present to and in the soul, with not a cloud or frown upon His smiling face—this is the fullness of joy I have had in Him for months and months together. Is it a matter of wonder, then, that my joy is full? In the very center of my heart sits my Savior, clothed in love, and there my smiling God.

Another source and element of this blessedness is the sweet spirit of adoption, crying, "Abba, Father," which God, by His Spirit, breathes into the heart. In the exercise of this spirit, the current of the thought, feeling, and affection naturally, sweetly, and continually flows out in sentiments of love, gratitude, and adoration toward God, and there it rolls in blissful fixedness about one changeless center. In the hour of temptation, the soul spontaneously looks to Jesus with the peaceful assurance that His grace will be sufficient. In time of need, however great or small the necessity, it naturally turns to God and casts its cares upon Him with the full assurance that He cares for us; that in Christ are provisions full and free for every want; that the ear of God is open when we pray to Him; that even before we cry He hears, and while we are speaking, He answers, "Here am I. Son, daughter, what is your petition?" To pray with the consciousness that God is thus present, that we are speaking to Him face-to-face as a man speaks to a friend—this renders our blessedness in God so great that the particular blessings asked for appear hardly necessary to the fullness of our joy. Thus my joy is fulfilled.

Another element and source of this blessedness is the perpetual and peaceful assurance that in and through Christ every real want, temporal and spiritual, may and will be supplied. Christ has promised that those who follow Him will not want any good thing—that is, anything that would be a real blessing to them, anything necessary to the perfect fullness of their joy. To have this truth perpetually present to the mind, to feel an entire assurance that this is the actual relation we sustain to Christ—causes us to rejoice with joy unspeakable and full of glory! Then we, being delivered from our enemies, serve God without fear, in righteousness and holiness before Him all the days of our lives. This is the relation I feel myself to sustain to Christ from day to day. While I remain here, I have no expectation or fear of wanting any good thing in time or eternity. All my interests lie secure in the hands of Christ. As the mountains are round about Jerusalem, so is the Lord round about His people, and I continually have the peaceful assurance that my soul dwells within that blessed circle.

Another source of this blessedness is the continued assurance that my way is so committed to the Lord that He does and will direct my steps. *"I will instruct thee and teach thee in the way which thou shalt go: I will guide thee with mine eye"* (Psalm 32:8). This promise is a living reality to my mind, and I find it realized in my experience from day to day in every time of need. When laboring in one place, almost up to the last moment when I am called to leave, I often know not where next to direct my steps. Yet when the time comes, the providences of God invariably make the way as plain as if a voice from heaven should tell me where to go. The firm confidence I have that this will be the case preserves the mind from all care about the future and leaves it at full liberty to expend its entire energies for Christ on the present field of labor. This state of peaceful trust, too, is itself, in the soul, a well of water springing up into everlasting life. Then, when called to act, to know that God has heard our prayer in making the way so plain that not a shadow of doubt remains that one is walking in the very path He has marked out, and when pursuing that path, to be able to say, "This is the highway God has cast up before me"—then, indeed, our fellowship is with the Father and with His Son Jesus Christ. Then we walk with God.

Another, and I may add, one of the chief sources of this blessedness, is the continued assurance that, through the grace of Christ, I am one with God—that my will is lost in the divine will and that I have no will to do what God would not have me do and that all that He would have me do, I will to do. Thus I live, *"yet not I, but Christ liveth in me: and the life that I now live in the flesh I live by the faith of the Son of God, who loved me, and gave himself for me*" (Galatians 2:20). This is the most blessed spot in the universe. Nothing can offend the soul when it is here. In this blessed spot, Christ seems to hold my soul from day to day. In this spot, no finite object has power to disturb the deep rest of the soul in God. God is its everlasting light, and the days of its mourning are ended.

I should here mention another fact in my experience, which I owe to the grace of Christ. It is this: a state of perfect contentment and an entire and peaceful acquiescence in the dispensations of providence in every variety of condition. As the soul retires under the shadow of the Almighty, no occurrence without has power to disturb it there. From that spot it looks out upon all the arrangements and movements of the surrounding universe with this sweet spirit pervading its whole being, trusting that in respect to all creatures, objects, and events, God's will be done. It then learns in whatever state it is, therewith, to be content. Every condition is best. So it appears to the soul, and that because our heavenly Father so wills. My dear ones, I desire you all to find this peaceful, blissful spot. No want unsupplied reaches the soul here. Never, it seems to me, did my soul dwell there so uninterruptedly as within a few months past. O that blessed gospel that has power to hold the mind in such a state! And O that blessed Savior who is the author and finisher of this *gospel* and is Himself its very substance!

Another element of this blessedness is this: an entire separation, in all my aims, purposes, and desires, from all objects but one—Christ and the interests of His kingdom. I do not know that I covet any man's silver or gold or apparel, that I have any desire for a name among men or any wish to pursue any object but the glory of Christ.

I have the witness in my own heart that, by the cross of Christ, I am crucified to the world and the world to me. In this blessed state, the soul can say, "Christ is all mine." Nothing interrupts its deep blessedness in Him. With what sweetness have I been able, especially during the present period of separation from you, to present my entire family as a whole burnt offering to Christ with this single desire and prayer, that we may all be entirely His, that we may be wholly separated from all that is unlike Him and have His entire image in all our hearts and that, as a family, we may all be able to say, "For us, to live is Christ." To entertain such desires and intentions is a foretaste of eternal blessedness.

I now come to speak of a source of blessedness, to the description of which, I fear, I will be able to make but a feeble approach. It is what, for want of better language to express, I would call those open, direct, and inconceivably sweet visions that, a great portion of the time, I have of the infinite beauty, loveliness, and ineffable glory of Jesus Christ and of the Godhead as manifested in Him. You will, doubtless, recollect that memorable era of my existence when, I may say, I received the first full baptism of the Spirit—a baptism in which the Sun of Righteousness shined out in cloudless light, beauty, sweetness, and glory upon my soul. We had just retired to rest. As I laid my head upon my pillow, in a moment the vision opened upon my mind. I had an apprehension of Christ, as He came out of the sepulcher after His resurrection. The work of redemption was finished, and Christ, having burst the bars of death, had come forth to present the offer of eternal life to a dying world. There was in His benign countenance such majestic sweetness and beauty, such mildness and love ineffable and infinite, and glory so divine and resplendent, and all mingled with compassion so tender for the sinner, that my heart melted in a moment. The fountains of the great deep of emotion were all broken up. My bosom was swelling and heaving with emotions to which no language could give utterance.

For seven years these baptisms have been more and more frequent till now they seem to be the dwelling place of the soul. At one time, I would view Him as He led the disciples out to Bethany and then lifted up His hands and blessed them and then, while He was blessing them, was taken up into heaven; at another, as He revealed Himself to weeping Mary at the sepulcher and to the two disciples at Emmaus; at another, as He met the weeping widow and with infinite love restored her son alive from the dead; at another, as He lay, the babe of Bethlehem, and yet the God incarnate, in the arms of the aged Simeon. At another, I apprehend Him as present to my soul, and I apprehend Him with the full and perfect consciousness that in Him I am complete, that there is not a demand of my being, in time or eternity, that He is not able and willing and present to meet. At first, I seemed to view Him at a distance from me, and yet, as I fixed the eye of faith upon Him, He approached nearer and nearer with a countenance infinitely benignant, saying, "If you will fix your eye steadily upon me, I will come to you, and make my abode with you." Thus He approached nearer and nearer till He shined upon me from every point. He is in the soul and yet all around. These views of Christ bring such sweetness and beauty into the soul that I have often thus described the effect to my own mind. The heart is a harp of a thousand strings, and all are unstrung and discordant by reason of sin. But Christ comes and puts every chord in tune, and then, with the fingers of infinite love, sweeping those chords, raises such notes of heavenly harmony that the soul lies all melted with the sweetness of its own melody. *"Yea doubtless, and I count all things but loss for the excellency of the knowledge of Christ Jesus my Lord"* (Philippians 3:8). In the study of the Bible, I seem to be walking along the banks of the river of life, at one time bathing in its waters and at another time plucking the fruit of the tree that grows upon either side of the river and has leaves for the healing of the nations.

Preaching the gospel has now an entirely different influence upon my mind from what it ever had before. In former years, when preparing and delivering a discourse, my feelings would be greatly interested. But when I was done, my own cup seemed to be almost empty. *Now,* while preaching the unsearchable riches of Christ, my own cup fills up and overflows continually, and I retire to rest at night with my soul afloat in an ocean of light, glory, peace, and blessedness that appears boundless and infinite. When watering others, none appear to receive so full draughts as my own soul. All the while, it appears such an infinite privilege to be a servant of Jesus Christ, to do and to suffer all His righteous will. With inexpressible sweetness, this passage and others of kindred character come home to my mind: *"Unto you it is given in the behalf of Christ, not only to believe on him, but also to suffer for his sake*" (Philippians 1:29).

Soon after I heard of the death of my mother, as I was meditating upon this event, this stanza passed with indescribable sweetness through my mind:

Hope looks beyond the bounds of time,
When what we now deplore
Shall rise, in full immortal prime,
And bloom to fade no more.[12]

For a whole night my soul lay all dissolved with that sweet thought without hardly closing my eyes to sleep. These sweet thoughts often flow on into my dreams, and then I sometimes hear music and singing that are perfectly unearthly. I will endeavor to give you some conception of one such scene. I was at T—— two years since, preaching this great salvation. One evening, as I retired to rest, I seemed, with infinite sweetness, to pillow my head upon the bosom of Christ. In this state, I fell asleep. I soon thought myself in company with some ten or twelve individuals before my father's dwelling, walking with them toward the door. As we were about to enter the door, the whole scene being inconceivably peaceful, they all stopped and commenced singing. The words and tune of all were in perfect harmony, which yet appeared undesigned, as each seemed to be singing, as it were, alone by himself. The perfect harmony seemed to be the spontaneous effect of the concurrent melody of each soul within. The words and the music were all unearthly, such as I had never conceived of before. I

12. Edwin Francis Hatfield.

looked at their countenances; each one beamed with a serenity so peaceful and heavenly that it appeared as if in each heart hope lay asleep on the bosom of bliss, and my own soul was as peaceful as theirs. One voice rose above all the rest. I turned to see from whom it came. It was from my departed father. One line they sung which I had before heard—

> Gently, Lord, O gently lead us.[13]

As they came to this, my feelings were so excited that I awoke, all dissolved in tears. When I awoke, the words and tune were distinctly in my mind. I attempted to sing them, but my voice was so coarse and harsh that the whole vanished in a moment. In thought only I remember it now. It has given me, however, such an idea of the harmony of heaven as I never conceived of before.

Such is an imperfect statement of what the Lord has done for my soul.

> Therefore praise him,
> Praise thy great Redeemer's name.[14]

From what I have written, you will not suppose that my mind has always been in the same state of ecstasy. This I could not endure. But my *peace* is as a river. Neither will you suppose that no feelings of sorrow dwell in my mind. I often weep over sinners and over Zion, weary, tossed with tempest, and not comforted, and as often I travail in birth for them. And what a privilege it is to weep with Jesus over a lost world! Such tears

13. Thomas Hastings, "Gently Lord, O Gently Lead Us," 1831.
14. Ibid.

are inconceivably sweet. God treasures them up in His bottle. In Him, however, there is perpetual rest.

Now, my dear ones, having told you the dealings of God with my own soul, permit me to say that my heart's desire and prayer to God, from day to day, for you is that you may all share with me in this fullness of joy. It is all for you. I have obtained it by the faith of the Son of God. If you will believe, you will also speak. May God, of His infinite mercy, grant that you may...

> *be strengthened with might by his Spirit in the inner man; that Christ may dwell in your hearts by faith; that ye, being rooted and grounded in love, may be able to comprehend with all saints what is the breadth, and length, and depth, and height; and to know the love of Christ, which passeth knowledge, that ye might be filled with all the fulness of God. Now unto him that is able to do exceeding abundantly above all that we ask or think, according to the power that worketh in us, unto him be glory in the church by Christ Jesus throughout all ages, world without end. Amen.*
>
> (Ephesians 3:16–21)

Such, reader, have been the dealings of God with one of the chief of sinners, consequent on his following the directions laid down for you in this discourse. Permit me simply to add, that if you will thus seek the Lord and thus believe on Him, you also will thus speak of "*the riches of the glory of this mystery among the Gentiles; which is Christ in you, the hope of glory*" (Colossians 1:27).